# CROSSING LINES

The Politics of Ethnic Pressure

# CROSSING LINES

*Histories of Jews and Gentiles
in Three Communities*

# Judith S. Goldstein

William Morrow and Company, Inc.
New York

The author is grateful for permission to quote from:
Cohen, William S. *Of Sons and Seasons.* New York: Simon & Schuster, 1987.
Morgenthau, Henry, III. *Mostly Morgenthaus: A Family History.* New York: Ticknor & Fields, 1991.
Material on the Seal Harbor, Maine, community courtesy of the Rockefeller Archive Center, North Tarrytown, New York.
Material from the Charles Eliot papers by permission of the Harvard University Archives.

It is the policy of William Morrow and Company, Inc., and its imprints and affiliates, recognizing the importance of preserving what has been written, to print the books we publish on acid-free paper, and we exert our best efforts to that end.

**Library of Congress Cataloging-in-Publication Data**

Goldstein, Judith S.
    Crossing lines : histories of Jews and Gentiles in three communities / Judith S. Goldstein.
      p.    cm.
    Includes bibliographical references and index.
    ISBN 0-688-08023-5
    1. Jews—Maine—Bangor—History.  2. Bangor (Me.)—Ethnic relations.  3. Jews—Maine—Mount Desert Island—History.  4. Mount Desert Island (Me.)—Ethnic relations.  5. Jews—Maine—Calais—History.  6. Calais (Me.)—Ethnic relations.  I. Title.
F29.B2G55  1991
974.1'3—dc20                                 91-22415
                                                        CIP

Printed in the United States of America

First Edition

1  2  3  4  5  6  7  8  9  10

BOOK DESIGN BY LYNN DONOFRIO DESIGNS

For
Deborah Ruth Goldstein

# Acknowledgments

I N RESEARCHING AND writing this book, I have been aided by a large number of people. Many residents of Bangor, Mount Desert Island and Calais answered my numerous questions and submitted to interviews about their communities. I am indebted to all of them for their accessibility and generosity in terms of time and interest.

Many librarians and archivists have given invaluable assistance in my research on this book. For their knowledge of sources and patience with repeated inquiries, I am deeply grateful to Cyma Horowitz and Michele Anish of the American Jewish Committee Library, New York; Tom Rosenbaum of the Rockefeller Archives Center, North Tarrytown, New York; Muriel Sanford of the Special Collections, Folger Library, University of Maine at Orono; the late Kay Littlefield and the entire reference staff at the Bangor Public Library; Dr. Abraham Peck of the American Jewish Archives, Cincinnati, Ohio; Nancy Howland at the Jesup Memorial Library, Bar Harbor, Maine; Gladys O'Neil and Debbie Dyer of the Bar Harbor Historical Society; and Robert Pyle of the Northeast Harbor Library, Northeast Harbor, Maine.

I have been enriched by the interest and guidance of many friends, old and new. They have discussed ideas and read the

9

manuscript at many stages of its development: the late Lucy S. Dawidowicz, Joseph Gilliland, Ronald Spencer, Catherine Cutler, Henry Holland, Janet TenBroeck, Mimi Stern, Marion Kirshenbaun, Margot Dotti Hoffmann, Rabbi Harlan J. Wechsler, Raymond Strout, David C. Smith, Jordan S. Alpert, Joan Dunlop, Jonathan Stein, Barbara Murchie Abercrombie, Suzannah Hadorn, Barney J. Goldstein, Linda Lewis, Ruth Eno, Judith Raab, Francis Brown, Nancy Unobskey, Sidney Unobskey, Martha Goldner, Seldon Ari Bernstein, Janet Galin, Earle G. Shettleworth, Jr., Rabbi Avraham Freedman, Lisa Cronin Wohl, Ernest Rubenstein, James B. Vickery, R. D. Eno, Lydia Vandenbergh and Neil Flax.

Two people have carried the often frustrating burden of following one revision after another of the manuscript: Sue Mercy and Rev. William Booth. For their unsparing criticisms and ever-present support, I am deeply and inexpressibly thankful. Harvey Ginsberg, my editor at William Morrow and Company, has been consistently wise and demanding. He has led me through the creation of this book.

# Contents

# Foreword

MAINE HAS ALWAYS seemed reassuringly different. Both within and without the state, Maine's publicists have sought to cultivate roseate views, emphasizing its pristine beauty, civic virtues, social order and strong, Anglo-Saxon, patriotic past. Even today, Maine's history strikes many people as magically removed from the most troublesome aspects of American life and history. This was especially true during the periods of intense national industrial and urban change from the 1880's through the middle of the twentieth century.

Maine's separation from mainstream America has been reinforced by a sparse Yankee population and an overabundance of acreage. Reaching far north to Canada and jutting sharply east to the Atlantic Ocean, Maine spreads over immense stretches of remote forests, uninhabited townships, mountains, rivers, lakes and offshore islands. These arcadian images exclude widespread and ugly industrial development, labor tensions, immigrant ghettos and ethnic infusions into the native culture. No crowded, decaying cities. Few immigrants. And fewer Jews.

The reality, however, was much different. Like every other state in New England, from the late nineteenth through the early twentieth centuries Maine experienced severe economic strains and significant changes in its population. Removed from large urban centers and little industrialized, Maine nevertheless attracted immigrants—French Canadians, Irish, Italians, Greeks, Armenians, and German and eastern-European Jews. To be sure, there were no horrific ghettos—separated by alien cultures and tongues—such as were found in the major cities of Boston, New York, Philadelphia and Chicago.

Powerful forces of economic change in Maine caused immigrants and the native Anglo-Saxon population to struggle with the competing forces of mobility, aspiration and privilege. Maine's upper-class populations firmly exercised their control. They promoted their culture over the immigrant minorities and native-born lower classes. Immigrants, for their part, mostly emulated American ways and adjusted to the hierarchical order. Many, however, felt the profound and painful conflict between maintaining their religious and cultural traditions and breaking into the patterns of American Protestant life.

This book focuses on the configurations of mutual accommodation—centered around religious, economic and social differences—between the Jewish immigrants and Gentile populations. Specifically, the story concentrates on Bangor, Mount Desert Island and Calais: the first, a city, in the Maine context, of lumber fame and wealth; the second, a nationally famous and exclusive coastal resort area, consisting of several villages and towns; the third, a small Maine city, once proud, prosperous and self-contained. These histories concern lumber barons and Jewish peddlers, Wall Street financiers and Main Street clothing merchants, local and national elites and immigrant Jews from Germany and eastern Europe. Some of the people who dominate this book are known only on the limited stage of local history: Dr. Lawrence Cutler and Henry Wheelwright of Bangor; Sarah Unobskey and Arthur Unobskey of Calais. Others, such as Charles W. Eliot, John D. Rockefeller, Jr., Henry Morgenthau, Sr., and Jacob H. Schiff, still command, many years after their deaths, national reputations.

What do these three places have to tell us about the tension between religious differences and competing cultures and traditions? And what do these three seemingly unconnected and dissimilar communities reveal about the nature of Jewish assimilation out of the large urban areas? Bangor, Mount Desert Island and Calais differed in size, economic strength, social complexity, and their state and national reputations. The three places also differed in their formative responses to the arrival of immigrants in America, in particular, to Russian Jews. As for the similarities, in all three places, Protestant leaders controlled business, politics, culture and education. Nevertheless, small groups of Jewish immigrants formed deep bonds to these local communities and to Maine. At one time or another in all three places, Jewish immigrants realized the democratic ideal of tolerance and acceptance.

Thus, the settings for the book which focus initially on the 1890's: two proud Maine cities, one large and one small, facing uncertain economic futures, open to the influx of eastern-European Jewish immigrants; and one of America's richest and most beautiful summer communities that closed itself off from any traces of the immigrant-filled Eastern cities. In probing new aspects of Maine's history, one finds the communal aspirations of Gentiles and immigrant Jews diverging and then fusing together in unusual patterns. This interaction of Gentiles and Jews can illuminate the varied and rich histories of assimilation in other American communities. There is, however, an intriguing local aura which derives distinctly from Maine's special history, culture and myths.

# I

## BANGOR

# CHAPTER I

## City Tides

PROUD AND PROSPEROUS, Bangor entered the 1890's in a spirit of vigorous self-assertion. "He that hath a horn and bloweth it not, the same shall sell no fish," proclaimed Henry Lord, successful shipping broker and president of Bangor's Board of Trade. Lord blew the horn loud and strong at the board's first annual dinner in March 1890. In the special style of Gilded Age grandiosity, the city's overwhelmingly Protestant business elite entertained two hundred people, including Bangor's most notable residents and distinguished guests from around the state.

Lumber magnates, merchants, lawyers, ship owners, statesmen, judges, doctors and politicians bearing Bangor's most familiar and respected names—Stetson, Strickland, Hamlin, Wheelwright, Parkhurst, Boutelle, Bass, Paine, Appleton, Robinson, Wilson, Merrill, Coe, Savage, Bragg, Nichols, Ayer and Hill—were present. The banquet hall at the renowned Bangor House Hotel overflowed with a sumptuous eight-course dinner, orchestral music, serious talk and formal speeches until late into the night. Festoons of laurels, a plethora of palms, a profusion of roses and other flowers formed a "tropical effect" such as Bangor had not seen before.

What was Bangor selling hard on that March evening in 1890? Certainly not fish. Nor lumber, nor shipping, nor the

things that had made her a rich city. No, Bangor, with its population of nearly twenty thousand people, was selling to herself
and others the elusive goods of potential and hope for the
future. To make Bangor a booming place, the city realized it
would have to promote itself just as southern and western cities
were doing. Prosperity would depend upon stemming the outward flow of men and capital, stimulating industrial growth,
and centering the trade of eastern and central Maine in the city.
A powerful economic current was moving away from Bangor,
exporting sons, daughters, money, and New England values
and traditions to other American states. "Think where we
would be today," Lord said, "if that outgoing stream could have
been stopped twenty years ago."

While Lord and his business colleagues spoke about the
tide going out, did they ever talk openly about the inexorable
and steady stream that flowed the other way, bringing
immigrants—Russian immigrant Jews among them—into the
city? Probably not. To Lord and the business class, the Jewish
immigrants appeared with a strange language, strange faces
and strange names: Cohen, Epstein, Kominsky, Goldberg, Hilson, Sarhazky, Bernstein and Goldman. In the dynamic cross-
currents of migration in the 1890's, Bangor was being marked
by consequential shifts: while losing Protestant native men and
women from the top and middle rungs of its society, it was
adding a new kind of immigrant to the bottom.

For those who were leaving the city and for those who were
first coming, Bangor was a typical, pleasing American city. It
was trying to shape its future while resting upon its legendary
past: a rich, pioneering, patriotic, lumbering and land-
speculating past. In the Queen City, as it proudly called itself,
there was Main Street, State and Center streets and Broadway.
Its early urban expansion was guided, in part, by the proverbial
planning grid, one supplied by the eminent Boston architect
Charles Bulfinch in 1801. Yet the physical layout had an un-
predictable configuration. The city, snug and walkable, was
pleasingly ensconced in hills, some steep, some gently sloped,
along the Penobscot River and Kenduskeag Stream. Churches,
irregularly tucked into hills throughout the city, dominated the
horizon in all directions.

Just sixty years before Lord's 1890 speech, Bangor had
been a sleepy settlement with a few modest houses, farms and

sawmills. But from the 1830's to the 1850's, Bangor soared to international fame as America's largest inland lumber port: first shipping white pine, then spruce, to America's coastal cities, the West Indies, and European and South American ports.

The Penobscot River was Bangor's crucial channel of communication and commerce to the outside world. Trading vessels sailed thirty-six miles into Penobscot Bay and twenty-four miles up the river, from the Atlantic Ocean to Bangor at tidewater. For decades, the Penobscot, above and below Bangor, served as a corridor for log driving, ice harvesting and carrying people and goods, by sailing vessel and steamship, in and out of the city. Over 8,200 square miles were drained by the Penobscot and its various branches. The river that begot the city was also an awesome physical threat that often menaced the city with spring floods.

Lumber-rich with a population of twelve thousand in the 1850's, Bangor had become a "wilderness acropolis" and a self-exalted city. Artisans threw up typical New England–style wood and brick residential and commercial buildings. Distinguished architects, one living in Bangor and several from Boston, created an impressive legacy for Bangor. Charles G. Bryant, a Bangor architect of remarkable ability, designed the Bangor House Hotel—a fine match of the Tremont Hotel in Boston— the Pine Street Methodist Church, the Mercantile Bank building and many homes in Greek Revival motifs. Bryant was also responsible for quelling an ugly three-day battle between Irish laborers and Yankee sailors in 1833. With its wild urban growth, Bangor's port was a social tinderbox. When the constables were unable to stop the fighting, Bryant led the militia and brought order with a show of guns and bayonets.

In the mid-1840's, Henry David Thoreau passed through Bangor on a trip that took him deep into the forests around Mount Katahdin, Chesuncook Lake, and the Allagash and Penobscot rivers. He later etched his memories of the vigorous city in *The Illustrated Maine Woods*. Bangor was "like a star on the edge of night, still hewing at the forests of which it is built, already overflowing with the luxuries and refinement of Europe, and sending its vessels to Spain, to England, and to the West Indies for its groceries—and yet only a few axe-men have gone 'up river' into the howling wilderness which feeds it."

Continuing through the 1860's and 1870's the name

Bangor automatically meant timber wealth and power. The river was filled with rafts of lumber: men moved the logs out of the woods, down the rivers, through the mills and onto native and foreign vessels that cleared the port. In those days of glory, hundreds of ships jammed the harbor at one time. In 1860, five shipyards were active in Bangor and across the river in Brewer, building ships to carry shooks and staves to Cuba and Puerto Rico and lumber to South America.

Bangor cultivated a special place—through commerce, society and culture—in the urban landscape in Maine and New England over the next forty-five years. Tranquil residential streets rested on hills above the jumble of the riverfront downtown, where immigrants lived or temporarily lodged in the mixed commercial and residential areas. In its mercantile-civic center, well-designed public and commercial buildings and fine shops alternated with wharfs and inexpensive stores. The city proudly claimed its own opera house, eighteen churches, a city poor farm, the Bangor Theological Seminary, a festival concert auditorium, a large Spanish-Romanesque passenger depot for the Maine Central Railroad, four hotels, a Normanesque city hall, a YMCA, a hybrid Greek Revival county courthouse, the annual late-summer Bangor Fair, market squares, a posh cycling club and Mount Hope Cemetery (Charles Bryant's fine example of the bucolic-extravagant style of the early nineteenth-century garden cemetery, modeled after Mount Auburn in Cambridge, Massachusetts).

To an observer, an unidentified Englishman with a superficial gaze, the city appeared most pleasing. He saw no poor people, no drunkenness, no severe sectarianism. People, he wrote, would be "astonished" at the "intelligence, refinement, culture and wealth of Bangor." He added his final reassuring compliments: "Nowhere have we encountered so many English-looking faces, nowhere had access to so many pleasant homes, nowhere met with such lavish hospitality."

Local drama still derived from living at the edge of a vast unknown territory. Much of that land in the 1890's and through the first decades of the twentieth century was traded, owned or controlled in Bangor: uninhabited townships, forests that had never been seen by their owners, millions of acres of timberland accessible primarily by rivers, streams and lakes. According to the 1888 report of the Bangor Board of Trade, Bangor men owned or controlled nearly one half of the nine million acres of wild lands, valued for their timber growth. "In other words," the author Edward Mitchell Blanding wrote, "nearly six thousand square miles of forest tract, one fourth of the total area of the state, or a territory as large as the states of Connecticut and Rhode Island combined, has its proprietorship in Bangor." In 1907, the reporter Frank Putnam calculated that six hundred individuals, families and corporations owned Maine's nine million acres of timberland.

John Prescott Webber was one of the ambitious men who founded a prominent Bangor family that thrived on lumber wealth from one generation to the next. The son of a sea captain, J. P. Webber came from Ripley, Maine. Without much education, he went on the road in the 1840's, selling firewood around Pushaw Lake. Slowly, he worked his way into the thriving, competitive Bangor timber market, moving in and out of the Exchange Street offices of timberland owners such as the Stetsons and the Stricklands. He started buying and selling large tracts of timberland in eastern and northern Maine.

There were no books, no accountants, and no taxes, and no collateral was provided to borrow from the Bangor banks. He needed only to develop a reputation for honesty, shrewdness and paying back loans. When enormous properties came onto the auction market at low prices during the depressed years of the late 1870's, Webber built his fortune. The Webbers became land-rich and, although sometimes lacking capital, they always lived well and at the top of Bangor society in those pre–income tax days. They thrived in the highly lucrative but volatile industry that between 1860 and 1910 was, according to historian David C. Smith, a "lottery."

Despite the popular impression that the timberlands were in their heyday in the mid-nineteenth century, Smith has written about the enduring lumber prosperity. "It is a statistical fact," he wrote, "that more lumber was cut in Maine after 1861 than before and the biggest years in the Maine woods were in the last decade of the nineteenth and the first decade of the twentieth."

Before the turn of the century, the demand for paper for city newspapers encouraged the growth of the pulp and paper industry and deeply affected Bangor's economic life. The center of the timber industry shifted from the lumber magnates in

Bangor to the interior mill-towns owned by large out-of-state paper companies. Land-hungry and requiring vast amounts of spruce, they strengthened Maine's forest industry despite the competition from the South, with its longer growing season, and the Pacific Northwest, where transportation rates were significantly lower than Maine's. In 1897, several Bangor men incorporated the Northern Development Company to develop water power around Millinocket on the Bangor and Aroostook Railroad line. Two years later, they sold their land to the newly formed Great Northern Paper Company, owned by financiers from outside the state. Within a few years of opening its mill, the Great Northern Company completely dominated the west branch of the Penobscot, reducing Bangor's influence.

The Webbers and other Bangor timberland owners had been the beneficiaries of the state's history that favored private individuals and corporations. Almost all of Maine's original holdings of forest areas came into private ownership at remarkably low costs. The journalist and lawyer William R. Pattangall, ever one to write about interesting political developments, penned an ironic portrait of the advancement of Edwin Chick Burleigh. Pattangall took on the state's mighty, rich and famous in a series of writings called the "Meddybemps Letters" and the "Maine Hall of Fame." Burleigh, a Bangor resident for several years, was a land agent, a governor of Maine and a congressman. To Pattangall, Burleigh's success was remarkably uncomplicated:

> Maine once owned large tracts of timberland. Maine does not own any now. Mr. Burleigh was once without any timberland. He owns considerable timberland now. Maine sold its timberland at a low price, a very low price indeed. It has since become very valuable. The men who bought it have prospered. It was sold, in part, through the land agent's office. Mr. Burleigh and his father had charge of that office for 11 years. Some of the land which Maine once owned and sold so cheap was afterwards owned by Mr. E. Burleigh.

Furthermore, Maine developed a system of taxation that assessed the wild lands or undeveloped townships (woods with no people) at a low rate in relation to their value. Remarkably, in 1890, the $9 million valuation for nine million acres produced a mere $30,000 in taxes. Prodded by pressure from reformers and critics in the state, the valuation climbed steadily after the turn of the century. But not too high and not too fast. In 1906, the timberlands rose in value to $36,000,000 but produced only $91,000 in taxes.

The lumber wealth would not have been there for the taking were it not for the inventive technical skills, the daring and the endurance of the men who worked in the forests and on the rivers. However, while wealth awaited the Bangor lumber barons, there were no fortunes for the men who cut and moved the timber on frozen ground and drove the lumber on the Penobscot River. Their return came, instead, in their legendary pride, skills and prowess, which Bangor prized as well. They were eulogized in *The Penobscot Man* by Fannie Hardy Eckstorm, the renowned authority on the history and folklore of Maine's lumbermen, Indians and hunters.

Each winter and spring, an army of three thousand to four thousand men worked in the timberlands and on the rivers. Year after year, many of the same men returned to extract wealth from the woods: men from Bangor and towns along the Penobscot, Maine Indians, French Canadians mainly from the Maritime Provinces and immigrants from Scandinavia, Ireland, Poland and Russia. Like all the other immigrants, those from Prince Edward Island came to Bangor hungry for work and money.

> Oh, the boys of the Island
> They feel discontent.
> The times they are hard,
> And they can't make a cent:
> So, says Rory to Angus,
> "Here we're doing no good.
> Let's go over to Bangor,
> And work in the woods."

Once in the woods, the men worked as choppers, cant dog men who placed the downed trees on sleds to be driven to the river, and river drivers who walked the waters on logs or rode in bateaux and canoes especially adapted to the work. They maneuvered over rapids and dams, floods and low water, breaking up jams and retrieving logs that jumped away from the flow. They lived and labored beyond the reach of ordinary life—subject to harsh cold and primitive conditions in the camps, removed in winter and spring from the fixed and predictable social order of family and religious life, drawn to the adventure and camaraderie of men working in isolation in the woods and on the rivers.

In Bangor, life was punctuated by seasonal arrivals and departures of the lumbermen. The city the men passed through in the 1890's was adapting to the latest technological changes. Rutted dirt roads, usable only by horses and carriages, barely by pedestrians and not at all by cyclists, were paved one by one. Sewage lines were extended. Electric lights were installed. Four telephone operators, placed at city hall, served five hundred users. Electricity, generated by water power from the Penobscot River, allowed the Bangor Street Railroad to install the first electric cars in the state.

At the turn of the century, Bangor appeared to be on the competitive edge of the national economy and culture. Capitalizing upon their lumber wealth, the city's leaders boastfully employed the rhetoric of expansion and industrial growth. The city's merchants, bankers and lumber lords seemed to be racing against other Maine cities to attract river-related industrial development and establish vigorous trade networks with adjoining counties. Bangor, after all, had the capital base for such expansion as well as an adequate labor supply.

Yet the constant talk about attracting major industrial developments led nowhere. In 1894, Francis H. Clergue, a native son, proposed taking over the Bangor waterworks, building a canal to create more water power and constructing additional electrical plants. Clergue intended to create enough power to supply a proposed pulp mill near the dam where five hundred Bangor men would produce paper for London newspapers.

Bangor's business leaders summarily rejected Clergue's proposal, as well as any other that would change their traditional use and control of the river for logging. Clergue left the city shortly and surfaced a few years later at Sault Sainte Marie. He formed a gigantic power and mill complex called Lake Superior Power Company—the Soo—serving both Canada and the United States. With some awe, Bangor's citizens tracked his financial and industrial exploits for the next few years. Article after article in the Bangor papers recorded the triumphs of the native son—until his downfall in 1903 when Clergue was over-extended and the company stock dropped drastically. In the midst of his crisis, one of Clergue's brothers returned to Bangor for a family visit. When questioned by a reporter about the recent events, he minimized the difficulties. The only problem at the Soo, he said, was the pressure from its New York invest-ment banking firm, Speyer and Company—"the Jew firm to whom we owe money."

Bangor's capitalists invested in hydroelectric power and other major industrial concerns—but always outside the city. In fact, Bangor's leaders regarded their city primarily as a pleasant and quiet place to spend their wealth. Their local investments were restricted to their banks and commercial and residential properties. They regarded establishing the city as a vigorous trading and transportation center as a more viable pursuit than industrial expansion. To keep up with other cities, Bangor's government and business communities (and often the two were indistinguishable) modernized their transportation and com-munication networks. Rail lines connected Bangor passengers and freight to Portland, Boston and New York, as well as to the Maine coast, downeast to Mount Desert Ferry, Calais and on to Canada. At the height of the summer traffic, seventy daily trains passed in and out of the city.

The most important of Bangor's hopes for becoming a pivotal trade and transportation center was focused on the Bangor and Aroostook Railroad, which started running lines northward in 1895 into the virgin territory of Aroostook County. A banner array of Bangor businessmen, connected solidly to state and lumber interests, became officers and board members of the new line. Investing $120,000 in the railroad, Bangor men had the mistaken expectation that the city would become the terminus for the new line. There was indeed an agreement between the city and the railroad, but the railroad reneged within a few years.

Like many American cities and towns, Bangor had a bit-tersweet romance with its railroads. Fluctuating rates and schedules as well as onerous debts were a constant source of tension for the city. And while the railroads helped to lessen Bangor's inland isolation, they also slowly ended the city's via-bility as a shipping port and shipbuilding center. In 1888, there were 178 vessels registered in Bangor; by 1899, there was less than half that number. Ten years later the port was moribund, as was much of the commercial life around the port. In 1905, Henry Lord's ship brokerage and insurance business had gone into bankruptcy with $50,000 in debts.

In fact, while the river trade was dying, people were dying from the river. In 1904, a chronic Bangor problem turned into a short-lived but highly publicized crisis. Five hundred to six hundred cases of typhoid were reported in Bangor, Old Town and Millinocket. The Penobscot County Medical Association concluded that the epidemic was directly attributable to Bangor's water supply—the Penobscot. Despite recommendations to use a different water supply, the public concern and epidemic abated when a new filter system was installed.

Still, the benefits from the railroads were enormous. They opened up new markets in the undeveloped interior areas and created jobs for natives and immigrants alike. Italian and Irish laborers built tracks for the Bangor and Aroostook and Maine Central lines as well as mills in new towns such as Millinocket. Jewish immigrants, too, spread along the lines, into places such as Milo, Brownville, Millinocket and Calais. Often they started peddling, and then they opened small stores for notions, clothing and dry goods.

The Bangor and Aroostook and the Maine Central railroads made Bangor a thriving, up-to-date retail and wholesale center for the surrounding counties. Bangor firms such as N. H. Bragg gained new markets for hardware, steel and iron products. Retailers such as Julius Waterman benefited from Aroostook's successful farmers and lumber operators coming to "downtown" Bangor to shop for clothing and other goods.

Downtown was centered around Main Street, with its tight concentration of buildings and businesses. The court and jail were nearby, on Hammond Street; the post office, straddling the two sections of the city, was situated over the Kenduskeag Stream. The city hall, on Columbia Street, towered over all. Wholesale and retail businesses, lumber offices, clothing stores, grocers, hardware stores, blacksmiths, employment offices for the lumber workers, tool manufacturers, a shoe factory, restaurants, a trunk factory, saloons and apothecaries were packed into Exchange, Broad, and Hammond streets. The Bangor Public Library and the Bangor Historical Society perched themselves on the upper floor of a commercial building next to the Kenduskeag.

Between the riverfront and its businesses and the hills and their high-toned residential life, Main Street, with its scramble of hanging signs, cut a north-south axis. There, shoppers enjoyed the better retail trade at department and specialty dry goods stores such as Freese's, The Fashion and E. C. Nichols. National food, clothing and theater chains also entered the city to compete with local firms as the small city began to tie itself to markets of mass production and mass consumption.

Downtown was also a circumscribed cauldron of social and economic problems. The immigrants—Irish, Turks, Syrians, French Canadians, Poles, Greeks and Jews—lived or temporarily lodged around the shallow valleys and hills along the Kenduskeag Stream and on the low hills above the Penobscot River. Most of their homes or boarding houses, in modest to run-down condition, had been built as rental properties for several families, or as rooming houses for transient laborers. Some were the modified, broken-up homes of wealthy merchants who long before had moved up to the hills away from the river and railroad traffic. Many of the immigrants lived on York, Hancock, lower Essex, French and Pine streets and the small streets that were cut in between.

The long shadow of the red-brick St. John's Catholic Church on York Street dominated the immigrant area. The large church was built in 1854 for the Irish Catholic community of 2,500 people. Having survived sieges of hostility in the 1830's and the Know-Nothing campaigns of the 1850's, a turning point came when the Irish community formed a regiment to fight in the Civil War. By the 1890's, the Irish had gained solid entry and status in the police, fire and other departments of the city government while many continued to labor in the timberlands, on the railroads, as well as in domestic service for Bangor's upper and middle classes.

At the turn of the century, the Irish in Bangor maintained a position of mutual accommodation in the social and political structure of the Protestant city. The official respect and recognition extended to the Irish community was evident at the observance of Rev. Edward McSweeney's twenty-fifth anniversary in the priesthood in 1895, when Bangor's Protestant civic leaders, along with the vicar-general of Maine and other leaders of the Roman Catholic church, honored the revered leader of St. John's at a series of celebratory events and services.

Outside the immigrant and lower-class areas, there were few overt social tensions within the city. At a time of intense urban change throughout the country, Bangor was a city in pleasing equilibrium. Business and professional leaders were in charge and immigrant communities were under control. No radical ideologies were running rampant through its native-born and immigrant labor population. There was, to be sure, an active labor force that made unprecedented demands concerning hours and wages. The lumber lords, merchants and real estate developers of old could no longer operate without regard to the demands of the labor market. By 1903, there were already twenty-eight labor unions in Bangor. Most union members were working a nine-hour day, reduced from the traditional ten or eleven hours. In 1903, the city witnessed its first Labor Day festivities organized by Bangor's Trades Council. They included a parade, an assembly at Maplewood Park, and a concert and ball at the auditorium.

Yet overall, the business and professional elite, at ease with its wealth, made little effort to hide that wealth except from the tax assessors. In the pre–income tax days of the nineties, many gave generous philanthropic support to the city's churches, religious organizations and associations—those dealing with poverty, intoxication and self-defined problems of so-called immorality among the lower class.

In a dry state, where temperance issues raged, Bangor went its own pragmatic, businesslike, defiant way: rich and poor had access to drink day and night. The rich shipped in alcohol from out of state and consumed it at their clubs and homes. The poor bought it at saloons. In the annual Bangor business directories, saloon keepers were listed in profusion—around sixty—from year to year. The listings stopped appearing by the late 1890's, but the saloons remained, as did the problem of intoxication. Throughout the 1890's, there were approximately one thousand arrests for drunkenness each year—a good two thirds of all arrests. Envied by some and condemned by others, Bangor's way of dealing with the state government and the temperance laws was known as the Bangor Plan. Once a year, the police arrested saloon keepers and imposed fines payable to the city. This was Bangor's way of getting a license fee for the privilege of operating illegally, at least according to state law. The rest of the time, the payment ensured protection from the city government.

Pursuing policies on behalf of their diverse interests, the city's leaders moved with assurance in and out of politics in the city and on the state level. Democrats and Republicans replaced each other with heated partisan rhetoric but without markedly rearranging or upsetting policies and interests. But if the differences between the parties were often irrelevant and misleading, the rewards of office were real. From the wards up, party involvement was one means of gaining mobility and job opportunities for natives and immigrants alike. In the city government, numerous offices were subject to the party test.

Decade after decade, the position of mayor was reserved for mercantile and lumber leaders. The Irish, with their large constituency and proclivity toward politics, were strongly represented as city councilmen and aldermen, but none of them rose to the top position. Unlike many American cities, Bangor did not have any real bosses. But it did have the Republican Flavius O. Beal, who thought of himself as one. In his nine terms as mayor, he aggressively promoted Bangor's municipal interests, along with his own investments in hotels, stables, railroads and the Bangor Fair.

Beal yearned for an impressive building to embody his city's image as a dynamic urban center. He realized his goal when he took $100,000 for a new city hall out of a fund that had been bequeathed to Bangor for educational endeavors. Many citizens had expected that the money would be used to build a new public library to house the collection formed by the Mechanic Association, an educational organization for the city's artisans. In 1893, Beal raided the library fund and took the principal, invested in bonds and stocks, and plunged it down deep into municipal real estate. While Beal talked of putting the library in the new city hall, no such plans materialized. Instead, the library remained in its precarious rented space next to the Kenduskeag Stream, supported by the city's fixed interest payments of $4,000 per year and sundry donations.

Beal's city hall, crowned by a sixty-foot tower with an outstretched winged eagle, peered over the city that was busy with work and a vigorous social life. The upper class, in particular, filled its lives with fancy rituals of etiquette and ceremonies centered around romances, marriages, teas and balls at home or at Society Hall downtown. Well-to-do families traveled frequently by train and steamship to other cities in America and to Europe. In the cool, blissfully green summer months, they entertained in their handsome houses, lovely gardens, and camps and cottages at nearby lakes and coastal havens such as Phillips Lake, Holbrook Pond, Pushaw Lake and Hancock Point. But most of the time, the cold climate that spilled over into spring, fall and sometimes summer, forced social life indoors, behind walls and windows.

On streets dense with elms and maples, the wealthy were still building elegant new homes in the 1890's, designed by local architects, such as Wilfred E. Mansur, or well-known Boston and New York firms. Many of the older homes, originally constructed with mid-nineteenth-century simplicity, were transformed into Victorian rococo, with modern plumbing and heating conveniences, mazes of rooms, heavy furniture and the weighty bric-a-brac of the new consumer society. Some were architectural extravaganzas in various styles—Greek Revival, Italianate, Queen Anne, mansard, shingle and Bangor idiosyncratic. Although often eccentric in design, sprawling and asymmetrical, they were never beyond the range of conventional architectural idioms. Most houses, however, were typical of those in other Maine cities: modestly styled and built from published building plans, usually without benefit of an architect. Home after home lined up in patterned predictability, compactly placed on narrow, deep lots along the numerous straight-lined streets.

On every day but Sunday, Bangor learned from its papers about happenings in the outside world, the city itself and, in detail, of the travels, trips and visits of recognized residents and their guests. The two leading papers were the Democratic *Bangor Daily Commercial,* owned by Joseph Bass, a wealthy timberland owner, real estate entrepreneur and ex-mayor of the city, and the Republican *Whig and Courier,* published by Charles Boutelle, a long-term congressman from Bangor. The *Industrial Journal* appeared on a weekly basis from the 1890's until 1918, reporting on business news of Bangor and the state. In the 1890's, the *Commercial,* the most ambitious and successful paper, consisted of eight to twenty pages. Edward H. Blake and

J. Norman Towle bought the small and little-read *Bangor Daily News* in 1895, built up its circulation and bought out the *Whig and Courier* in 1900. After the turn of the century, the *News* and *Commercial* engaged in close and vigorous competition that lasted for half a century.

The papers, with circumspection and confidence, reported on the proper and pleasurable social life—by invitation only—of the upper class in the 1890's. Typically, as front-page news, the *Commercial* wrote in flattering detail about a long-awaited tea and dance when all three hundred of the invited, the "society people of the city," visited Mrs. William H. Strickland's home on Broadway.

Despite its own carefully constructed social order, society in Bangor was not necessarily society elsewhere. Just forty-five miles away in exclusive Bar Harbor on Mount Desert Island, Bangor society did not meet the acceptable social standards. A writer for the *Commercial* and a man of self-proclaimed standing in the resort was asked why Bangor people in the 1890's no longer vacationed in Bar Harbor. "It seems," he stated, "as if the people from the other middle, westward and southward states in selecting this glorious spot as their favorite 'hunting ground' were determined to keep natives of the whole state in due subjection." Despite the snubbing, Bangor papers gave front-page attention to glittering diplomatic and naval visits, receptions, musical and sporting events, and the building and sale of cottages on Mount Desert Island. Readers also found weekly listings of everyone staying at the hotels and cottages in the island's fanciest villages.

In the Gilded Age, Bangor well understood the culture of the robber barons, many of whom vacationed at Bar Harbor. The city's sense of importance was satisfied primarily by periodic surveys and profiles of leading business people. Unfortunately for its later inhabitants, Bangor entered the 1890's without a historian or chronicler for the city. Judge John Edwards Godfrey, the preeminent local historian and author, had died in 1884. His absence meant that controversies, transitions, achievements, failures and gossip were to vanish from the city records, except for meager stories picked up by reporters and editorial writers for the newspapers. The only efforts at contemporary self-reflection were through the reports of the business elite's Board of Trade, founded in 1872. It provided annual summaries of trade statistics and business events and issued publications selling Bangor's business opportunities and virtues as one of Maine's most desirable places to live.

One of those virtues was to be found in the realm of music. By the turn of the century, it had become the outstanding proof of the city's culture and status. In part, the interest rested solidly upon a widespread, multiclass, folk- and church-inspired musical tradition. Pullen's Orchestra, which had been providing background music for Bangor's social functions, transformed itself into the Bangor Symphony Orchestra in 1896. According to one Bangor critic, it was a courageous enterprise, given the response of Bangor audiences. When unfamiliar music was played at one concert, no one applauded at the end. "I felt," the critic wrote, "as if I had been sitting in an icehouse for a week. If I had been leading that orchestra I would have come to the front of that platform and told that audience to remove its cold carcass to the hot end of the North Pole."

Ambitious as it was, the Bangor Symphony Orchestra did not put the city on the cultural map. Bangor made its reputation by merging its enterprise and financial support with the verve of William Chapman, a Maine-born, dynamic music director and conductor. Chapman started his annual Maine Music Festival in October 1897 with an enormous chorus of eight hundred singers from Bangor and other towns and cities in the state, an orchestra of sixty local musicians, and a group of soloists including the Maine-born prima donna and musical heroine, Lillian Nordica. The festival, held in a newly constructed auditorium with seating for four thousand people, lasted for three days in Bangor and then moved down to Portland. A local architect, Victor Hodgins, designed the acoustically superb auditorium when Bangor supporters raised $12,000.

The indefatigable Chapman trained the local chorus and orchestra, set the programs, promoted the festival and lured the world's greatest artists to perform operatic, choral and symphonic works. Blauvelt, Gadski, Ian Williams, Sembrich, Campanari, Schumann-Heink, Calvé and Nordica were among the stars who brought dazzling fashion and drama to the city. Oversized front-page pictures in the press heralded the arrival of the artists. Stories about their careers, performances, marriages and divorces were avidly followed. Personal appearances, contacts on and off the stage and any recognition of Bangor's special qualities were treasured and reported at length.

A reporter from the *News* was overwhelmed by his interview with Mme. Schumann-Heink—"the living, breathing personification of truest womanhood." The reporter asked if she liked to come to Maine. " 'I love Maine,' she cried ecstatically. 'I go to New York and it is cold and stiff and formal. . . . I come to Bangor and when I come out to sing I laugh, and the chorus laughs, and the audience laughs, and then they all applaud, and we are good friends right away.' " Gingerly, he wondered if "at times, the cause of grand music is not irrevocably lost amid the wilds of eastern Maine?" With enthusiasm, she replied, "I think that the finest singers in all the world are to be found in Maine and California."

Like the rest of America, Bangor started to live in the fantasies of the silent-movie world. In the early 1900's, the city went on a splurge of theater building to serve the popular demand for plays, vaudeville and movies. With seating for hundreds of patrons, the theaters were exotically decorated. The Graphic, Keith's Nickel, the Union and the Bijou were Bangor's versions of the "Cathedrals of Kitsch" built all over America. The theaters, some locally owned and some belonging to national chains, mixed popular and serious entertainment.

For entertainment, Bangor turned to movies, theater and the Maine Music Festival. For its moral and spiritual direction, Bangor anchored itself to its numerous religious institutions. These included three Congregational, two Methodist, one Episcopal, three Baptist, one Universalist, one Unitarian, two Catholic churches and one synagogue. Over eight decades, Bangor had established, adorned, embellished and enriched its handsome churches. In architectural styles from modest to ornate, using simple woods or expensive stone, the churches reigned over the Bangor landscape.

The churches led the city in its dutiful observance of the Christian religious calendar as well as in the abortive crusades to control drinking in the city. Temperance issues served as the religious catchall for social ills such as poverty and criminal behavior. But, according to the clergy and lay leaders, fervor for the temperance movement declined in the 1890's, as did religious devotion and disciplines.

Those active in the churches supported missionary work as well as programs to aid the city's less fortunate. Bangor's leaders assumed responsibility for the moral behavior and order of the city. An underlying premise of the charity movement, which Bangor shared with other cities, was that the poor were personally immoral and needed to be elevated. Each of Bangor's churches had its own group, run by women, providing money, clothing and rent support for the needy. Frequently, these church groups generated ideas for educational and social change, such as the kindergarten movement.

The burden of charity relief fell to private efforts, except for the city's almshouse and poor farm, where indigent persons lived and worked, and the nonsectarian city missionary. Apart from the church groups, there were organizations for the Home for Aged Women, the Home for Aged Men, the Children's Home, the Kings Daughters' Home and the Fuel Society.

The needs of Bangor's rich and poor, Protestants and Catholics, were joined in a major effort in the early 1890's to establish Bangor's first hospital. The initial assumption was that the hospital would encompass "all kinds of religious, medical and political beliefs and a broad catholic belief." Soon afterward, plans for the hospital became bogged down in a controversy between allopathic and homeopathic physicians. The dispute continued even after five allopathic doctors took the initiative in 1892 and opened the Bangor General Hospital at Mace House on State Street overlooking the Penobscot. With a matron and one patient, its purpose was to treat the ill, with the exception of the insane and those with contagious diseases. Despite the continuing internal struggles, the Eastern Maine General Hospital, as it came to be called, began to receive financial backing from the city and state in addition to the donations of private benefactors.

Ecumenical effort such as that on behalf of the hospital was an unusual occurrence. Routinely, Bangor's private organizations were composed of rigidly separated ethnic groups. The Masons, Elks, Knights of Pythias, Ancient Order of Hibernians, Knights of Columbus and Odd Fellows had local chapters. Protestants, Catholics and Jews had their own separate clubs, some of which offered educational and cultural enrichment through literary and musical pursuits. Others offered mysterious rites and ceremonies of fraternal connections or gave burial and other benefits. Most mixed social, educational and philanthropic aims. A few built handsome, distinguished buildings for the city's leading Protestant merchants and professional leaders. The Tarratine Club offered fine food and a businessman's refuge, modeled on men's clubs in Boston and New York.

Social conventions and a rigid separation of responsibilities blocked almost all women from nondomestic activities, except for church, charitable and educational associations. The very few Bangor women who worked were doctors, teachers or store owners. The women's clubs provided one of the very few opportunities for learning, self-improvement and a structured community of friends. Enthusiasm for the Athene Club, which had over 140 members in the late 1890's, lifted its secretary in 1899 into a state of verbal frenzy:

Alas! how much unwritten history never sees the light. There can be no expression of the present intercourse—the friendly discussion—the revelations of character and unexpected ability—the scintillations of wit—the interchange of sympathies—perplexities and discouragements—the broadening of opinion—the curbing or annihilation of differences—the expansion of the mental forces and the development of the spiritual—a clearer insight into the needs of humanity and a broader outlook towards their amelioration.

Public education in the 1890's also elicited deep commitments and passions. Dr. Daniel Arthur Robinson, longtime chairman of the school board, and Mary Snow, the first female superintendent of the system, made fervent appeals for educational innovations and improvements in antiquated facilities. Their objectives included getting more money for the system to meet the needs of a growing student population and a restless, underpaid group of teachers. Both native and immigrant children were creating complex demands, especially as increasing numbers of students went to high school.

Both Robinson and Snow correctly perceived that under the gloss of stability, contentment and success, there were reasons for pessimism and concern for Bangor's future: inadequate industrial development and a stagnant population. Charles Bartlett, head of the city's Citizens League, also found distressing omens. Addressing his fellow members at the first meeting of the Chamber of Commerce in 1910, he candidly said: "We are poked away in the northeastern corner of the United States, not on the line between anywhere and anywhere else, and must work out our own salvation."

The same concern was evident four years later, when Bangor's leading citizens proudly gathered in the handsome rooms of the newly constructed public library to celebrate the fiftieth anniversary of the Bangor Historical Society. Bangor appeared "prosperous and happy," according to the venerable Henry Lord, who addressed the gathering of fellow members. It was a larger and wealthier city than in 1864, but, he added with obvious sadness and nostalgia, Bangor was no longer famous or boldly enterprising.

Lord's regrets were not just for the transformation of the lumber trade and the death of a vibrant commercial life on the river. He was thinking about his fellow citizens, too. "The strong, able, virile men of that day, most of them native born, like the rafts on the river and the ships on the docks, are gone forever," he lamented.

Emigration of the natives was taking its dispiriting toll. William Pattangall, the ever-acerbic observer of Maine politics and society, had found Maine people everywhere he went outside the state: "on the cars, in the stores, in hotels, everywhere you meet Maine men, doing everything from running million-dollar factories to trying to light their two-cent cigars at the electric light bulb." The depths of native flight could be exaggerated, as Pattangall was wont to do, but it could not be ignored. "If everybody who had left Maine had stayed there," he wrote, "we would have had a population of about seven million and Meddybemps [Maine] people would have been going up to Boston to get out of the crowd and rest a little. . . ."

Like Henry Lord and many of Bangor's other leaders, Pattangall, the lawyer, politician, editor and writer, never cast his lot outside the state. He fulfilled his restless needs, first by sailing around the world before going to the University of Maine, then by moving from Machias to Bangor to Waterville and then Augusta as a journalist and writer.

For others, however, who left to make their careers elsewhere, Maine's nostalgia industry started to grow. It dwelled upon the roughness of big-city life; it inspired the publication of the *Pine Tree Magazine* for Maine people living in other states, carrying news of natives who had left; it led to the creation of the Pine Tree State Club in Boston. At one of the Club's gathering of "ex patriots," Julia Harris May read a poem before an audience of eminent Maine daughters. It included Sarah Orne Jewett, one of the state's favorite writers, who had moved to Boston herself. In the singsong meter of traditional sentiment, May spoke fervidly for those who were left behind:

> O wanderers from the land of Maine
> the perfume of the pine
> Is mingled with your memory. Her violet vales
> entwine;
> Memorial wreaths, she calls for you, O, must
> she call in vain
> Come back to her who calls for you, O!
> wanderers of Maine. . . .
>
> Come back! There's room enough, O hear the
> voice of Kennebec.
> The ocean calls; She looks for you on every
> home bound deck,
> The long Penobscot murmurs, Come, Aroostook's fertile plain
> Is beckoning her wanderers to the motherland
> of Maine. . . .
>
> Dear wanderers who wander yet if we no more
> may meet,
> Until the Land of the Beyond shall press your
> weary feet.
> We still will lift our banner high, and sing the
> old refrain,
> For you are ours forever more O! wanderers of
> Maine.

# CHAPTER 2

# *The Wanderers*

WHILE JULIA HARRIS MAY pined for the wanderers from Maine, immigrant wanderers, including Russian Jews, were moving into Bangor. They came with fragile, pressing hopes for making a living in a seemingly prosperous city. The immigrants were poor and work-hungry. "Nobody came down with a pack of gold," was the way one Bangor Jewish woman described the journey of her father to the city.

Bangor's Russian Jews established themselves near the tail end of the glory days of timber and shipping, taking their lowly place at the bottom end of the city's trade in junk, trinkets, clothing and dry goods. Ignorant of the tide going out of the city, the immigrants did not know that the departing natives were looking for their "pack of gold" outside the state. Unlike the Protestants from Maine, however, the Jewish wanderers were not wanted back where they came from.

They had been pushed out by the violence and poverty in Russia and Russian-dominated Poland. Bangor's eastern European Jews, who started to arrive in the city in the early 1880's, came primarily from the Lithuanian vicinities of Vilna (Vilnius), Kovno (Kaunas), and Minsk and Grodno, in Russia, which were places of severe overpopulation and minuscule economic opportunity. Forced into one area by government fiat, all

40

but 300,000 of Russia's 5.2 million Jews lived in the Pale, a wide strip of Russia broken into twenty-five provinces that lay between the Baltic and the Black Sea.

For Jews, existence had become increasingly problematic from the time Russia began ruling Poland in the late eighteenth century. One hundred years later, new and cruel regulations severely contracted not only the areas in which Jews could live but their educational and business opportunities, too. Generally, Jews could not own land. They were almost completely excluded from state schools—from primary grades through university—by means of small quotas. They could not be employed in numerous trades, as state teachers, judges, or elected officials. They were forced, however, into one type of service for the state: all Jewish males between twelve and twenty-five were subject to long army terms, while irrevocably assigned to the lowest ranks.

The government-sponsored formula for handling Jews was simple: some would be converted, many would emigrate, and the rest would be killed off through violence. There were Jews who converted, but they were comparatively few in number. The emigration of two million Jews, of whom over one million went to the United States between 1891 and 1910, left millions still in Russia. The Jewish population continued to explode as a result of early marriages, high birth rates and low death rates. Despite the Russian formula, masses of Jews remained Jews, fixed in a system of unrelenting hostility, violence and sustained uncertainty.

By the late nineteenth century, large numbers of Russian Jews were following the European pattern of moving to towns and cities, gaining employment in commerce or as skilled workers. Almost all of the Jews who settled in Bangor had originally come from shtetlach, small centers with a few hundred Jewish families. They had lived in cramped, wooden houses with dirt floors, on unlit, unpaved streets surrounded by farms and forests. In a story by the Yiddish writer Sholem Aleichem, one of the characters described the tenuous and intimate character of his village life:

> We have, knock wood, a few Jews, we have a synagogue, we have a study house, we have a rabbi, we have every-thing. In fact, there are only two things that God for-

got to give us: a chance to make a living and some
air. Well, as far as a living goes, we've worked out a
system: we all, the Lord be praised, manage to make
one from each other. And air? For air we go to the
manor grounds; you'll find as much of it as you want
there.

Aleichem's most well-known and sympathetic character,
Tevye the dairyman, described his poverty in ironic God-
inspired terms. Tevye hooked God into his plight, for who else
was there to help him? In the days before he got lucky and got
a horse, he was "with God's help . . . poor as a devil. No Jew
should starve as I did! Not counting suppers, my wife and kids
went hungry three times a day. I worked like a dog dragging
logs by the wagonful from the forest to train station. . . ." As
was his need and his desire, Tevye prayed to God: "Master of
the Universe, what have I done to deserve all this? Am I or am
I not a Jew like any other? Help! . . . See us in our affliction—
take a good look at us poor folk slaving away and do something
about it, because if You don't just who do You think will? . . .
Heal our wounds and make us whole—please concentrate on
the healing because the wounds we already have. . . ."

Before they left eastern Europe and settled in Bangor, the
Jews were deeply immersed in a detailed and traditional calendar of religious observance filled with daily prayers, Sabbath
rest and study, holiday fasts and celebrations. They lived under
rabbinic domination and superstitious rites. In his autobiography, the philosopher Morris Cohen recalled the place of
belief—ritual and ethical guidance—amidst the piercing poverty of his early life in eastern Europe. Jews made life tolerable,
he wrote, because of an "inner life and religious devotion which
ennobled its joys and sorrows and provided strength and dignity for meeting the tasks and perplexities of the day."

Religious dictates governed communal responsibilities for
social mores, business practices, health and welfare institutions
and education. It was in the cheder, the religious school, where
boys, but not girls, between five and six years old started to gain
a rudimentary education in reading and sometimes writing Hebrew. Boys prepared for bar mitzvah by studying prayers, the
Torah and Jewish law. While most boys ended their schooling
with the ceremony, some went on for more religious study in

yeshivas. The isolated, religious Jewish communities imposed their own taxes and settled their own disputes, with as little recourse as necessary to Russian governmental institutions. Ultimately, communal authority was imposed on Jews through the powers of excommunication from the synagogue and community for violations of Jewish laws.

Nevertheless, in the late nineteenth century, the primacy of religious thought and control was under challenge from Western secular thought and radical political and economic doctrines such as Zionism and socialism. Many Jews were already looking toward the languages of opportunity—Polish, Russian and especially English—and new countries of promise. One immigrant who settled in Bangor explained: "Every Jew in Russia knew that there was nothing left for him in the Old Country. For a young man there was no future to which he could look forward. America seemed to offer the only salvation."

In their historical memory, the Jewish immigrants knew how to move their human capital and activate the mechanisms of adaptation. Intuitively, they sought ways to fit into the economic crevices of a new host society. Importantly, they knew that they belonged to a group that had a separate identity in the Old World and could continue to have one in the New. Those wandering Jews arrived in America with limited skills, in turmoil from leaving their closed worlds of isolated Jewish communities. Almost all of them, and especially those who went to Bangor, were from the enlarged lower class of Russian Jewry. Often they came alone, even as young as thirteen or fourteen years old. Yet they were committed to bringing their families to America despite the horrors of traveling across Europe and the Atlantic in the inexpensive but sickening closeness of steerage. Wives, children, sisters and brothers, mothers and fathers were needed in America: this was an emigration of a people for posterity, not for an interlude.

In America, the Jews first entered the turbulent, compressed currents of the East Coast ghettos in New York and Boston. Some of the immigrants restlessly broke away again, blown by the winds of chance, rumor or family ties. A few heard flimsy tales of work in Bangor, a small, thriving Maine city. Others followed the jagged tracks of family, friends and acquaintances who had already made their way to the city.

The Jews who went to Maine were few in number. Between 1890 and 1910, only 1,835 Jewish immigrants moved to Maine. Their numbers were minuscule compared to those who went to three other states in the East: 66,023 Jewish immigrants settled in Massachusetts; 108,534 in Pennsylvania and 690,291 in New York. Between 1899 and 1920, 1,074,442 Jews constituted 11.2 percent of all immigrants. Considerably larger in number than the 439,724 Irish, the Jewish immigrants were exceeded only by the 2,000,000 Italians.

When the eastern-European Jewish immigrants came to Bangor, they settled in a city that had had limited but positive experiences with two groups of German Jewish immigrants. The German Jews who had settled throughout America in the 1840's differed markedly from the Russian Jews who came fifty years later. The historian Paul Johnson wrote that those German Jewish immigrants were "liberal, optimistic, sober, rational, patriotic and unostentatious and highly respectable." They were also relatively few in number, part of the 150,000 Jews in America in 1850. Bangor's group, which had come in the 1840's, consisted of a small number of dry-goods merchants, peddlers and tailors. Immediately and ambitiously they tended to their Orthodox Jewish needs by establishing a synagogue, Ahawas Achim ("Brotherly Love"), with approximately thirty members.

From their meticulous minutes written in German, it is known that the congregation received a charter from the city in 1849, established the burial ground on Webster Avenue as a permanent legacy to the Jewish community, employed a shohet for the proper ritual slaughter of animals, planned for a school with instruction in German, English and Hebrew, discussed building a mikveh (ritual bath) and prepared for the time when they might need to disband. That moment came in the late 1850's, when Bangor's economy soured. The Jewish community dispersed, and its few sacred ritual objects, including a Sepher Torah, were sent to Boston for safekeeping.

When Bangor again prospered in the 1860's and 1870's, another set of German Jewish immigrants came to the city, among them Julius Waterman, William Engel and Louis Kirstein. Although they came as peddlers, they soon started building careers that would place them in eminent positions. Engel, the only Jewish immigrant to go into the timber business, became a lumber baron and mayor of the city. Kirstein went into insurance and real estate, and developed two new residential areas of the city, Little City and Fairmount. Waterman opened one of Bangor's most successful men and boys' clothing shops and became an officer of the Board of Trade. The German Jews were included in the social life of the Protestant middle and upper classes by participating in the social activities of the Board of Trade, and their entertaining and travels were reported in the social columns of the newspapers.

They were also generous to the city. In 1896, when the new Palm Street School was established, the *Commercial* called for private gifts to complete the school. Julius Waterman donated a large American flag. The paper acknowledged the gift, calling Waterman one of the "warmest friends of liberal education" who believed in encouraging "the principles of patriotism in the hearts of youth." Waterman's biggest and most appreciated acts of generosity started in 1897 and lasted several years. He treated all Bangor boys—over one thousand of them in 1903—to a day, at his expense, at Riverside Park, the amusement park at the end of the electric trolley line in Hampden. The *Commercial* described the annual event in great detail.

Much at ease with Bangor's upper social and economic class, the second wave of German Jews made only meager attempts to identify themselves as religious Jews. They did revive Ahawas Achim in 1874 by bringing back the ritual objects from Boston and adding to the original synagogue minutes, but their record keeping was as minimal as their religious practice was problematic. Each year the small group, numbering no more than ten people from Bangor, Ellsworth and Bar Harbor, hired a hall for celebrating the New Year and the Day of Atonement. Although they took responsibility for the Webster Avenue cemetery, they made no efforts to attract other German Jews to the city.

Thus the first group of German Jews, who arrived in the 1840's, disappeared by leaving the city during the economic reversals of the late 1850's. The second group, coming in the 1860's and 1870's, disappeared as Jews while staying in the city. This they did by means of intermarriage, conversion, or by not marrying at all. In her study of the formation of the Bangor Jewish community, Lucille Epstein traced ten members of the second generation of German Jews. Six were living in Bangor at the time of her study. Five were unmarried and one was married to a non-Jew. Three of the six had converted. Four other German Jews had moved from Bangor. Three of them married Jews of "comparable economic and social status," and one married a Gentile.

Little is known of the interaction between the German and Russian Jews, although the new immigrants, indubitably, admired the success of the established German Jews. According to Epstein's study, the German Jews had an attitude of "benevolent interest and protection" toward the later arrivals, offering guidance and extending credit.

> On one occasion a Russian Jewish peddler made an attempt to board a train leaving Bangor. With him he carried, of course, his peddler's pack of dry goods which he intended to sell in some other part of the state. The conductor of the train refused to allow him to board because of his excess baggage, and the peddler, bewildered and insecure, turned to leave the station. Coincidentally, a well-established older Jewish resident of Eastern German origin happened along at the station. He saw what had happened, and although he had not known the peddler, heretofore, he immediately used his influence with the railroad authorities to regain passage for him.

Acts of generosity and kindness notwithstanding, the Russian Jewish immigrants had to establish their own forms for safeguarding the past and adapting to the native Protestant society. Bangor's earliest Russian Jewish immigrants, such as Ezriel Lemke Allen, Nathan Cohen, Jacob Altman, Joseph Byer, Joe Bernstein, Hyman Epstein and Simon Kominsky, started rebuilding their lives out of scraps and tiny beginnings.

Survival and work were the first tasks to face. With few skills and no capital, the Russian Jews peddled among Gentiles in the city or at country farms, traveling by foot with packs on their backs. They bought or exchanged whatever they could carry: trinkets, needles, lotions, matches, clothing, threads, pots and pans, leftover fabric, buttons or tops from sardine cans. With piecemeal success they obtained carts and horses. Sylvia Alpert Duze described the arduous daily existence of her father, Israel Alpert, when he worked as a peddler around 1910:

My father had a team and a horse and he went to homes and commercial areas where he bought up scrap metals which he in turn sold to junk yards. Papa got up very early in the morning. In the winter he had to stoke the furnace, add enough coal to last all day, and build up a good fire in the stove. He also shoveled snow and took care of the horse before hitching him to the team, and made sure his family was set for the day before leaving for outlying areas to buy and sell as he went along. In the winter he left before dawn and returned after dark. He was a small slim man, barely five feet tall, and how he handled all those heavy metal parts by himself, I'll never understand. The side of the wagon used by my father in his business had the name of its former owner, "Bunker," on it. Not knowing his real name, everyone who did business with him called him Billy or Eddie Bunker.

Five days a week and every week of the year, except for Jewish holidays, the peddlers went out from Bangor in Maine's harsh winter days and the warmer months of late spring, summer and early fall. They walked on the dirt roads, trekking up and down long hills, looking for farmhouses placed on tidy strips of cleared land. Often screened sedately behind a straight line of planted maples or oaks, the small white houses stood in the peaceful and lonely landscape.

The farm wives looked out onto the quiet roads with mixed feelings of anticipation and dread: they welcomed the peddler carrying needed goods but they feared the odd-looking, undernourished, foreign-speaking stranger. Lura Beam, the Maine-born sociologist, wrote about the unnerving differences between the Yankee peddlers and immigrants. The Yankee might be invited to dinner, she wrote, "a familiarity possible only because his town was known, he drove through annually, and he was entertaining." But "the rag man was on a lower social rung. He was vaguely dark, a foreigner from no-one-knew-where; he was never offered hospitality. He was greedy over the rag-bag which hung in the wood shed, a huge calico bag stuffed with all the worn-out clothes not good enough for rug making. He took the year's rags and paid in two tin dippers."

While Beam's family and village recoiled from the Jewish

peddler, he was received with cautious tolerance in many other hamlets and farms. At first, the peddler was usually housed in the barn for twenty-five cents a night; over time, with regular visits he might be allowed to stay in a room in the farmhouse. Most peddlers ate little and kept strictly kosher, carrying fruit, bread and kosher salami. Some shared tea or potatoes with the farm family. After being on the road from Sunday to Thursday evening, they returned back to Bangor for Friday-evening Sabbath observance.

The farmers helped the peddlers in many ways: by trading, by increasing the immigrants' knowledge of English, and by building special friendships which often lasted many years. Some farmers also helped in speeding the naturalization process, a requirement for getting a legal peddler's license, which cost between $10 and $25. Often Bangor immigrants sought out a special judge in Ellsworth who was reputed to be lenient on the residency requirements. One of the Jewish peddlers, a young immigrant boy, asked a few farmers with whom he stayed on the road to appear as witnesses for him. By producing worn tablecloths to show how long he had been selling to the farmers, they stretched the truth about his time in Maine and the United States.

Bangor's Jews followed the typical economic patterns of other Jews throughout the Northeast. Slowly, the Bangor immigrants accumulated enough capital to establish little dry-goods, clothing or confectionery stores. Some became shoemakers or tailors, and a few began working in the sawmills and harvesting ice. The economic difficulties of the petty entrepreneurs were apparent early. Sometimes, the immigrants piled up too many debts. The *Commercial* reported that Isaac Goldsmith, "a dealer in clothing, which he sells upon the road outside of Bangor," owed $2,000 to Bangor merchants. He had "extensive dealings with Bangor firms who have found him full of integrity and business sense." Those qualities, however, did not prevent him from expanding too fast and using the same real estate as a mortgage for several different creditors.

In the 1890's, at least half of the Jewish immigrants lived in the areas between Spruce, Broad, State and Washington streets, in small, run-down houses sited on tiny plots. Their homes were among the boardinghouses where the lumbermen spent time when they came in from the woods and near the clothing stores and saloons where they spent their money. The Jews lived amid the other displaced and disoriented immigrants—Italians, Irish, Syrians, Tucks, Finns and Russians. Slowly, and with unrelenting effort, the Jews began to buy houses, mostly from the Irish immigrants. Sometimes, they established stores on the first floor, lived on the second floor, rented apartments on the third, and acquired cows, chickens and horses, which were placed in the backyard. Others, such as the large Cohen and Epstein clans, settled in the 1890's in a better neighborhood, on Essex Street, over a mile away from the Penobscot River.

What inspired the immigrants' heroic efforts at self-preservation and self-improvement? Above all, the Jews welcomed the miraculous differences between the New World and the Old. There were no fears of wars and extended army service, no pogroms and no massacres. There were no legal restrictions on occupations or on residential opportunities. Work in and around the city was hard, but the Jews were no longer immobilized at the bottom of an economic system as they had been in Russia. There were no limitations on their hopes in the free, enterprising, democratic air. No longer did the Jews have to tax themselves and provide singlehandedly for their education. In Bangor, the Jews did not need to set up their own welfare institutions, such as orphanages, old age homes or hospitals.

The immigrants found an environment and a climate that was similar to that of Russia: a landscape of forests, rivers and farms beyond the city; cold winters with frost thickly layered on the windows and warm summers with masses of flies blocking the sunlight into their houses. The lumbermen, with whom the Jews did most of their business, were in many ways similar to the peasants they had left behind in eastern Europe: rough-living, sometimes hard-drinking, and of a different religion from the Jews.

The immigrant Jews struggled through the process of "ruthless underconsumption" to move slowly up the economic ladder. While they ate little and rested less, except on the Sabbath, they always looked for opportunities they had never had before. Month by month, year by year, usually taking from two to seven years, they conserved enough money to bring over the rest of their families. The stingy living and the deprivations made possible the slow accretion of family, relations and friends, allowing the small Bangor community to re-create a viable religious world.

In Bangor, the immigrants looked longingly for a new balance to their lives—one that inevitably loosened the ties to the old language and religion. The task of remaining Jews while securing the respect of their American-educated children and the larger Gentile community was not easy. The immigrants learned to survive the discomfort of the greenhorn image. One young boy, using rudimentary English when he wanted to stay over at a farmhouse, wrote on a sign: "Can I sleep with you?" The same boy, only fifteen years old, was mortified by his ignorance of social customs. Unfamiliar with the practice of setting the plates face down to await the next meal, at supper he placed his food on a plate turned upside down.

According to Epstein's study, the Jews were often treated with "sheer curiosity." One immigrant recounted that in Bangor "people on the street used to stare at his boots, perhaps snicker at the pack he carried on his back, but never failed to ask him ... about life in Russia, the Czar's policies, or the meaning of some ancient religious custom of the Jews." The questions were not unfriendly, but the "immigrant became increasingly self-conscious."

John Higham, a historian of immigration, wrote that the English settlers, the ancestors of most members of Bangor's middle and upper classes, considered themselves founders, not immigrants, in America. "Theirs was the polity, the language, the patterns of work and settlement and many of the mental habits to which the immigrants would have to adjust." In Bangor, the opportunities to meet Gentile culture came faster than in the larger urban areas. Concomitantly, there was a stronger tendency to fashion manners, attitudes, inflections, dress and social habits to follow the new ways.

Bangor's small Jewish population faced conditions markedly different from those of their counterparts in Boston and New York. For Bangor's fifty-seven Jewish families in 1899, there was no ghetto. There were no groups of foreigners or ethnic walls to break through to get to the native economy. In New York or Boston, once the Jews stepped beyond their own community, they did not find the native Protestant middle class but the Irish who had arrived before the Jews or the Italians who came at the same time.

How did Bangor's upper and middle classes regard the Jewish influx? In the 1890's, when unflattering stereotyped images of Jews, black Americans, Italians and Irish were an accepted part of public discourse, ethnic groups were treated with curiosity, amusement and insensitivity that would become publicly intolerable in a later time. Stereotypes evident in the press, literature and on the stage, did not usually denote serious anti-Semitism. But as Oscar Handlin has written, they "made Americans acquainted with a distinctive pattern of physical features, clothing, forms of expression and language associated with the Jews. Most important, it ascribed to that figure a pervasive concern with money."

An item in the *Commercial* in 1890 included a full menu of stereotyped images: "Lazarus Goldstein—I love your daughter and would like to marry her. Isidore Goldfogle—You may have her, my poy. Mit Rebecca, who is 16 years old, I give $5,000, mit Sarah, who is 24, $10,000, mit Loweza, who is 30, $25,000. Vich one do you vant? Goldstein—Haven't you von about 40?" William Pattangall, when writing about F. Marion Simpson, a political figure Pattangall little respected, referred to a nasty exchange of accusations between two Maine newspaper editors. One reported about a "masked ball, giving the name of each of those present" and closed the account as follows: "Frank Dingley, Jew peddler, no mask." Pattangall added that had Simpson been at the ball, one could have written of him: "Political failure. No mask." Camouflage would have been equally ineffective for the Jew and the politician.

Stereotypes aside, the Bangor newspapers wrote about the religious practices and celebrations of the Russian Jewish population with curiosity, interest and respect. The Jews were treated as uniquely biblical "exotica" and received a degree of attention not given to the Greeks, Irish or Italians. Religion provided the only way to connect with the Jews, other than through business relations.

Unlike Bangor's few German Jews, the Russian Jews were determined to establish an identity of their own. Those efforts began as early as the 1880's with religious needs: a synagogue to observe the daily and monthly religious calendar; a Chevra Kadisha for the proper burial of the dead; a Jewish cemetery; and shohets (ritual slaughterers) and kosher bakers to adhere to dietary laws. In 1884, the Independent Order of Benjamin was formed and bought a burial ground. Curiously, this one, as well as the one on Webster Avenue, never received official recognition from the city. All city reports listing the number of deaths were divided into only two categories: Protestant and Catholic. Obviously, Bangor's Jews died like everyone else. But how the Jewish deaths were accounted for is not discernible from the official records.

The nucleus of Beth Israel, Maine's first permanent congregation, was organized in the 1880's. A small group borrowed a Sepher Torah from Ohabei Shalom of Boston, the same synagogue that had kept the Torah of Ahawas Achim. In 1888, the formal organization of the synagogue took place. Services were held in people's homes or rented spaces. In 1892, the *Commercial* reported that the New Year was celebrated at çity hall services with Morris Golden, the religious leader of the congregation.

> Rosh Hashonoh, as the Jewish New Year is called, is a time of mutual good will, when all variances are forgotten, for the first day of the new year is the beginning of the ten Penitential days, at the end of which all human beings are supposed to stand in judgment before their creator, and he who seeks pardon for his sins must first forgive those of his fellow beings against him.

The paper further reported that there had been a large attendance and all were "made welcome without regard to their religious belief. . . ." Perhaps with some exaggeration, the report added: "Today many of the other religions have been present and manifested earnest attention during the services."

A year later, the New Year was again heralded by the paper with instructive descriptions about the services. "Wherever Jews are throughout the world, the race observes the holiday. Although the descendants of the children of Israel are widely scattered they never forget their peculiar customs and religious ceremonies." The paper reported about sixty people at the services led by Rabbi Golden, who over the past five years had done much to "unite the Jews in the city." The readings were from the "costly bible," the five books of Moses, written in parchment in Hebrew. "The rabbi and his faithful followers

were in their praying robes, and after the reading was concluded, prayers were said. The rabbi leads and the congregation joins in on certain passages and then they all pray in concert
with a rhythmic swaying motion. . . . One of the most notable
things is the absence of the women in the tabernacle proper.
The women, led by one of their own number, worship in an
adjacent room."

In May 1894, a Hebrew wedding was announced in the
*Commercial* as "a Grand Ceremony." Rabbi Golden would offi-
ciate at the marriage of Annie Goldberg, sister of the tailor
Louis Goldberg, to Max Franklin, "a young man well known in
Hebrew circles." The paper reported that "the services at the
synagogue will be public and those of Mr. Goldberg's friends
who have not received invitations are invited to attend." So
many friends came that some had to stand outside on the street.
Inside, a canopy was held up and the groom appeared. "The
melodious chanting of the rabbi in Hebrew was entirely new to
many of those present and very interesting," the *Commercial*
wrote. The bride entered and a prayer was said for her. Surrounded by two women, she "passed around and around the
groom" and then stood next to him. While little girls stood,
holding lighted candles, "the ceremony proceeded, the rabbi
chanting the service, and occasionally those around him joining
in the final words of a sentence." Following more prayers, both
the bride and groom drank from a glass of wine. "After drinking it was thrown to the floor and crushed beneath the foot of
the groom, which forms a very important part of the ceremony.
The men all wore their hats during the services and at the close
all kissed the bride and groom." The couple received "many
valuable presents."

By 1897, the Jewish community was able to build a permanent synagogue of its own. The board of directors consisted of
Max Cohen, Joseph Byer, Israel Goldman, Lemke Allen, Joe
Bernstein, Harry Cohen, David Snyder and Simon Kominsky.
The congregation bought property on Center Street, reputedly
for $1,000, and hired the architects Hodgins and Packard, de-
signers of the festival auditorium, to draw plans for the building. The cornerstone was laid on August 23, 1897, with Mayor
Joseph F. Snow and F. H. Parkhurst representing the city. According to the newspaper, Rabbi Goldenkop of Bangor led the
prayers in the "Hindoo language." Rabbi Shasher of Boston

spoke, as did Snow and Parkhurst. Snow guided the cornerstone into place. Under the cornerstone were records of the
synagogue and information about the community.

Hodgins and Packard designed a simple, unadorned
wooden synagogue, containing a gallery and basement, raised
double entrance doors and a sanctuary with a pulpit in the
front. The ark, also designed by Hodgins and Packard, was
made by Bangor's fine woodcraftsmen, Morse and Company.
The *Commercial* reported that "in the center, raised by several
feet, is the sacrificial altar." There was seating for several hundred people and a gallery for women. Fifty incandescent lights
were installed, as was steam heat. Under the easterly corner, a
granite stone bore the inscription in English, "Congregation
Beth Israel." On the other side was "a legend in Hebrew characters which have so far defied the utmost attacks of newspaper
reporters."

The dedication of the synagogue took place upon its com-
pletion on December 20, 1897, with one hundred people, including "prominent Gentiles" present. The synagogue was
decorated with "festoons of laurel, lilies, chrysanthemums and
cut flowers in profusion." Pullen's Orchestra played musical
interludes before, during and after the ceremonies. The flowers and music were, of course, a reflection of the way Bangor's
elite celebrated public events.

For the supporters of Beth Israel, it was a moment of glory,
achievement and unaccustomed extravagance. According to the
Bangor tax records for 1897, Joe Bernstein, Morris Golden,
Philip Hillson and Max Cohen each had one horse. Louis Goldberg had $1,350 in real and personal property, Lemke Allen,
$1,600, Simon Kominsky, $405 and Joseph Byer, $115. And
Harry Cohen, Solomon Harris and Morris Rosen had no assets.
Although Beth Israel appealed to wealthy Jews outside the city
to help pay for the $4,000 synagogue, Bangor's Jews relied
overwhelmingly upon their own contributions, as well as a bank
mortgage for the financing.

The newspaper reports of the dedication, the only ones
that survive, give the impression that the Jewish congregation
opened itself to the Gentile community. During the dedication,
however, either the Jews stopped being traditional Jews for two
hours or the Gentiles did not understand what was going on
and used standard reportorial expressions to describe the

event. The *News* stated that "From a Gentile's standpoint the services were differed [*sic*] but little from the ordinary Christian worship. The ceremony was impressive and decorous. The custom of the congregation as well as all connected with the service wearing their headgear seemed rather odd at first but was soon forgotten." The reporter finished off his impressions with a plea for support for the congregation: "The church is still in need of aid and it seems not a great remove from true charity to help a sect who in all sincerity are striving for a suitable place in which to worship in the faith of their fathers."

Like Russian Jews throughout the country, Bangor's Jews would respond to the challenge of being in America in contradictory ways. The community would become both idealistic and narrow, trusting and paranoid, generous and petty, unified and discordant, cohesive while divisive in its emerging class and social differences. It would try to adapt to Bangor's ways, but would keep some ties to eastern Europe and the Lower East Side. Although the Jews would open themselves to broad aspects of Protestant culture, many immigrants would remain fearful of losing their Jewish identity, especially through their children in the second generation.

# CHAPTER 3

# *A Humble Niche*

To THE DISMAY of the Jewish population in 1906, or Hebrews as they were generally called, Abraham Jacobs became a one-day sensation in Bangor. The *Bangor Daily News* appeared with a bold, eye-catching headline: JACOBS DISAPPEARS! POSSIBLE MURDER IN MIDDLE OF NIGHT. The paper presented a tale of neglect, religious conversion, mystery and putative violence. The *News* tried to work its local story, involving Hebrews and Gentiles, into a tale of acute drama and pathos. Excitement built but collapsed within a day. Jacobs and the Bangor Jewish community returned to their customary places, tucked away in a small corner of Bangor's life.

Jacobs, the father of five children, had lived in Bangor for fifteen years. With a loan from the Bangor Building and Loan Association, he had bought a house for his family and boarders. Despite the investment in real estate, the *News* wrote, the family lived in "utmost misery, privation and squalor." Rosa, the fifteen-year-old daughter, ill-clad and ill-fed, nonetheless did her schoolwork with "dogged determination." Sympathetic neighbors and teachers at the Union Square Grammar School had taken heed of her plight. In desperation, Rosa had appealed to her neighbor, Mrs. Samuel Fellows. Mrs. Fellows had fed the child and for three years had let her live in the Fellowses' home in return for domestic service. The Fellowses had also introduced Rosa to the Second Baptist Church.

When it had appeared that Rosa might convert to Christianity, her father had intervened and had castigated Mrs. Fellows. Mrs. Fellows had replied that Rosa was not attending church but the Baptist Sunday School, "a good, pure place," she assured him, "where they make girls respect their elders, and give them good books to read, and teach them to be honest, upright women." The reporter wrote that Jacobs, despite his "quiet, morose manner," understood "American institutions and ways" and had acquiesced in what Mrs. Fellows had said.

The *News,* however, presented Mrs. Jacobs in a vastly different manner. She exemplified "the lowest type of Russian Jew—ignorant, uncouth, saturated with all the prejudices but blessed with none of the virtues of her people." To get Rosa away from the Fellowses' home, Mrs. Jacobs had induced her rich brother from Newark to come to Bangor. Rosa, refusing to be swayed by her uncle's appeals to leave the Fellowses' house, had turned to her father for help. He "took her in his arms in a manner surprising for one of his unemotional race" and had told her, "I am going to protect you."

Then Jacobs disappeared. Although the Jews in the city said Jacobs was in Boston, Chicago, California or St. Johns, New Brunswick, the *News* suggested foul play. One lady informed the paper that Jacobs had been killed, hauled off in a horse-drawn cart in the black of night and hurriedly buried in the Hebrew cemetery beyond Mount Hope. Those Hebrews who knew what had happened pledged themselves to "secrecy," wrote the *News.* The city missionary and neighbors fed the children and, along with Mrs. Fellows, asked the police to investigate the disappearance.

In subdued contrast, the *Commercial,* guided by facts from an informed source in the Jewish community, told a different and tamer tale. The Hebrew community, it reported, was much "excited" by the accusations of foul play. But the foul play was false. Two Bangor Jews had seen Jacobs in Boston.

Jacobs, it was reported, had never been able to make a living in Bangor. With a passion for real estate, he had borrowed money to buy a tenement. The income did not support his family, forcing his wife to take in wash and cook for others. When Rosa had moved in with the Fellowses and had gone to

the Columbia Street Baptist Church Sunday School, the Hebrew community had been deeply concerned. It had tried but
failed to induce Jacobs to interfere with Rosa's Christian education.

Mrs. Jacobs had appealed to her brother in Newark for
help. When he had come to Bangor, he had joined Rabbi Selzer
and Max Cohen, president of Beth Israel, in offering Jacobs
$200 or sufficient goods to start peddling again. When Jacobs
had refused to cooperate, Cohen had threatened to get a warrant against Jacobs for nonsupport of his family. Jacobs had
simply disappeared to avoid arrest. Eventually, he had made his
way to Boston. Dispassionately, the *Commercial* brought the
story to rest: Jacobs had no money, Rosa was well, and her
religion was "something to be settled between her and her relatives." A few months later Jacobs returned to Bangor, rejoined
the Jewish community for Passover and went back to peddling.

The Jacobs episode showed that, with stunning and shocking rapidity, the traditional Jewish life of eastern Europe was
already being turned upside down. Jewish boys and girls were
educated in Bangor's public schools; Jewish families owned
homes in Gentile neighborhoods; Jews secured loans from Gentile institutions; they had easy access to Gentile reporters from
the city's newspapers. Compared to the familiar and tightly
controlled Jewish worlds in the Russian Pale, Bangor's Jewish
community lacked authority and power over its members. Excommunication, humiliation, shame, social isolation and the de-
nial of burial rights were powerful tools of control in eastern
Europe. But they were far less effective in Bangor.

And what did the story reveal about Gentile attitudes toward the new Jewish immigrants? It showed a sharply etched
racial-religious scale of images and stereotypes. Jacobs and his
wife fell heavily on the negative side. She was the "lowest type
of Russian Jew—ignorant, uncouth, saturated with all the prejudices but blessed with none of the virtues of her people."
(Those virtues, whatever they were, remained undefined.) Jacobs, an irresponsible failure, was "unemotional," like his
"race." And the Bangor Jewish community, set apart by religion
and language, seemingly had something to hide when it swore
itself to "secrecy" about mysterious and violent events.

The Jacobs story exposed some of Bangor's firm racial and
religious boundaries, which applied also to Irish Catholics and

blacks. Except for major events, which called forth encomiums from Protestant civic leaders, Bangor's two thousand Catholics also lived in their separate religious and ethnic worlds. Like the twenty-fifth anniversary of Rev. Edward McSweeney's ordination, the fiftieth anniversary of the founding of St. John's Church, celebrated in 1906, was an occasion when attendants "breathed in an atmosphere of religious indulgence and religious brotherhood." The whole city celebrated the growth of the Catholic community: the building of the church in 1856; the addition of twenty beautiful stained glass windows in the 1880's; the installation of the bell that tolled over the riverfront; and the establishment of religious schools and residences. No one recalled, however, that anti-Catholic feelings had prevented St. John's from building a school on Broadway in the 1840's. Nor was mention made of the strong strains of social superiority that Bangor's Protestant community harbored decade after decade.

While Catholics held a conspicuous but separate place in the city, Bangor's small black population was unobtrusive. The city, still moved by Civil War memories, was receptive to campaigns to aid victims of antiblack violence and injustice in the South. But Bangor clearly held to stereotypes that were frivolous, insensitive and humiliating. An advertisement for safes in the *Bangor Business Directory* in 1901 showed a picture of a black boy, the large whites of his eyes turned upward and a wide grin on his face. "ALL COONS LOOK ALIKE to some people—the same might be said of safes."

When a black baseball team from Philadelphia routed Bangor's nine, the black players were depicted with huge protruding lips, and the *Commercial* fired off a series of shibboleths: "There was a race war on at Maplewood Monday afternoon and when the smoke of combat had cleared away the colored gemman [*sic*] were discovered to be the whole thing. They had cut a watermelon and thoroughly enjoyed the operation. It was one of the cases when the white man's boasted superiority was not apparent."

The assumed nature of the white man's superiority hardly affected the thinking of Bangor's Jews. They were totally immersed in the arduous tasks of working and rebuilding their lives and communal institutions. After 1900, the Jewish population in Bangor began to grow steadily: from 57 households, including 289 people, to 168 families with 838 individuals in 1910. The numbers were a small reflection of the extraordinary surge of immigrants coming to the United States from eastern Europe.

The *Commercial* took note of the impact of Jews in New York: "The extent to which the city of New York is influenced by its Hebrew population is little realized by Americans who do not live within that city. . . . All attempts to restrict communities and keep Hebrews out have been abandoned. The only way that any Christian congregation could get out of a Jewish neighborhood would be to remove from the city altogether." Jews uptown and downtown are "well-bred and well-behaved beyond anything Christians dreamed concerning them."

The area around Hancock Street was Bangor's equivalent of New York's Lower East Side. Only half of the Jews lived there in 1899, but by 1910, it was the home of 70 percent of the city's Jewish immigrants. Marriages within the small Orthodox community pulled together intricate familial webs. Weddings were grand occasions when hundreds of invited guests— sometimes as many as eight hundred—celebrated in a rented hall downtown. Too poor to hire caterers, the immigrants rented dishes and brought food from home. The Epsteins, Cohens, Rosens, Goldens, Kominskys, Striars and Alperts consolidated and reinforced one another. Leaders such as Max Cohen, Myer Minsky, Morris Rosen and Simon Cohen emerged to direct the synagogues and philanthropic organizations.

Slowly, the Jews moved up the economic scale. An occupational profile of the Jews shows that transformation. In 1899 there were thirty-two Jewish peddlers, while only ten Jews worked in clothing and dry-goods stores. Just eleven years later, the economic picture had considerably improved: among the male population, there were fifty-three shopkeepers, sixty-one peddlers, five in manufacturing, and sixteen in clerical occupations. Eighteen were tailors, one was in professional service, nine were skilled laborers, and five were unskilled laborers. In a striking change, many women also worked. There were five woman shopkeepers and ten women in clerical positions.

With apartments in single houses as opposed to compressed rows of city tenements, Bangor's Jews initially lived more comfortably than their counterparts in Boston or New York. They also moved more quickly to buy their own homes, usually from Irish neighbors at a cost of $1,000 to $3,000. However, Bangor's economic opportunities were more limited than those of larger cities. Often, the most restless and entrepreneurial of the Jews moved away.

As petty entrepreneurs, the Jews worked for themselves or for other small businesses. None stayed for long, if at all, working as laborers in Bangor's small industries. As a result, they did not develop outwardly sympathetic views towards labor organizations, and only a few adhered to socialist or radical political doctrines brought from eastern Europe.

The transition from itinerant peddlers to established merchants with stores on Exchange or Broad streets did not escape the notice of Bangor's Gentile population. Various myths about the trading Jew ran through the city as he sold cheap, inexpensive clothing or dry goods to the lumbermen or laboring class. The behavior of the Jewish shopkeepers was a source of fable, wariness and amusement. Vignettes appeared in the papers about Jewish traders trying, and often failing, to outwit their Gentile customers. Drawings of Jews with long, hooked noses were sometimes included.

Incident after incident disclosed the differences between the demonstrative, awkward Jews and their unflappable Yankee neighbors. A reporter from the *News* described pandemonium at the opera house when people rushed to get seats for a show. One incident best illustrated the chaos. "A Hebrew lady, with about a dozen small children, made a charge up the stairs. When the little Ikeys couldn't be drawn through the crowd in the wake that she left, they came over the heads of all through the air. It made no difference how they came, so long as they got into the theatre on time—and they did. In the crush of the woman and her brood the young man who was helping to collect the tickets lost his wits and nearly fell down the stairs."

The distinctive appearance and dress of the poor Orthodox Jews attracted heckling and unpleasant attention. "If you were clean-shaven and dressed in American style, you could walk down any street in the city with complete safety," one immigrant in Bangor stated. "But if you had a beard or a skull cap on your head, that was different." As a result, the Bangor Jews, seeking to adapt, shed the Orthodox insignia of skullcaps worn by men and wigs worn by women.

The *Commercial* reported in 1908 that tensions were high

around Hancock Street where there were fights and brawls among the different nationalities. When a young boy threw a rock through the window of the "Jewish baker," Isaac Dvorin, the matter was brought to municipal court. A reporter wrote: "Hebrew witnesses were greatly excited over the matter and were inclined to wander from the subject. Party politics, payment of taxes and American citizenship figured in their testimony much to the amusement of the large crowd which had gathered in the courtroom to hear the case."

Yet Bangor never knew any violent or sustained anti-Semitism. For the Jewish immigrants, discrimination never blocked low-scale occupational choices or access to most residential areas. The courts worked for Jews and Gentiles alike, as did the expanding school system.

American historians have debated whether the Jewish traditions of Talmudic study and idealization of the religious scholar were responsible for Jewish dedication to educational pursuits. Indisputably, Jewish immigrants valued educational opportunities for their children as the singularly most effective way of realizing the American dream. Emelyn Peck, in *New England Magazine,* described the importance of the public schools for the young Jewish immigrant at the turn of the century. The school, she wrote, "forms the transcendent influence; for it is the centre of his social interest, the open highway of his ambition, and the fountain for his quenchless thirst for the new American ideas."

Immigrant hopes converged with the dedicated fervor of the Bangor teachers who worked during the days and evenings with the foreign population. Mary Spratt, a teacher at the State Street School that served the Jewish section, was primarily responsible for teaching foreign children—nearly two thousand between 1905 and 1920. "Many children have entered my school immediately upon their arrival in this country," she said. "Reaching Bangor on a Friday, perhaps, a little girl comes to me on Monday. One little girl apologized for the dress of a little newcomer who had just arrived because she had worn the dress all the way across the Atlantic."

Appalled that foreign-speaking adults had to pay for private lessons to learn English, Spratt got permission to start free night classes in the State Street School in 1907. She and other teachers worked mostly without pay, aided by volunteers from the Kings Daughters and Athene Club. Finally, in 1912, when there were approximately fifty students, the public school system took over full responsibility for adult education. Spratt taught in a spirit of generosity and solicitude. "There is no way," she said, "by which we can make anyone feel that it is a blessed and splendid thing to be an American, unless we ourselves are aglow with the sacred fire—unless we interpret Americanism by our kindness, our courage, our generosity and our fairness."

As part of their own interpretation of "Americanism," Bangor's Jews used the press to enhance and validate the status of the community. It also sought to display a view of Jewish life which, in fact, was part facade, part wishful thinking, and part exhortation. Beth Israel, the "Jewish church" as it was often referred to in the newspapers and official city publications, sought attention as the only Jewish voice in town. When lay leaders and rabbis—accurately and inaccurately—informed the papers about religious observances, the press gave detailed explanations to the Gentile community. These early forms of news releases served not only as public notices to educate Gentiles but as exhortations to Jews to conform to Orthodoxy.

No other immigrant group enjoyed such coverage. Year after year, Rosh Hashanah, Yom Kippur, Succoth, Chanukah, Passover and Tisha B'Av were described in long explanatory articles. Religious tales were simplified and popularized, rituals were revealed, and religious duty was lauded.

On Rosh Hashanah in 1902, an editorial in the *Commercial* stated that "Bangor citizens may not have noticed for the past two days the companies of Jewish people who have thronged our streets at early morning and late evening wending their way to or from the modest little synagogue of Beth Israel on Center Street. Quiet and orderly they have been, dressed in generally gay attire, red colors predominating, and walking with sedate or gay pace upon the streets." The editorial continued with highlights of Jewish history, ritual and meaning centering on the special Jewish calendar, the blowing of the ram's horn and the obligation to renew "friendships, the forgetting of personal differences of the past and a desire to begin the coming year in the attitude of contrition."

In 1907, the *Commercial* proclaimed the arrival of Yom Kippur with a sense of urgency. "Every Hebrew is expected to lay aside all business cares and all pleasures and spend the 24 hours between sundown of the day preceding and sundown of the day of the feast in fasting and prayer." Notice was given to Jews and Gentiles alike: "Bangor Hebrews will observe the feast to the letter. Every Hebrew's place of business will be closed all day Wednesday and not a sou's worth of business will be transacted."

Kashrut, the Jewish dietary laws, was impressed upon the Jewish and Gentile public through several articles. "There are nearly 600 of the Jewish faith in Bangor all of whom observe the law of their religion with respect to Kosher meat," the *Commercial* announced in 1906. "The orthodox Jewish public . . . depends entirely upon the honesty and 'true faith' of the butcher. That is, if a butcher who stands well in Jewish circles announces on his window that he sells 'Kosher' meat, his word is taken and no attempt is made to verify it." The paper explained that a "schochet" guarantees that meat has been prepared in a procedure that is based on "the most approved scientific and hygienic principles."

According to the *Commercial,* the shohet does not look like a butcher. "Instead, there stands before the beef a figure most commonly slight, bearded, Oriental in his make up." He examines the meat to make certain that the slaughtered animal was healthy in all of its organs. Highly educated and thoroughly versed in religion and theoretical science, the shohet must pass an examination before a rabbinical board. No such body, either in this country or abroad, "ever takes any chances in these men."

The realities about kashrut and other Jewish practices were, in fact, deeply problematic in Bangor. Notwithstanding the article in the *Commercial,* Bangor's Jews, such as Simon Kominsky and S. E. Rudman, frequently and fiercely contested the shohet's authority and skill. Issues of competency caused schisms in Bangor's synagogue life. The rabbinic boards might not have taken any chances with the shohets, but the Bangor Jews disagreed. All too often, a Bangor shohet, who served also as a hazzan (cantor) and mohel (authorized to perform circumcision), was fired for incompetence and negligence. One shohet, a Mr. Rubenovitz, left because he was "grossly insulted" in the "public market." Desperate at one time, members of the synagogue pleaded with a Boston rabbi for help: "Situation is open. Have no meat. Send *shohet* at once."

While the synagogue was at the center of Jewish institutional life, it was no longer the epicenter. The religious strictures of the tight, static Russian Jewish world dissolved in America, and Bangor was no exception. Jewish men in Bangor could not hope to spend their lives exclusively in religious study. Women, who in Russia would have supported and honored their husbands engaged in study, would no longer do so.

Traditional roles for women were also undergoing severe change. In Russia, Jewish women had been excluded from participating in religious services and in a lifelong study of the Talmud. They worshipped separately from men, primarily in Yiddish. Their marriages were arranged by a matchmaker; they endured as many as ten to fifteen pregnancies, often losing several children at birth.

In Bangor, as elsewhere, all of this changed. Ritual observance through the home became the primary source of Jewish identity. It was the locus of domestic rituals of the Sabbath: lighting candles, distinctive Jewish food and Sabbath visiting from family to family for a little cake, tea and a "lump sugar." As rates of infant mortality dropped dramatically along with the number of children women bore, women were less in need of rabbinic authority. Marriages were by choice. Girls received the same secular education as boys.

In this period of intense change and adaptation, it was a constant and arduous effort for Beth Israel to find, hold and pay a rabbi. Between 1900 and 1912, the synagogue succeeded in attracting three rabbis—Louis Selzer, Mordecai Klatchko and Louis Plotkin—pious and learned men who were steeped in traditional Jewish observance, as well as modern Hebrew, and Zionist beliefs. Fresh from Russia, each of the rabbis stayed a few years in Bangor and then moved on to serve other, usually larger, Orthodox congregations in America. In photographs we see them immersed in traditional piety with long beards, top hats, black frocks and formal and severe facial expressions.

Throughout these years, Beth Israel not only had difficulty in ensuring Sabbath observance, since many men felt compelled to work on Saturday, but also had to struggle to meet its financial obligations. At Rosh Hashanah services in 1905, the congregation was informed that those who did not pay their dues and assessments "shall be deemed as not belonging to our chevra either in public or private nor shall they be noticed in any concerns peculiar to the Rites and Ceremonies thereof on any occasion."

Equally difficult was transmitting religious traditions to a recalcitrant second generation. Originally, Jewish boys in Bangor were taught by private tutors. Then in 1902, a Hebrew school started in the basement of one of the public schools. Weekly efforts were made to secure money to pay the Hebrew teachers. Each Sunday Robert Cooper, Philip Hillson and Israel Ratchkovsky went from home to home collecting money. Two years later, the Jewish community bought a house on Carr Street for a Hebrew school. By 1907 there were over eighteen children, including two girls, who studied Torah and Hebrew after public school.

Inevitably, the students resisted the traditional way of learning by rote and the restrictive aura of Old World piety and authoritarian methods of their non-English-speaking teachers and rabbis. "For the most part," Lucille Epstein wrote, "the students learned without understanding and had difficulty in making an adjustment between their public school training and their religious education. The Hebrew school was the institution which clashed most violently with the American institutions with which the second generation came in contact."

With equal inevitability, after 1900, new immigrants arrived adhering to different rituals. Unwilling to give up familiar and traditional forms of prayers and services, these newcomers sought to hold separate services at Beth Israel. When the leaders of the synagogue found the demand intolerable, ten men, including Eli Striar, David Pinchos Striar, Shel David Striar, Sam Gass, Harry Viner and Gimpel Morris started Beth Abraham synagogue. At first, in 1902, they rented rooms for their services. In 1906, they bought a modest wooden house on Carr Street and converted it into a synagogue. The group also bought a burial ground behind Mount Hope Cemetery. The official history of Beth Abraham, written in 1983, succinctly states that from the early years, "little is known about the spiritual leaders of Beth Abraham. Most of them were not ordained Rabbis, but Hazans, Shohets, Mohels or a combination thereof."

The existence of several synagogues is not surprising, given the schismatic nature of Jewish worship and the American proclivity to reorganize whenever disputes arise. Similar splits occurred all over New England and throughout the country—Portland, Maine; Burlington, Vermont; Keene, New Hampshire; and Haverhill, Massachusetts. Often the different synagogues were situated right next to each other, locked into jealousy, suspicion and competition.

To some people in Bangor the divisiveness seemed unnecessary. But given the tensions of immigrant life, Bangor's Jews were expecting the impossible from themselves. Adjusting to a new economy, political system and secular society produced a contentious Jewish community under severe strain. Discord was acceptable within the Jewish community but hardly possible vis-à-vis the host society. Within their own group, the disputatious immigrants would "fight at the drop of nothing," one of them recalled. Differences over ritual observance were magnified precisely because many aspects of Jewish life and identity— dietary laws, language and community control—were under siege.

The Jews in Bangor divided generally along the lines of those who came from Lithuania and Latvia and those from other parts of Russia (Lithuania and Latvia having been annexed by Russia some decades before). The Lithuanians—the "Litvishe" or "Litvaks"—tended to become shopkeepers and professionals and liked to think of themselves as superior to the newly arrived "Russishe." In fact, though the Russians were poorer and possibly less educated in Jewish learning, they carried deep strains of Hasidic influence and were hardly less religious than the Lithuanians. The differences over ritual merged easily into issues of class, authority and power, superiority and inferiority, acceptance and rejection. The joke about the Jew stranded on an island by himself has a deep ring of truth for Bangor. When he built two synagogues just for himself, he proudly reasoned that he needed both: one was the shul he went to and one was the shul that he wouldn't go to.

The Jewish community transcended its religious differences and united in philanthropic, educational and fraternal organizations that provided social activities as well as health and death benefits. Some of the organizations were short-lived, such as the Independent Order of Benjamin and the Young Men's

Hebrew Association; some, such as the B'nai B'rith Pine Tree Lodge and Young Judea, lasted for many years.

Looking to Bangor's established fraternal organizations, the Jews also organized Jewish units, such as the Zion Lodge of the Modern Woodmen, since, for many years, the Gentile counterparts did not invite Jewish membership. Emulating Gentile organizations was considered a satisfactory alternative. A few men, such as Max Cohen and Myer Minsky, first became Masons in Brownville and then, years later, in Bangor. Initially, organizations in the smaller towns were more receptive to Jewish members than was Bangor.

The Jewish community also united fervently in support of Zionism and relief activities to aid the Jewish masses left behind in Russia. The activities connected Bangor's Jews to national organizations and national issues. Year after year, under the leadership of Myer Minsky, Bangor's Zionists brought in speakers from outside the city to lead meetings dedicated to fund raising and Zionist education. One such speaker, Julius Meyer, the president of the Boston Zionist Council, spoke in 1908 about the precarious situation of Russian Jews. Emigrating to Europe and America, he said, would not be the answer to the Russian problem. "Even in this country," Meyer maintained, "a slight prejudice often exists against our people, which is showing itself in the restrictive immigration laws which have been proposed in Congress."

The anti-immigrant sentiment to which Meyer referred had little impact on Bangor. Nationally, however, it generated an intense debate between restrictionists and American Jewish leaders. The restrictionists regarded the "new" immigrants from eastern and southern Europe as racially, economically and socially inferior to the "old" immigrants from northern and western Europe.

The *Commercial* reported on the findings of Prof. William Z. Ripley of Harvard, author of *The Races of Europe*. In part the headlines read: FOREIGNERS OUTBREED US, FUTURE AMERICANS WILL BE SHORT, DARK AND BROAD HEADED—ENGLISH TYPE GOING. Ripley concluded that the Yankee type would disappear as had the buffalo and Indian. "The United States is not a 'melting pot' as Israel Zangwill has termed it, so much as it is a great uncooked or half-cooked racial stew to which the various ethnic elements are still in an unblended state." Unlike many of his fellow restrictionists, Ripley was not totally dismayed about America's future. "Even if the Anglo-Saxon stock be physically inundated by the engulfing flood," he concluded, "the torch of its civilization and ideals may continue to illuminate the way."

Senator Henry Cabot Lodge of Massachusetts, fearing racial and political corruption, led the campaign to raise effective legislative barriers. To end America's traditional acceptance of nearly all European immigrants (severe restrictions already applied to Orientals), Lodge sought first to bar all illiterate persons. The senator gained considerable support and public recognition when a congressional study, undertaken by the Dillingham Commission, was made public in 1910. Confirming the concerns and assumptions of the restrictionists, the study supported the literacy test; endorsed the validity of eugenics, the tool of racial categorization; and pronounced the racial superiority of the old immigrants and the inferiority of the new ones.

Congressional action lagged well behind the accelerating process of social and economic discrimination. Many native Americans took refuge in exclusive academic institutions, high-status professions, and resorts and clubs which did not welcome Jews. Where both German and Russian Jews were concentrated in large cities, discriminatory patterns were the most severe. John Higham, a historian of American immigration, determined that social and economic changes in the Gilded Age—beyond the unsettling aspects of massive immigration—caused "status panic." American society, subject to urbanization, industrialization and unsettling mobility (both up and down the social and economic ladder) needed new status lines. Beliefs in the primacy of the Anglo-Saxon past, genealogical purity, and the political, cultural and physical inferiority of the new immigrants offered a means of reforming and stabilizing the social hierarchy around the turn of the century.

Struggling as peddlers and small merchants, Bangor's Jews had little occasion to worry about the new economic and social restrictions. Instead, their concern over anti-Semitism jumped across the East Coast to eastern Europe. The frightful pogroms at Kishinev, Bialystok and other Russian cities, which were compared by the *Commercial* to the "blackest deeds of Nero's regime," prompted a swift and outspoken reaction in Bangor as well as other communities of American Jews. In 1903 and 1905,

leading Jewish philanthropists—Jacob H. Schiff, Jacob Seligman, Adolph Lewisohn and what the *Commercial* called "a committee of Hebrew bankers and merchants"—led the outcry and
raised relief funds. In 1905, the group met with Sergius Witte,
Russia's delegate to the Russo-Japanese peace conference in
Portsmouth, New Hampshire. They told him "that the million
or more Russian Jews who have come to the United States have
become good citizens, notwithstanding their sudden emergence
from the greatest darkness into the most intense daylight of
political and civil liberty, and that they have shown themselves
entirely equal to the responsibilities which have been placed
upon them as citizens of this great republic."

Reportedly, Schiff, the famous Jewish philanthropist who
had visited Bangor on several occasions when he summered
in Bar Harbor, asked Max Cohen to raise relief funds. In any
case, the Bangor Jewry organized a Central Committee for the
Russian Jews and held mass meetings that brought together
most of Bangor Jewry as well as a few sympathetic Gentiles. "A
Jewish rabbi," it was reported, "speaking from the pulpit and
almost sobbing forth the soul cry of his down-trodden race in
Russia, was the spectacle which presented itself to a large
audience."

Did that gathering include any of Bangor's German Jews?
Most probably not. Amid all the seething action of Bangor's
Russian Jewish community, Julius Waterman, Louis Kirstein,
William Engel and the handful of other German Jews continued to belong only in a nominal way to their nearly defunct
Ahawas Achim synagogue and to maintain the Webster Avenue
cemetery. To the minute book, so meticulously begun in the
1840's, they added skimpy data about infrequent meetings, tiny
assessments for caring for the cemetery and sporadic observance of the high holidays, Rosh Hashanah and Yom Kippur.
Disinclination, surely not a lack of money, was at the heart of
their failure to maintain any religious practices.

Their immigrant roots, however, did not escape public notice. Before Engel served his one term as mayor of the city,
William Pattangall, in his nominating speech, made oblique reference to Engel's immigrant past. "I have as little reverence for
wealth as any other man in America," Pattangall said, but "nothing but admiration for the man who by his cunning hand, the
breadth of his brain and by his own ability, industry and

strength of character, rises from a humble station to affluence and prominence."

Although Engel, Kirstein and Waterman could never serve as religious models, they did demonstrate the rich promise of success, mobility and acceptance into the Gentile middle and upper classes. It would be many decades, however, before any of the Russian Jews would attain comparable affluence and stature in Bangor. In the first years of the twentieth century, they were still in their "humble station."

# CHAPTER 4

# *Converging Worlds*

IN THE EARLY SPRING of 1911, three perilously warm and dry weeks created the potential for catastrophe in Bangor. On the afternoon of April 30, a small fire started in a hay shed downtown on Broad Street, and strong winds caused it to spread. Suddenly, "blazing brands, sticky torches of tarred paper and sparks blew across Kenduskeag Stream and started fires in the great broadside of modern structures, in half a dozen places all at once—almost half a mile run from the first fire."

Unpredictably and uncontrollably, flames flew to the Universalist church and started feeding on one building after another on Exchange and State streets. When the seven-story Morse-Oliver Building came crashing down, the fire moved to East Market Square, up Park Street and on to Harlow Street, razing the central fire station, Windsor Hotel and the public high school. The post office burned and with it $100,000 stored in so-called fireproof vaults. The Tarratine Club was saved, but the fire lurched up the hill to the west side of Broadway, destroying more and more houses. Beth Israel Synagogue fell in the fire's path, as did Central Church and St. John's Episcopal Church. Hour after hour, well into the night, the fire continued. Light from the inferno of a city, now without electricity, gas or water, except to fight the fires, was seen eighty-five miles southwest in Brunswick.

After the fires were finally stopped, the tragic count began. There were two deaths and many injuries. Three hundred and eighty-five buildings, including 289 homes—from the shabbiest to the finest in the city—and nearly a hundred businesses were consumed. Many of Bangor's most important civic and religious buildings were destroyed: Norumbega Hall, the high school, the post office, customhouse and courthouse, the central fire station, six churches and one synagogue. The public library with seventy thousand volumes was gone. The entire collection of the Bangor Historical Society disappeared: Indian artifacts, photographs, Indian jewelry, letters, books, journals, surveys, pamphlets, business records, deeds, surveys, newspapers, lawbooks, guns, uniforms, paintings, minutes of meetings, music, maps, club records, speeches, magazines, genealogical charts, and engravings. The University of Maine Law School and its library were in ruins. Innumerable old trees burned on the residential streets, especially on French Street and the west side of Broadway.

Adolph B. Friedman, who tried to save the "Sefer Torahs and other holy books," described the last moments before Beth Israel was destroyed. He saw Tom Gibbons, a lineman, rush into the "synagogue to dynamite it as a barricade to the advancing flames. . . ." The lineman "hauled himself through a cellar window with half a dozen sticks of dynamite in one hand and the fuses draped over his arm. In a matter of seconds there was a muffled explosion inside and the building collapsed like a house of cards."

Firefighters came from cities and towns all over Maine to end the conflagration. Despite the magnitude of destruction, there was no panic, rioting or unruliness. Four hundred and fifty soldiers and policemen were quickly brought in to patrol the devastated areas. For the first time, the police chief called for soldiers from G Company of the National Guard.

Ever sensitive to its reputation in the rest of the country, Bangor was shocked at the sensational and false descriptions that appeared in newspapers throughout New England. With great headlines, Boston papers called Bangor stricken and paralyzed. Untrue! The conflagration was a calamity, but Bangor was never immobilized or completely disabled, although it lost

$3,600,000—one-eighth of its property valuation in the fire—
and recovered only $2,000,000 in insurance. Fifty thousand
dollars was quickly raised for the relief of victims. Reacting
swiftly, local businessmen fought off vulturous retail invaders
from other cities who tried to grab sales out of the devastation.
Temporary buildings were erected for local merchants to carry
on their businesses—not one of which failed to resume opera-
tions.

Bangor handled the fire with imperturbability and courage. Mary Robinson, Dr. Daniel Arthur Robinson's sister, saw
her church, the First Congregational, burn and then the high
school where she went as a child and now taught. "I walked
home," she remembered, "in darkness to which the still burn-
ing fire added some light, waked mother who had peacefully
gone to bed and to sleep and reported what I had seen. She
made the obvious remark that there would be no school next
day and resumed her slumber. Mother didn't believe in getting
worked up over something you couldn't help."

The fire presented challenges and opportunities that
would previously have been unthinkable. Mayor Charles
Mullen promptly appointed a special committee consisting of
Phillip Coombs, the city engineer, John P. Frawley, a druggist,
and Franklin E. Bragg of the N. H. Bragg company. The Committee on Civic Improvement hired Warren Manning, a Boston
architect, landscape designer and a founder of the American
Institute of Landscape Architects and, just one month after the
fire, boldly presented its recommendations to the public and
the city government.

In its most radical proposals, the committee called upon
the city to purchase property in the burned-out district, develop a broad avenue of civic buildings consisting of a new
library, high school and federal building, and create a waterfront park and promenade with "business frontage" along the
Kenduskeag Stream. Through impressionistic sketches, Manning suggested an aura of Venetian elegance, unified through
classically styled buildings set back from the Kenduskeag. The
model was European. The justification was rebuilding a city of
commercial vitality on the foundations of refinement, culture
and beauty. The hope was visionary: "You can make your city,"
the report stated, "one of the most beautiful in the world, and
this well within your means. . . . You have made Bangor well

known as a musical center. Why not make it better known as a center of city and country beauty and of good city planning."

Unexpectedly, Beth Israel was the first to respond to the plan. Before a citywide debate split Bangor into opposing camps, synagogue leaders adopted Manning's European vision and rehired Victor Hodgins, the Bangor-based architect of its first synagogue, to design a new building in an appropriate style. Synagogue members now wanted a building with a dome, ornamental columns, large windows and a handsome entranceway.

The congregation bought a piece of property at the opposite end of York Street from St. John's Catholic Church. The new location, overlooking the Penobscot River, placed Beth Israel in the heart of the residential community of Orthodox Jews. While dominated by the graceful spire of St. John's, the synagogue itself would tower over its immediate neighborhood. Soon after the purchase, Beth Israel proudly presented Hodgins's plan in the *Commercial*: "The members of the congregation Beth Israel . . . are to build a new synagogue . . . which will be one of the most attractive church edifices in the city. . . ." Hodgins envisioned a lofty, imposing and highly detailed synagogue in Corinthian style, with four large terra-cotta columns flanking three arched doors and windows.

While Beth Israel seemed to be moving confidently toward erecting its new synagogue, Bangor embarked on a contentious debate over aesthetics, costs and architectural styles in rebuilding the remainder of the city. A series of mass meetings revealed the factions and spelled out the issues: immediate, unfettered rebuilding by property owners versus a planned redevelopment controlled, in part, by the city government. The objectives of the Committee on Civic Improvement found instant allies among Mayor Mullen, the Twentieth Century Club, the Federation of Women's Clubs (representing over five hundred women), the Bangor Theological Seminary and former mayor Beal. Joseph Bass, publisher of the *Commercial*, led the outspoken opposition of many of Bangor's businessmen. Repeatedly, Bass warned that the proposals would mean higher taxes, would curtail building activity and would cause financial burdens for future generations.

Despite traditional political and social impediments to participation, many women eagerly engaged in the controversy.

When a hearing was scheduled in the city hall auditorium, it was announced that "the balcony will be reserved for ladies and their escorts—although it will be entirely proper for ladies to attend without escorts." According to the *News*, this meant that while the ladies were seated in the balcony, the "brains and brawn of the city" were on the main floor. An overwhelming vote of approval for the Civic Improvement Committee plan occurred in early June, and a few days later, the city council endorsed the plan, including a $250,000 bond issue to cover the expenditures. Construction immediately started on commercial blocks with the expectation that banks, the post office and federal building, the library and several theaters would soon follow. By October 1911, forty houses had been constructed. At a slower pace, many of the churches were rebuilt, including the First Baptist and St. John's Episcopal. Central Church and First Congregational Church merged to build All Souls, which was completed in 1912 and 1913.

Bangor continued its tradition of using many fine architects. Some, such as Wilfred E. Mansur, C. Parker Crowell and Victor Hodgins, were Bangor-based. Others, such as Jardine, Kent and Hill, Carrere and Hastings, Warren Manning, and Peabody and Sterns, came from New York and Boston. Nonetheless, Mansur, who had achieved national recognition when he was elected to the American Institute of Architects in 1901, remained the most prominent.

The new high school, designed in a plain, classical idiom, was built to accommodate over nine hundred students. The new library and historical society, adjacent to the high school, had a more ambitiously detailed classical style, with a dome, a brick and granite facade, and finely detailed windows. Both structures, designed by Peabody and Sterns, were placed next to each other on the east side of Harlow Street to form Bangor's most impressive public statement of civic commitment and adherence to the city beautiful. Manning had originally envisioned the two buildings as more grand than they turned out to be. He had also designed gardens and detailed landscaping for the library and had hoped to open the area across Harlow Street down to the Kenduskeag Stream to lend scenic splendor.

This was but one of many ways in which Manning's grand visions faded away under financial pressures and differences over aesthetics and urban design. In fact, one of the very first signs of disaffection came from Beth Israel. As Joseph Bass and his supporters subjected Manning's ideas to attack and ridicule, the synagogue summarily dropped Hodgins as its architect along with his distinctive classical design.

In late June, Beth Israel announced, for the second time, that it would rebuild its synagogue, this time with Henry Lewen, a New York engineer and designer of fireproof structures, as architect. A month after the fire, Lewen had arrived in Bangor promoting his patents. In a city acutely sensitive to the need of fireproof structures, Lewen placed a major advertisement in the *Bangor Daily News* on June 1. Then he waited for business to come his way. Beth Israel responded first. (The Keith cinema followed soon thereafter.) The new synagogue would be constructed of fireproof, reinforced concrete in a unique pastiche of many influences: Byzantine, classic, and art nouveau. With a dome extending fifty-two feet high, the synagogue attained the height and dominance that its leaders desired. Lewen proudly maintained that his minaret-style dome with twisting columns was "something absolutely new in this country."

In a development of far greater significance to Manning's goals, the proposed setbacks on the Kenduskeag Stream were soon ignored. Building after building was placed at the edge of the water and any commitment to urban planning and architectural excellence was forgotten. The new Bangor, except for its line of civic buildings, looked much the same as it had in the late nineteenth century. Those who supported Manning's idea for redesigning and landscaping the area around Kenduskeag Stream focused on creating the Norumbega-Kenduskeag promenade and park. Within two years after the fire, the Citizens League, headed by Charles Bartlett, and the Bangor Federation of Women's Clubs raised $12,000 to purchase the land formerly occupied by Norumbega Hall. But it would take nearly ten years to complete the mall.

Clearly, Bangor businessmen sought to continue their old ways of investing and building at will without government restraints, design guidelines or higher taxes. But the fierce reactions against the 1911 plan may also have reflected strains over the deepening vulnerability of Bangor's economy. Bangor's small-scale industries were facing increasing difficulties with the demise of the shipping industry, reduced logging opera-

tions on the river and the disappearance of the sawmills. In
only one respect was the market unchanged: thousands of laborers still poured into the city, the entry and exit point for
work in the timberlands.

While boosterism remained standard fare at the Chamber
of Commerce, any big dreams had vanished by 1915. No entrepreneurs treated Bangor to visions of hydro-industrial
wealth. No one tried to place the city on the fantasy map of
dramatic economic growth, power and importance. In place of
making power from the river's flow or prodigious manufac-
tured goods, Bangor viewed its economic assets in terms of
trade with the surrounding areas and the high quality of its
residential living.

A year after the fire, the controversy over rebuilding spilled
into demands for political reform. The agitation came from local
issues that meshed into the nationwide Progressive and woman
suffrage movements. Bangor's reformers in 1912 and 1913,
such as Mayor Mullen, Franklin E. Bragg, the Twentieth Century Club and the Bangor Federation of Women's Clubs, had
been among the most prominent supporters of the Committee
on Civic Improvement in 1911. In their new campaign, based
upon Progressive models in Des Moines and St. Paul, the reformers called for a government of five commissioners who would
exercise both legislative and executive responsibilities, replacing
the mayor, councilmen and aldermen elected by individual
wards. The political tools of initiative, referendum and recall
were also proposed to serve as checks on the commissioners. Jobs
would be attained on the basis of merit and examinations.

Mayor Mullen joyfully envisioned the end of the "collection of wards," which he described as one "of diversified interests . . . harmonized by a logrolling legislative body." Among
those "diversified interests" were various ethnic groups who
gained city jobs from political patronage by electing councilmen and aldermen from their communities. The *Commercial,*
the *News,* many business and political leaders, and the immigrants all strongly opposed the reforms. When Mayor Mullen,
a Democrat, ran for reelection in March 1913, he clashed with
Flavius O. Beal, campaigning for his ninth term in office. Beal's
influence carried when he routed the reform proposals, Mullen
and the Democrats.

Just one day before the city rejected Mullen and the reform proposals, he attended the dedication of Beth Israel Synagogue. "For those who duly estimate the happy equality of our religious rights, and the prevailing harmony among our religious sects, the scene was productive of higher emotions," the *News* reporter wrote. "Among the audience and in conspicuous stations on the floor of the building, we observed several members of the Christian clergy and many other distinguished citizens, all manifesting by their presence and demeanor, that, however we may differ upon certain points, the greatest truth is recognized and acted upon, that we are all children of a common and Eternal Father."

The mayor accepted the key to the synagogue, ceremoniously opened the door and led the congregation and invited guests to their seats. An orchestra played between speeches made by Beth Israel's president Morris Rosen, the mayor, and several Jewish leaders from around the state. Rabbi Moishe Shohet, new to the synagogue, led the congregation in a "religious ceremony . . . invested with all the solemnity of the Jewish church" through chants, prayers and the placing of the Torahs in the new ark.

The *Commercial* described the "splendid" building in the "heart of the Hebrew colony on York Street and vicinity," noting the conspicuous illumination from electric lights and a chandelier. There was seating for 620 people, including 220 seats in the balcony for women. The celebratory day at Beth Israel ended with a banquet in the evening for the members of the congregation.

The directors of Beth Israel bore the responsibility for raising $38,000, the final cost of the new synagogue. A 1913 photograph of Beth Israel's directors shows a group of seventeen sturdy men of varied ages: some wore suits, others frock coats; some wore hats, some skullcaps; most had beards or mustaches while four of the younger men were clean-shaven. All bore serious, even stern, expressions.

While the directors secured a $10,000 bank loan, they relied mainly upon fellow congregants and on benefactors for donations. Fortunately and fortuitously, they could call upon the New York financier Jacob H. Schiff for help. The most renowned American Jewish leader in the early twentieth century, Schiff was reputed to be the single largest contributor to Beth Israel with a gift of $1,000. His interest in Bangor was

based on proximity and happenstance. Over a period of many
years, Schiff appeared in Bangor from the nearby resort of
Mount Desert Island for a two-day stay to attend synagogue
services on the anniversary of his father's death. Honored by
his presence, Bangor's Jews treated Schiff as a dignitary of the
highest rank, as did the Bangor papers.

The Jewish community upon which Schiff bestowed his
gift was making its own economic progress. Several Jewish merchants who owned wholesale and retail businesses in clothing,
dry goods and furniture were prosperous enough to make their
way on to the list of taxpayers who paid more than $50, rein-
forcing economic and social differences among Bangor's Jews.
The *"leitesche menschen"*—the relatively more comfortable Jews
such as the Epsteins, Cohens, Allens and Friedmans—had
moved to better sections, leaving behind the Jewish peddlers,
cattle dealers and owners of little confectionery or grocery
stores—tiny businesses called "storkeles." Max Cohen, the
owner of a jewelry store and long-time president of Beth Israel,
emerged as an influential stalwart of the Republican party in
the city and state. Meyer Epstein, a graduate of the University
of Maine Law School, served on the city council. Mike Pilot, also
a lawyer, became an active Democrat and unsuccessful contes-
tant for Bangor mayor.

By 1915, the Jewish population had swelled to over three
hundred families. Uniformly, the modestly comfortable and
the poor alike turned their unceasing work and limited financial resources to the benefit of their children. Members of the
second generation grasped educational opportunities in Bang-
or's high school and colleges and universities outside the city
in a move toward the economic security that their immigrant
parents would not be able to achieve for themselves.

But that same ascent through the Bangor educational system had exposed Jewish children to a new set of conflicts. From
elementary school to high school—with usually no more than
three to five Jews in an entire grade—they straddled two
worlds: one emanated from Jewish values, traditions and the
Yiddish language that filled the homes; the other derived from
the ideas and manners of the secular American culture, per-
sonified by non-Jewish friends and teachers.

Bangor High School had sororities and fraternities that
were divided along Gentile and Jewish lines. These divisions,

which were regarded as a natural consequence of the different cultures, carried no stigma of rejection. But the tension between the two worlds—immigrants' homes versus American Protestant society—intensified when Jewish students entered colleges and universities, such as Colby and the University of Maine at Orono. There, along with the promised educational opportunities, Jews first met pervasive social discrimination and the growing prejudices of the society at large. After the turn of the century, Protestant college fraternities, sororities and social clubs handpicked their members in a whirl of competitive social life. Indubitably, Jewish students were not solicited for the prestigious—or any—Gentile social clubs.

To ease the sense of dislocation and vulnerability, a small number of Jewish men and women from Bangor turned to the Intercollegiate Menorah Association at the University of Maine. Henry Hurwitz had started the nationwide organization in 1912 to encourage Jewish self-respect and the study of Jewish culture and religion on college campuses. (It was estimated that out of 350,000 college students in the country, there were no more than 10,000 Jewish students.) By 1915, fifty-one Menorah societies were connected by the energetic Hurwitz and his publication, the *Menorah Journal.*

It was through the *Menorah Journal* that many Jewish students shared their anguish over discrimination and rejection: they dissected its causes; they examined its manifestations; they tried to come to terms with the painful contradictions of democratic expectations and religious and cultural rejection. In 1916, in "A Gentile's Picture of the Jew," Harold E. Stearns, a former Harvard student and afterward a contributing writer to *The New Republic,* shared his understanding of the Jewish dilemma. Stearns described his own prejudice against the "objectionable Jew." Annoyance with Jews, he wrote, "was always there waiting to be stimulated. It diminished and died away in exact proportion as Jews became un-Jewish, so to speak, as they became imitative of current standards and manners, as they shared certain points of view, as in appearance they more and more approximated the Anglo-Saxon."

Stearns's confession evoked a strong reply. An anonymous Jewish physician wrote of the inconsistent and tormenting complexities of Gentile attitudes that encompassed both repulsion and need. "The cultured and liberal Gentile has two distinct and contradictory attitudes toward the Jew," he wrote. "The one is toward the individual. That individual is his friend, his companion, his confidant. The other is his attitude toward the race. From the race he turns with a feeling of repugnance." That aversion "bars" Jews from Gentile clubs. "He refuses our children his schools. He keeps us from the places where he and his women-folk gather, and yet—Let him suffer deeply in his purse, health, reputation, let him stand in great peril and his most intimate doors are thrown open and he calls aloud for help."

At Orono in 1915, no one was calling for help among the 1,269 students except for a handful of 25 Jews on campus. Just nine miles from Bangor, the state-supported college was started in 1865 under the Morrill Act. Predominantly an agricultural school, it had slowly developed a liberal arts curriculum. By the turn of the century, it had become a university with strong departments in forestry, engineering and the sciences. Many Bangor students naturally gravitated to it along with faculty members, donors and trustees from the city.

A. I. Schwey, one of the Menorah Society's organizers, reported with guarded optimism on the newly established branch. "Conditions on the campus were such that it made all of the Jewish students feel the necessity of the right kind of Jewish organization." The first job involved placing "the Society in the right light on the campus by emphasizing the absolutely non-sectarian, academic, cultural nature of the Menorah Society and the fact that membership is invitingly open to all members of the University." Several successful meetings were held with university president Robert Judson Aley. "All of our activities have caused favorable interest," Schwey concluded, "on the part of both the student body and the college authorities, and a great change has come about in the attitude towards the Jewish men."

After colleges and universities, the First World War provided a second source of secular exposure for Jewish men from Bangor. Patriotism, preparedness and the romance of war infused the city as it recruited local men into the United States Army. After the German invasion of Belgium in 1914, the Allied cause captured the hearts of Bangor citizens who, in a matter of weeks, raised $2,000 for Belgian relief.

Two and a half years later, in June 1916, 170 Bangor

Guardsmen of the G Company left the city to prepare for the possibility of a war in Mexico. Ten thousand people honored the soldiers in a resounding send-off parade. Article upon article in the local press followed the route of the boys in G Company to Texas for training. A few months later, some of the soldiers returned home to emotional and enthusiastic crowds. It was the first of many parades, receptions, joyous and sometimes mournful homecomings.

The war fed on Maine's old competitive spirit, reviving the battles of city versus city and state versus state. If Maine, and Bangor in particular, were no longer distinguished by dynamic economic growth and a growing population, at least their patriotic responses could equal or surpass any other place. These hyperpatriotic sentiments brought French Catholics, Jews and the Irish into community efforts in unprecedented ways.

Along with other cities in the state, Bangor created a Committee of Public Safety to evaluate local industrial capacity—particularly in lumber and shipping—encourage recruiting for the National Guard and Maine regiments, organize a "home guard, special police force, or committee for the 'investigation of enemy aliens,'" promote 100 percent Americanism and suppress pacifists. Anxious searches were conducted for German spies, who were presumed to come off U-boats plying the Maine waters. Mount Desert Island was considered particularly vulnerable, given the government's radio transmitter at Otter Creek. Closer to home, soldiers guarded the Kenduskeag Bridge.

Bangor's most grandiose parade took place on April 3, three days before Congress approved President Woodrow Wilson's request for a declaration of war. Between five thousand and seven thousand people joined in the greatest local public demonstration since the Civil War. Governor Carl Milliken presided over a flag-bedecked city. The Committee of Public Safety offered a resolution to the four thousand people gathered in the festival auditorium calling for a declaration of war: "In the midst of the existing international crisis in which the liberty of mankind is at stake and Christianity is doubted . . . our peace loving and peacefully inclined communities filled with spies, and peccant conspiracies set afoot in our land, our duty is, as clear as the blue of a noon-day sky, to defend human society against military aggression."

Over the next months, intense efforts were made to give financial support to the war and to foster enlistment in the army. By June 1917, Bangor had subscribed $1,953,500 in Liberty Loans, exceeding the goal set for the city. Bangor raised another $1,709,000 in a second Liberty Loan drive in October 1917. By March 1918, recruiters had sent two thousand to the army, more than any other district in Maine and New Hampshire.

"Bangor Blazes up for Liberty" was one of the mottoes as Bangor pleaded to raise another $1,000,000 in 1918. Through their own separate "Hebrew committee" of the Chamber of Commerce, the Jewish community gave $35,000. The newspapers publicly lauded immigrant communities for their contributions, reporting that 100 percent of the Greek community had given to the campaign and that the Jewish people in Bangor showed "wonderful enthusiasm" compared to the "feeble" effort of the American-born.

Bangor organized its own National Security League to uncover any deviation from total support for the war. Under the encouragement of the Committee of Public Safety and the vigilante spirit of anti-German suspicions and intolerance, Bangor High School dropped the study of German, as did the University of Maine. Bangor's most conspicuous example of anti-German sentiment occurred in 1918, when University President Aley fired Dean William A. Walz of the University of Maine Law School in Bangor. Although many of the dean's students supported him, they were not able to overcome the pressure from the *Commercial*, the zealously nationalistic Aley and the university trustees. The latter judged the dean harshly: "There are times which demand especially from those who impart instructions to the youth of the Country . . . the most disinterested patriotism."

Another episode revealed the depth of hysteria. A well-known Bangor artist was sketching in Haymarket Square. A Bangor man, characterized by the *Commercial* as one with "an inbred hatred of German," asked the artist what he was doing and whether he was a German. When there was no reply, according to the paper, "the questioner aroused by the growing conviction that something was wrong, kicked the easel over and the drawing fell into the mud." The artist was angered that his painting was destroyed, while his accuser wanted to have the artist "arrested as a possible German spy."

In the midst of all this furor, the Jewish community carried the added burden of concern over the carnage in eastern Europe; many family members and friends still lived in the center of the war zone, trapped by opposing Russian, Polish, Austrian and German forces. Bangor's Jews could do little to help but raise money for relief through house-to-house solicitations on Jewish Tag Days in 1916 and 1917.

These were minor efforts, however, compared to those made in the fall of 1917 in conjunction with the national American Jewish Relief Committee. For the first time, Bangor's Jews were brought deeply into the web of national Jewish relief efforts, joining forces with some of America's most philanthropic and prominent Jews, including Jacob H. Schiff, Louis Marshall, Henry Morgenthau, Sr., and Julius Rosenwald. "New blood was infused into the civic and philanthropic leadership of scores of cities," the historian Marcus Eli Ravage wrote. "Men and women without number and in every part of the country who had never before been active in communal affairs were initiated into the ways of social usefulness, and came away feeling that there were responsibilities for them which they could never again disregard."

Throughout November, Bangor's Russian Jewish leaders met every evening, in Louis Kirstein's office, to plan their campaign. Kirstein served as the treasurer of the Bangor drive, publicly identifying himself for the first time with Bangor's Russian Jews. His involvement helped the immigrants—led by Simon Cohen, A. B. Friedman, James A. Cahners, Myer Minsky, James Striar and Samuel Kurson—to reach out to the Gentile community for financial support. Henry Morgenthau, Sr., a former ambassador to Turkey, may have been responsible for Kirstein's sudden change of heart. According to one version, Morgenthau learned from Myer Minsky that Kirstein was not active in the relief efforts. Subsequently, Morgenthau may have invited and pressured Kirstein to participate. Another view was that Kirstein had, for reasons of his own, wanted to identify himself in Bangor as a Jew rather than as a German.

In a public letter reprinted in the *Commercial*, the Jewish relief committee expressed its indebtedness to Kirstein: "Mr. Kirstein is very much interested in the work and although not in good health, still is putting all his energies into the work. The members of the committee feel a deep gratitude to Mr. Kirstein for the generous part he is playing in obtaining the required amount from the district."

The New York headquarters established fund-raising goals and sent speakers to Bangor to address mass rallies. Pledges were given to help raise $10,000, the goal set for Maine's eastern district. At Beth Israel, $3,000 was pledged. In addition to cash contributions, Bangor women offered their wedding rings and other jewelry.

In December 1917, through a large notice in the papers— "An Appeal to the Public!"—Bangor's Jews called for help from the entire city. "The Jewish Relief Committee of Bangor, cooperating with the central committee in New York which includes some of our best patriots and greatest philanthropists in the world, makes this plea to our benevolent and patriotic American people." The direct appeal raised $6,000. Names of contributors were printed in the newspapers, and daily articles demonstrated how the fund was painstakingly increased by small donations of $5 and $10. The largest individual contribution was made by Max Striar, who gave $145; thirty-eight people gave $10, and more than fifty gave $5.

Immigrants were appreciated and praised as never before. In words that went beyond the pro forma expressions of respect, Mayor John F. Woodman told a Jewish group that "the city was proud of its Jewish citizens." He conceded erstwhile differences when he assured the Jews that "every one now recognized that the Hebrew was a most desirable member of the community."

The Jews did not draw praise for all that they wanted to do. Beth Israel asked permission to build a one-story "receiving house for the dead" on York Street. Morris Rosen said it would be used only once or twice a year for deceased Jews who had lived outside the city but would be buried in Bangor. "When a Hebrew dies in an isolated country place," he explained, "and is brought to Bangor for burial, his body must first be washed and prepared for interment." This had been done in a private home in Bangor. Several aldermen and Mayor Woodman strongly objected to the building, calling it a "dead house," suitable for a cemetery. Permission was denied.

In June 1918, two hundred Jewish representatives from all over Maine gathered in Bangor to plan another statewide relief campaign, which set Bangor's goal at $15,000. A succession of city officials welcomed the participants and again praised Bangor's Jews. Colonel F. H. Parkhurst, chairman of the Public Safety Committee, concluded that "one of the results of this war for America would be the elimination of race ancestry and every man would be taken for what he was worth."

The importance of the meeting was underscored by the appearance of Louis Marshall. A brilliant and indefatigable strategist and champion of Jewish causes, Marshall showed the intensity of his concerns on his visit to Bangor. The renowned Jewish leader spoke to his large audience about the positive efforts of American Jews during the war: "after 20 centuries of oppression the Jews had at last found a place giving them opportunities . . . that were nowhere to be found in any other land." He asked his audience rhetorically: "Why then should we not contribute, give our last dollar, and even our last drop of blood for America and for what she stands?" Passionately, Marshall described the suffering of Jews in the war-torn areas. "Unless help comes to them, our brethren, they are doomed to utter annihilation. . . . It is for us then to come forward and give."

One episode during the war became part of the lore of Bangor Jewry. Myer Minsky received news that the Jewish Legion, including David Ben-Gurion, would pass through Bangor on its way to Halifax. (The Legion, organized to fight in Palestine, was part of the British Army.) In the middle of the night nearly the whole Bangor Jewish community, accompanied by a band, walked to the railroad station to greet the soldiers, a procession that took place in one Maine town after another. Portland gave a "royal reception," wrote one soldier:

> But the town that we will remember to the end of our days, the town that will be present before our eyes even in the smoke and thunder of battle is the little town of Bangor. It was 4 a.m. We were trying to sleep as best as we could in our seats for we were traveling second class. Suddenly, through the night came the strains of "Hatikvah." Instantly we were on our feet. The train pulled in. Jewish, American, and British flags swayed back and forth in the cool breeze. Then came a resounding cheer, and men, women and children invaded our quarters. They brought sandwiches, and smokes, and fruit, and heart-warming smiles. Ev-

ery one of them, even the girls, wore bands across their breasts. "Sons and Daughters of Zion." Upon inquiring, I found that was the name of an active young men's and young ladies' society of Bangor. The train stopped there for only a few moments, so we had little time to speak.

What a wonderful few moments they were! Then came the last moment. Again, there was the wishing of all good things, again there was the exchange of kisses.

A bit carried away, he continued:

But somehow, the girls of Bangor and their kisses were different from those of other places. In fact, I make bold to say, unless you were with us that night you cannot know what a real kiss is. A pretty maiden runs alongside the train, she stops and puts her foot on the rod underneath, she jumps up and catches hold of the window sill, then you look into a pair of big black eyes full of light and feeling and sympathy, and red lips meet yours. Only an instant it lasts, but those lips are with you forever. No ordinary kiss is this. This is a kiss for the forerunners of the Messiah! Off! to our land! Take it and hold it and keep it forever.

With eight hundred Bangor men in service, Bangor followed the war, campaign by campaign, battle by battle, and then sadly took account of the local injuries and deaths. Bangor's first fatal casualties in Europe were Norman Dow and Kenneth Klein, whose parents lived on Essex Street. Abe Goldberg wrote to his parents in Bangor about giving Klein a religious burial at the front after walking twelve miles with ten other Jews to retrieve Klein's body. "We buried Kenneth Klein as a good soldier and as a Jew," he wrote. "I said the prayers in Jewish and a thunderstorm broke before I finished repeating them in English. That did not interfere with my saying Kaddish and we planted flowers on his grave."

Beyond the war efforts, sacrifice and privation bore down heavily in Bangor for two years. Few people would forget the frightfully cold winter of 1917, when the city was reduced to a two-week supply of coal, and the following winter, the most severe on record. Readings of thirty to fifty below zero virtually immobilized the city. Because the Penobscot River was frozen and impassable, only the railroads could bring coal at a time when the war strained the state and national transportation system. Although the city was never cut off from a supply of coal, the isolation, cold and vulnerability were deeply frightening.

Ten months later, an outbreak of influenza held Bangor in its deadly embrace. Initial reports in October identified only two hundred cases and little danger to the city. Soon, however, it was clear that the city would not escape the severity of the international pandemic. Dr. Daniel Arthur Robinson, chairman of the Board of Health, canceled all public gatherings, including the Maine Music Festival, and closed schools, churches, theaters and clubs for five weeks. Ultimately, 1,600 people were afflicted and 110 died.

The city sadly sustained many more deaths of Bangor soldiers at the front, including Hyman Hillson, Sam Marcus and Henry Lait from the Jewish community. When, on November 11, 1918, peace was declared, Bangor went wild. Headlines roared with joy: BANGOR'S HAPPIEST, NOISIEST MOST GLORIOUS CELEBRATION—CITY IN PANDEMONIUM FROM EARLY MORNING UNTIL PAST MIDNIGHT—ALL BUSINESS SUSPENDED—THOUSANDS IN GREATEST PARADE EVER KNOWN HERE.

The city had survived deep personal strains, economic challenges and social transformations. Mary Robinson, who feared that World War I—like the Hundred Years War—would go on forever, described how it had changed her life. When news of the armistice burst through the city, school was canceled and an impromptu parade of young and old was formed. "Though conscious of being a staid old maidish person, past fifty," she wrote, "I simply had to do something, so with the rest of the teachers and the rest of Bangor, I entered the procession and marched through town. Five years before I should have supposed that nothing on earth would have led me to forget my dignity."

Bangor Jewry also had been transformed by the war. Its contributions in men and money had created a new and respected connection to the city itself, as well as to the state and national Jewish organizations. Jews joined the armistice parade feeling proud, thankful and equal—in sacrifice—to their Protestant neighbors.

A reporter for the *Commercial* described the Jewish celebration as solemn and majestical:

> For the first time in the history of the Jewish race in Bangor, the sacred Bibles of the Jews were taken from the inner recess or place of keeping in the synagogue on York Street, the mother church of the Carr Street synagogue, and in the care of Rabbi Shohet and Rabbi Kaprow were placed beneath the magnificent crown of gold. . . . The Bibles . . . still held and guarded by the rabbis, never for a moment out of their clasp . . . took their place in the parade for world peace, driven in the car of Simon Cohen. . . .
>
> In days of old when the Jews were persecuted, kings or governors or conquerors inflected [*sic*] as a last punishment the obligation that they take the sacred bibles to the city gates. But this time, in Bangor, the bibles have been taken out in what Bangor Jews recognize as the most wonderful and most momentous event in their history for not only has it meant the occupation of Jerusalem by the allies, but it means that the country of their adoption, the America they claim as the one country where Jews are allowed to live as others live, in peace and happiness, is triumphant over oppression. . . .
>
> The Jews of Bangor have been prominent and active in all war work. Mr. Cohen, whose car carried the rabbis with their priceless books of religion, has a son in the service and is himself one of the most untiring of workers in the interests of the allies.

If the war was a triumph for the immigrant Jews and their children in America, the following twenty years of peace would prove to be different.

Broadway, one of Bangor's most fashionable
residential streets, circa 1910

JORDAN S. ALPERT

Marked by a multitude of
hanging signs, Main Street,
circa 1900, was the center
of Bangor's commercial life.

Hyman Epstein in his clothing store on Exchange Street
in Bangor, circa 1900

JORDAN S. ALPERT

*BANGOR DAILY COMMERCIAL*, OCTOBER 7, 1897

Victor Hodgins of Bangor designed Bangor's first synagogue for the Beth Israel congregation. It was completed in 1897.

*BANGOR DAILY COMMERCIAL*, MAY 18, 1911

After the fire in 1911, Victor Hodgins turned to a classical idiom for the new Beth Israel Synagogue. Shortly after its presentation in the paper, the congregation abandoned the design and replaced Hodgins as their architect.

Beth Israel Synagogue, dedicated in 1913, was designed by Henry Lewen, an expert in fireproof construction from New York.

Members of Congregation Beth Israel bring a new Torah into their synagogue, circa 1930. The picture, taken from the steps of Beth Israel, shows Beth Abraham Synagogue across the street.

Henry J. Wheelwright was Bangor's most powerful and influential citizen for many decades.

Judge Abraham W. Rudman inscribed his picture to Henry J. Wheelwright, "To my friend tried and true, Henry J. Wheelwright, With sincere regards."

Rabbi Avraham Freedman headed Congregation Beth Israel from 1949 to 1969.

Rabbi Henry Isaacs has revitalized Beth Abraham Synagogue since his arrival in Bangor in 1961.

Catherine Cutler and Dr. Lawrence in 1941 at Camp Blanding in Florida

Rev. Arlan A. Ballie on the steps of All Souls Congregational Church
in the early 1950s

# CHAPTER 5

---

# *Passage Between the Wars*

IT TOOK THE EYES and ears—and the indignation—of a non-native to be the first author to write about Bangor in the 1920's. Mildred Wasson moved to Bangor with her father-in-law, the highly regarded writer and artist George Savery Wasson, after the premature death of her husband. With ease, she entered Bangor's social elite and became privy to its family histories, values and prejudices. In but a few years, this outspoken woman became the premier novelist and social critic of upper-class life in the Queen City.

*The Big House* and *Churchill Street,* written in the late 1920's, reworked Bangor into Hamlin and Broadway into Churchill Street. They were conventional novels—contrived in their fictional complications and resolutions—about romance, deception, rebellion, family decline and renewal. But the novels came straight out of Wasson's knowledge of Bangor's old order in decline. Her themes mirrored its state of mind: nostalgia for the disappearance of the daring, acquisitive, tough lumber lords; contempt for the financial ineptitude of the spoiled and wasteful second generation; irritation over the weakening of upper-class privilege and domination; and annoyance with the competitive and encroaching presence of aspiring immigrants—especially Jews.

In *The Big House,* Victoria Price was the rebellious, or-phaned favorite of her aging, autocratic grandfather. Born into Hamlin's upper class, she lived at the top of society in a stuffy provincialism reinforced by rigid rituals. She was educated at Hamlin High School and further refined by the "faded spinster culture in town"—a culture attained through dancing, French, and art and nature classes taught by women. Bound to Hamlin, her grandfather insisted that she finish at the local high school: "If the Jew girls down on Hancock Street could graduate from High School, she could stay right there till she did likewise." She prepared for Vassar "in keen competition with shrewd little Jews and Syrians. . . ."

Decline spread through the city as the lumber fortunes dissipated. "We're just parasites living on the dead," Victoria said. "Even dear old Hamlin lives on her past." The river was dead and the old mills closed up. With disdain she remarked: "Hamlin had deteriorated into a wholesale grocery and grain mart for the thriving potato country round about."

Even for the Prices in *The Big House,* wealth and the sense of social superiority were severely diminished. The family lum-ber business didn't "amount to anything," a friend of Victoria's commented. "I agree with you," Victoria said. "James A. Price and Son is history." When Victoria and her cousin met down-town, they sat on a park bench in the promenade. "Ever sat in the park before?" Victoria asked. "Two Prices sitting on a park bench, discussing their finances! We might be a nurse-maid and policeman. . . . Wouldn't the family die?"

Although more capital was needed to keep the family afloat, Victoria's grandfather refused to sell his timberlands. His deceitful son and daughter-in-law cajoled the patriarch into selling the Big House. There were buyers aplenty, including the Catholic church, which was interested in converting the house to a lying-in hospital. Unaware of the identity of a po-tential purchaser, Victoria's uncle inquired: "Who is this party, if I may ask? Some Jew trader who wants to start a synagogue on Churchill Street?"

Fixed upon a saga of Bangor's declining elite, Wasson was curiously selective in unmasking signs of a city in transition. While she could refer to the "Jew trader" who was pressing upon the territory of the middle and upper classes, she ne-glected to note many of the more significant and deeply disruptive changes that were occurring: the passage of the income tax; woman suffrage; frenzied consumer spending in newly created national markets; speculation in stocks and real estate; the rapid proliferation of automobiles and radios; popular infatuation with films; Prohibition; the antilabor, anti-Catholic, anti-Communist, and anti-immigrant campaigns.

Her disdain, so casually expressed, accurately reflected the growth of anti-Semitism throughout the country in the 1920's, even as it ignored the fact that the city's Jews and their children were mostly English-speaking, conservative and Republican. Certainly, the number of Jews was not increasing in a way that could overwhelm Bangor's native population—a threat that seemed palpable to many Protestants in large cities, despite the dramatic decline of immigration from eastern Europe. Under the specter of a postwar flood of refugees, restrictionist sentiment finally prevailed in Congress. After years of sustaining presidential vetoes, Congress, in 1917, passed a literacy test over President Woodrow Wilson's opposition. Although the test prevented the entry of illiterate immigrants from eastern and southern Europe, Jewish lobbyists, led by the American Jewish Committee, were able to secure an exemption for those fleeing religious persecution, a clause designed specifically for Russian Jews.

By 1929, Congress had implemented severe restrictive measures based upon quotas and demographic profiles. The schemes allotted modest quotas for "old immigrants" from western Europe and virtually none for the "new." The immigration laws thereby effectively ended the possibility of further reunification of families from eastern Europe. For Bangor, the implications were clear: Bangor Jewry would not grow significantly beyond its few hundred families.

In many respects, however, negative national stereotypes fitted Bangor's Jewish population. Although they still lacked real wealth and conspicuous success, the Jews were hardworking merchants, expanding modest and middle-sized businesses. They were also ambitious, self-sacrificing parents who resolutely promoted educational and professional achievements for their children. That strong dynamic of unrelenting mobility, gained through economic and educational achievement, was abrasive and disconcerting. John Higham described the stinging tension: "As assimilation improved their status, the Jews reaped more and more dislike as they bettered themselves. The more avidly they reached out for acceptance and participation in American life, the more their reputation seemed to suffer."

As American Jews became educated and eligible for professional and managerial positions, they discovered numerous places where they would not be employed and many areas where they could not live. Bangor proved no exception with its own habits of social segregation. While Bangor maintained few residential restrictions in the 1920's and 1930's, there were no positions for Jews in Bangor's banks, in the prominent Protestant law firms or on the hospital staff. Nor were there openings in the Penobscot Valley Country Club, founded in 1924 with 350 members, or in the high-status social and service organizations such as the Athene and Shakespeare clubs.

Bangor's patterns of discrimination, however, never bore the cold, implacable rejection that they did in larger cities and resort areas. A few exceptional Jewish women crossed the club lines in the late 1930's. Helen Golden, a leader in Jewish women's organizations, also belonged to the musical Schumann Club and the Community Concert Association. Lena Ginsberg served on the Girl Scout Council and was a member of the Bangor chapter of the American Association of University Women. At the all-male Tarratine Club there were also a few exceptions. Among them were Dr. Lawrence Cutler, Nathan Sanders, the proprietor of a dress shop on Main Street, Barnett Landon, a tailor of fine men's clothing, Abram Kirstein, the owner of one of Bangor's largest real estate and insurance firms, and the lawyer Abraham Rudman. Bangor's Jews had Gentile neighbors, clients and customers. There was civility and often congeniality, but few social friendships.

The barriers to acceptance were both subtle and abrupt, locally and countrywide. Public figures and newspapers quickly dropped their high-pitched recognition of immigrant contributions to the war effort. By the middle of 1919, appreciation had given way to fears of foreigners breeding radical ideas, revolutionary movements and anarchic behavior. Labor unrest and antilabor crusades caused a narrow, exclusive redefining of Americanism. There was a frenzy of deportations to try to rid the country of unwanted foreigners. Intense pressures for conformity were fostered by Americanization movements, the Red Scare and the Ku Klux Klan.

Anti-Semitism, in particular, was nourished and solidified by diverse forces: congressional restrictionists cut the flow of Jewish immigrants; Henry Ford promoted the scurrilous *Protocols of the Elders of Zion,* which posited a Jewish conspiracy to dominate the world; college and university administrators imposed religious quotas that severely limited the number of qualified and aspiring Jewish students; and the KKK, which instigated political turmoil in the South and Midwest, agitated in Maine.

With its antiblack, anti-Catholic and anti-Semitic campaigns, the Klan's membership in Maine swelled. Centered in Portland and led by F. Eugene Farnsworth, the Klan fed on the state's long-standing suspicions of its Irish and French-Canadian Catholic populations. Fictitious assertions of support surrounded the Klan's activities as it claimed a membership of 20,000 to 23,000. According to Portland papers, there were 1,500 members in the Bangor area in early 1923. The Klan built a following among Methodist and Baptist ministers and fraternal clubs, such as the Masons, the Odd Fellows and the Knights of Pythias. Barred by local officials from using public facilities, the Klan bought houses for meetings in Bangor and across the Penobscot River in Brewer. Entering the political arena, it forced some Catholics off of school boards and out of teaching positions and tried to end aid to parochial schools through a constitutional amendment. The organization successfully endorsed many state legislators and mayors; most conspicuously it promoted State Senator Owen Brewster for governor.

Although there were no recorded anti-Semitic incidents, a threatening aura surrounded Bangor's Jews. They looked to Gentile religious and political leaders to defend their values and contributions to their city and America. The Reverend Samuel C. Beane of the Unitarian church was one who spoke up on their behalf in 1923. "There are no more remarkable, more distinguished or more wonderful people than the Hebrews," he told the congregation at the Unitarian church.

As the Democratic nominee for governor, William Pattangall became the state's most outspoken critic of the Klan. The Brewster-Pattangall election caught fire over that issue. Pattangall took his fight into the national forum at the Democratic National Convention in June 1924. Gaining nationwide attention, the fiery Maine politician sponsored a resolution condemning secret societies. The opposition, led by William Jennings Bryan and delegates from the South and Midwest, defeated the resolution by one vote.

Pattangall again met defeat, this time in his fight for the governorship in the largest voter turnout to date in Maine's history. But the Klan phenomenon expired quickly. As governor, Brewster distanced himself from the Klan; Farnsworth was indicted for embezzling funds; and the Klan's influence, membership and financial base were eroded by 1925. At the same time, Brewster appointed Pattangall to the state's highest court, removing the feisty lawyer from the elective arena for good. The intense and demagogic spasms of Maine's anti-Catholic and anti-Semitic fervor were exhausted.

In fact, by 1925, politics had became a sideshow to the fast-moving, heady, speculative, acquisitive consumer culture that was transforming the city as well as the nation. Bangor was now promoting itself as the center of automobile and truck traffic for eastern and central Maine and became "Bangor, a Motor Center," according to the Chamber of Commerce's new slogan. In the emerging automobile culture, the city appealed to tourists to drive through on their way to Maine's scenic coast, lakes and woods. Bangor residents were also on the move to resort areas. Although the Bangor newspapers had long since lost interest in the social life of Mount Desert Island, the once exclusive resort town of Bar Harbor now advertised in the Bangor papers for visitors to watch the Fourth of July parade, races, dances and airplane flights.

The advent of the automobile broke the proud and carefully constructed web of distinctions that had previously graced the city. High Street, Broadway and State streets, which had stood in lofty residential separation above the railroads, harbor and commercial downtown, were suddenly closely connected to the city. Main Street changed: it was not only the best place to shop, but also a passageway through the city at a fast impersonal pace.

Even Bangor's beloved annual circus parade could not survive the onslaught of the automobile. In 1929, the Sparks Circus, the last of many to come to Bangor in the summer, gave up its parade of animals and performers. Every year, to the delight of the whole city, the circus had slowly circulated through the town from the railroad station to the fair grounds. The *Commercial* lamented the break with tradition. "The time has come when in a city of metropolitan scope, the parade is no longer possible. Swift-moving modern life, twentieth century traffic, simply will not stand aside for the half-hour that it passed. They want the thoroughfares—they want all the room and the time and the attention and so the parade is doomed."

Bangor's economy was tested and transformed during the 1920's. The city held its own as a retail and wholesale center in the nationwide buying fling. While wages remained reasonably steady, profits increased substantially. Incessantly, people bought into the signs and symbols of an improved standard of living. Thousands upon thousands of buyers flocked to Bangor for its fairs, including the traditional August livestock fair, and shows of new goods—ranges, refrigerators, vacuum cleaners, washing machines, radios and automobiles. Leading them all in sales and civic pride, Freese's department store maintained its preeminent position, but lower-priced national chain stores were moving in. When Newberry's opened in 1920, the papers reported that thirteen thousand people jammed into the store on the first day.

Feeding the buying spree, the banks surged into competitive prominence. No longer relying on understated images of gentility and stability, they brazenly advertised for business on the front pages of the *Commercial* and *News,* replacing the quiet domestic piano advertisements of yesteryear. Even the *Commercial* momentarily lost its stability to a giddy investor in 1924. The Bass family sold the paper to Dr. Frank Gordon, a Bangor-born dentist and promoter of silver fox furs. His ownership of the *Commercial,* however, was even more short-lived than his guardianship of a chain of fox farms. Within a year of his purchase of the paper, Gordon's fur business failed. Before he declared bankruptcy, five hundred people converged on Bangor's City Hall to try to recoup their losses, amounting to $3,000,000.

Along with rampant consumerism, Bangor also joined the nationwide craze for speculation in real estate. When Lucerne-in-Maine, a development in Swiss Alpine style, opened on almost six thousand acres on the outskirts of the city, people rushed to buy lots in the fancy, tastefully designed resort. It consisted of Swiss chalets and attractive log cabins, a twelve-mile park, an eighteen-hole golf course and a fine clubhouse.

While speculation in foxes and real estate were hot items in Bangor, industrial development remained stagnant. In the early 1920's, the Chamber of Commerce organized the Real Estate Associates to buy properties and build factories to promote industrial use. But by 1925, Dr. E. E. Pullen, the president of the Chamber of Commerce, conceded that his organization had not been "very active" or effective. The inertia, he maintained, came from a "belief that conditions did not warrant such promotion in the past, [and a refusal to acknowledge] that conditions had changed." Pullen was referring to the decline in the timber business. Each year, as fewer men were employed in the woods, Bangor profited less from its former source of wealth. As if to signal the end of an era, Charles Tefft executed a handsome, dramatic sculpture which was placed next to the public library. It boldly commemorated the combination of timber, the Penobscot River and the river drivers from which Bangor drew its strength.

To many in Bangor, the city's prosperity in the 1920's may have paled in comparison to the riches of the past. But prosperity is always relative. To the Jewish population, the city was teeming with possibilities even as the last logs were brought down the river in 1927. When old merchants and owners retired, the Jewish merchants (and a few Greek and Syrian immigrants) avidly seized opportunities to buy the downtown properties. The Jews expanded or started shops and businesses and bought properties in the inflated real estate market. The number of peddlers dropped dramatically: in 1921 there were 34, in 1930, only 9. By 1930, there were 153 Jewish shopkeepers, 12 professionals and over 60 in clerical work.

The papers recorded the activities of many of the Jewish merchants. James Cahners and A. B. Friedman, owners of the Eastern Furniture Company, claimed to have the largest retail furniture establishment north of Boston. Cyrus Schiro established the Standard Shoe Company on Main Street. Myer Segal, formerly an instructor at the University of Maine, opened Cortell-Segal, a women's store of fine quality on Main Street.

Outdistancing them all was Simon Cohen, a long-standing purchaser of Bangor stores and buildings. His first venture on Main Street, around 1910, was the New York Syndicate Store. At discount prices he sold men's clothing and shoes that he bought up from firms that were going out of business. In the

1920's, he pursued major landmark commercial properties downtown: the Bass Building, the Parkhurst Trunk Company factory, and the Pickering Building were among those that old Bangor families and estates were willing to sell. Local wags maintained that Main Street was being "Simonized." Working with his three sons in his several stores, Cohen thrived. A leader of Congregation Beth Israel and an active philanthropist, he enjoyed his heady success by driving through Bangor in a large chauffeur-driven touring car and frequent travel abroad.

Encouraged by their success in business, the Jews started to settle in better parts of the city on both sides of the Kenduskeag. In 1910, 70 percent of the Jews lived in the poor sections around Beth Israel and Beth Abraham. By 1920, 53 percent of the Jews were still living there. Just ten years later, the Jewish population was sufficiently spread out so that only 27 percent remained around Hancock and York streets.

Many of these Jews were becoming increasingly lax about religious observance. Beth Israel had difficulty maintaining a permanent rabbi. Poor Sabbath attendance was a continuing problem. Some Jews abandoned kosher laws and the use of a mohel to perform circumcisions. Jewish family structure was dramatically transformed through a falling birth rate. The second generation had significantly smaller families than their immigrant parents, as birth-control practices reduced families to an average of two or three children. Despite intense pressure— from within the Jewish community and without—marriages between Jews and Gentiles took place. In fact, by 1940, Lucille Epstein counted thirty-one intermarriages among Bangor's Jews, many of whom had moved away from the city. Notwithstanding his leadership in the Jewish community, two of Simon Cohen's children married non-Jews. (Many years before, the first Cohen to marry a non-Jew was Simon's sister, Ann. Her family ostracized her for marrying a non-Jewish man.)

Beth Israel, the largest synagogue, with 120 members in 1923, jealously guarded its leadership among the Jews and its role as spokesman to the Gentile community. It continued to flood the press with descriptions of all the holidays, maintaining the image of a highly observant and disciplined Jewish community. Despite continuing financial difficulties, Beth Israel proudly retired the debt taken on to build the new synagogue in 1913. In a symbolic gesture in 1923, derived from the example of All Souls Church, the synagogue burnt its mortgage of $10,000. At services and a banquet, three hundred people celebrated the event in the presence of two former rabbis, Louis Selzer and Moishe Shohet.

Intermarriage made the old lines separating Russian and Lithuanian Jews less distinct. But divisiveness within the community was still strong, and the synagogues experienced two more schisms during the 1920's and 1930's. Differences over ritual and observance as well as personal feuds fostered the splits. A small part of Beth Abraham's congregation started Toldoth Yitzchak in 1920, buying a house on the corner of York and Essex streets. In 1937, a fire destroyed the Beth Abraham Synagogue on Carr Street. A year later, it was rebuilt on York Street, directly across from Beth Israel. Seven hundred people attended the dedication ceremonies.

Led by Myer Segal, another group left Beth Israel in the late 1920's to found Beth El in an attempt to make their religious observances more accessible to the second generation of Americanized Jews. They affiliated with the Conservative movement and conducted services in Hebrew and English. Although unable to afford buying a building, the fledgling congregation was able to maintain an English-speaking rabbi for two years in the mid-1930's, taking great pride in his efforts to reach out to integrate the congregation into the city as a whole.

Prosperity made possible new levels of institutional growth and philanthropy under the leadership of Myer Minsky, A. B. Friedman and Morris Rosen. Bangor's Jews unceasingly promoted philanthropic and educational activities through the synagogues, Zionist groups and organizations such as the Free Loan Society and the Bangor Hebrew Ladies Aid Society. The Kirsteins were the most generous Jewish philanthropists. When they celebrated their fiftieth wedding anniversary in 1922, they provided for a large number of charitable gifts, including a $5,000 award for excellence at the high school. They also gave $500 to each of nineteen Gentile and Jewish charities.

In 1920, the Jewish community organized the Bangor Hebrew Institute and hired a principal from New York to direct daily and Sunday classes for seventy children and a night school for adults. The institute was the successor to the Hebrew school organized in 1907 and housed, since 1913, in Beth Israel Synagogue. The Bangor Hebrew Institute attempted to modernize the teaching of religious subjects and, for the first time, to use teachers who spoke English. Within a year, the Bangor Hebrew Institute Realty Company purchased a former boardinghouse on State Street for $10,000. In 1919, in response to Jewish requests, the Bangor Public Library began to purchase works by Yiddish writers as well as American and European classics translated into Yiddish.

The Zionist cause remained central to the community's efforts. Bangor was on the circuit of Zionist appeals, as a long parade of famous Zionist spokesmen, such as Abraham Goldberg, sought out financial support. Every year the community raised thousands of dollars at meetings, luncheons, dinners and conferences. City officials, political leaders and Christian religious figures were asked to endorse these efforts for Jewish settlement in Palestine. With rhetorical grace, the officials usually provided the approval that Bangor's Jews sought. On one occasion Robert A. Jordan, secretary of the YMCA, remarked "that he had attended so many Jewish affairs that he was asked by one person whether or not he was a Jew himself."

The Jewish community entertained itself—more and more comfortably—with a succession of formal dinners, musicales at city hall, concerts and outings under the auspices of B'nai B'rith, various Zionist clubs and the all-male, all-Jewish Veritans Service Club. With increasing affluence, the Bangor Jews ventured beyond Beth Israel and the Bangor Hebrew Institute for meetings. In 1921, the local Zionists held a luncheon at the nonkosher Bangor House for a small number of Jews and Gentile guests.

When cantor Josef Rosenblatt gave a concert for six hundred people in the city in 1923, his presence brought pride to the Jews and superlative praise from the *Commercial*. The cantor "chose those numbers that contained the greatest appeal to move the human heart and delight the ear of his countrymen. The words of the Hebrew numbers were followed with delight by the older or Orthodox Jews and the faces of those who use Yiddish could be seen to brighten when the great cantor's voice was heard in the Yiddish words of a familiar folk song."

The Rosenblatt concert was the first Jewish contribution to Bangor's distinguished musical heritage. The musical—and verbal—love affair between Bangor and William Chapman, director of the Maine Music Festival, remained a permanent part of the city's cultural life. In 1921, the Bangor Symphony Orchestra and Maine Music Festival celebrated their twenty-fifth anniversaries with a banquet at the Bangor House at which speakers recalled the names of over 150 major artists who had come to Bangor. Only Caruso was missing from the glorious list.

After many supporters lauded Chapman's achievements and Bangor's generosity and high culture, George W. Chadwick, a Boston musician and composer, gave the principal address. Amid his praise for the festival, Chadwick told his audience that as he looked over the list of the members of the Bangor Symphony Orchestra he found commendable names—"Sprague, Sawyer, Smith and Robinson. No doubt you have Jones too. It is the only orchestra in the United States with names like that. Most of them have names ending in 'isky' or something like that. It shows that Americans can be good orchestra players. . . ." After sudden applause he continued: "To my mind it takes more than a scrap of paper and three or four years' residence in New York to make a good American."

Ultimately, praise and glorious recollections did not increase audience attendance or reduce the festival's mounting deficits. The high costs of performers, extensive repairs for the auditorium and competition from radio and the movies caused Chapman to resign in 1926. For his glorious exit and final festival concert, the charismatic conductor brought Beniamino Gigli to sing *Aïda* before a crowd of four thousand people.

With Chapman's departure, the festival continued as an annual one-day affair, featuring renowned musical groups that were often joined by a local chorus of several hundred. But Bangor dropped off the ambitious and expensive map of musical distinction. Never again would the city's pride come from its high musical culture. Bangor became another American city, connected by radio and movies to the circuits of national entertainment and periodically visited by theatrical stock companies and vaudeville groups.

The transition—from active participation in the local musical culture to passive enjoyment of national radio shows and Hollywood fare—occurred in the same era when many of Bangor's long-time social and political leaders passed away. In most instances, they left no heirs to carry on their particular styles of philanthropy and leadership, honed in the late nineteenth century. These were men who had shaped the social institutions of middle- and upper-class Bangor life without having had to consider or contend with the force of a powerful mass culture. Their authority and values derived from service to the city and its organizations, church morality and family probity. They were endowed with varying degrees of talent, eccentricity and moral aspiration. Some were born to great wealth; some, without independent means, succeeded by vigorous work and ambition. Their public and private lives brought order, distinction and some drama to the city.

Edward H. Blake was the last member of his wealthy and long-established family to live in the city. When he died in 1922, he was president of the Merchants National Bank, which had long been controlled by his family. Since 1894, he had been a co-owner with J. Norman Towle of the *Bangor Daily News.* A recognized expert on admiralty law, Blake also owned one of the finest yachts in Maine. Conversant in seven languages, he was a poet, musician and composer who built a great pipe organ in his handsome house on Court Street. Upon his death, the *Commercial* praised him in discreet words that defined the ideal Maine personality: "Of quiet, undemonstrative manner, behind his natural reserve there glowed the warmth of true and wholesome geniality for those whom he counted as friends."

The paper discreetly stated that behind the public and social person was a man of "most delicate sensibilities." In reality, Blake was a man of some eccentricity who demanded the steady attendance of his local physician, Dr. Everett T. Nealey, in Bangor and during Blake's travels. The doctor's heirs sued the Blake estate to recover $168,000 for unpaid services allegedly dispensed over a period of twenty-eight years. The suit, one of many contesting the estate, was settled for $78,000. Out of the estate of over $2,000,000, Blake left $150,000 to Bangor institutions and $500,000 to Bowdoin College. The bulk he left to Frederick Adams, an officer at Blake's bank.

Not all of those in Bangor who appeared to be wealthy, like Blake, died with their fortunes intact. F. H. Parkhurst was one who did not. Although he inherited the Parkhurst Trust Company, a small but highly prized Bangor industrial enterprise, his ambitions revolved around Republican politics. (In steady pursuit of the governorship, he appeared consistently at Jewish functions.) His dream was fulfilled when he was finally elected governor in 1921. Unfortunately, just thirty days after taking office, he died. It was discovered that his estate was bankrupt, burdened with debts of over $200,000. The factory, which failed to sell at auction, was the one purchased by Simon Cohen.

In 1917, James C. Stodder, one of Bangor's leading social figures, bequeathed $500,000 to the Bangor Public Library and $500,000 to the Eastern Maine General Hospital. The gifts would go to the institutions upon his wife's death. His was one of two large gifts to public institutions from donors who, fortunately for the city, had no children or close heirs. Frederick Hill, another Bangor banker, left $476,714 to the public library and an equal amount to the University of Maine in 1920.

Flavius O. Beal, after a long career of leading Bangor as a nine-term mayor and enterprising businessman, died in 1922. The towering stone city hall was his monument to Bangor's stature in eastern Maine. The Bangor Fair and Maine Music Festival, both of which he ran, were his means of attracting crowds to the city. He was a feisty, wily, manipulative and powerful Republican politician who took equal pride in cultivating friends and in outwitting enemies such as Dr. Daniel Arthur Robinson and Joseph Bass, the long-time publisher of the *Commercial*.

Dr. Robinson, or DAR as he was popularly known, succeeded at almost every task and challenge, save that of beating Beal in several mayoral campaigns. He exemplified an extraordinary set of traits, including moral certitude and a sense of unselfish responsibility toward his community. He served as president of the Maine Medical Association; he was on the Board of Overseers of Bowdoin College for over forty-six years, chairman of the Bangor school board for over forty years, head of the Bangor Board of Health, long-term trustees of the Bangor Public Library, deacon of a Congregational church and Mason, par excellence, as a Knight Templar in St. John's Commandery.

When he died in 1930, a boulder from his summer home in Hancock Point marked his grave at Mount Hope Cemetery. His daughter, Fannie Harlow Robinson, described its peaceful setting and moral message: "It stands under native evergreen trees, now so overgrown that they almost hide it, but nature can never obliterate the solid qualities which that stone symbolizes."

By the time of his death, those "solid qualities" had fallen under economic siege. After 1929, the Depression crept slowly into the city, creating a bleak new world in which the prices for Bangor goods and services—from lumber to law to bread—plunged. Unlike many places in the rest of the country, the city was at least able to maintain a low rate of business activity and a stable population. Some professional and business people actually moved to the city, finding more opportunities in eastern Maine than in other places. The Jewish population, in fact, grew by over a hundred families from 1930 to 1940.

For some individuals—from lumber merchants to local wholesalers and retailers—the losses were tragic and irreversible. Many, such as Simon Cohen, who had feverishly expanded their businesses in Bangor and investments in Wall Street, never recovered from their losses. Most of the Jewish businessmen and professionals who suffered from overextending themselves in the 1920's refused to go into bankruptcy, even at the urging of their Bangor banks to whom they owed money. It became a matter of honor and pride not to default. This was the case with Simon Cohen as well as Harry Epstein, who had a prosperous wholesale dry-goods business until the Depression.

Retrenchment occurred everywhere. The number of city government jobs was cut back. Salaries were lowered. Teachers were asked to remit 12 percent of their salaries to the city administration. Many hundreds of families were forced, for the first time, to go on relief, receiving money or food or living at the city's Poor Farm. In addition to aid provided by the city, church groups and the Family Welfare Society (formerly called the Associated Charities) worked to relieve the distress of the unemployed and indigent.

Economizing became a profound and overriding concern. For the upper and middle classes, the first and most obvious target was municipal spending. Business leaders moved to take control of what they regarded as the indecisive, scandal-ridden, partisan and ward- and ethnic-dominated form of government. In 1931, the League of Women Voters called for drastic reform, proposing to replace the traditional, partisan bicameral system of aldermen and councilmen and elected mayor with the election of nine representatives at large who would appoint a nonpartisan, professional city manager.

Within a year, the city voted to convert to the new form of government—in fulfillment of reform hopes nourished by many members of the upper class since 1912. Bangor's nine elected representatives, most of whom were sponsored by the nonpartisan, patrician Citizens Charter Committee, came over-whelmingly from the mercantile and professional classes. Emma Godfrey, head of the League of Women Voters, was among them. The others included a bank president, a prominent retailer, the general manager of the Bangor and Aroostook Railroad, one of the city's best-known lawyers and a leading builder. With extraordinary speed, the new city manager, brought from Pennsylvania, and the elected representatives reorganized many of the government offices and drastically cut the budget and the number of office holders.

Bangor's greatest moment of alarm arrived with the national bank holiday called by President Franklin D. Roosevelt soon after his inauguration. In April 1933, the Merrill Bank, with fifty thousand accounts and eleven branches, was in dire trouble. To avert its collapse, a committee was hurriedly formed to take over the bank's affairs and arrange for an infusion of capital. Immediately, it began negotiations with the Reconstruction Finance Committee in Washington for a loan of $2,000,000. Simultaneously, a campaign was launched to raise another $1,000,000 locally, accompanied by appeals to patriotism and city pride.

The *News* reported that the resulting spirit of cooperation was similar to that of World War I, when men "discussed the ways and means of serving their city, country and fellowman without regard to personal gain. . . ." There was an "appreciation of what it means to a city to have all its banks open, when many communities are suffering from closed institutions, and not overlooking the fact that Penobscot County is perhaps one of the very few counties in the whole country where every bank is open. . . ." Finally, after weeks of negotiations, reorganizing efforts and appeals to the community, the public subscription raised the necessary $1,000,000. Bangor came through the nationwide banking crisis without losing any of its financial institutions.

Day by day, the public looked for signs of renewal from both the private and public sectors. The Roosevelt administration helped the staunchly Republican city to survive. (Bangor voted for Herbert Hoover, although wards 1 and 2, with their heavy Irish and Jewish constituencies, voted for Roosevelt.)

Bangor's former mayor and current congressman, Democrat John G. Utterback, an avid supporter of the President, was able to bring thousands of jobs to the city and area. By November 1933, Bangor had three projects sponsored by the Civil Works Administration which employed over five hundred men.

The announcement of a new Sears facility in Bangor brought forth proud boasting that the store would be the second largest in New England. Fifteen hundred people applied for positions in the store in 1933. The papers gave unqualified praise to Cyrus Schiro's son, Albert, one of the leading merchants in the Jewish community, when he expanded and remodeled his Standard Shoe Company. Finally in 1935, a long-awaited, city-subsidized shoe factory started operating in the plant of the defunct company of Parker and Peakes. The Philco Shoe Company, run by Philip Lown and Max Kagan, two Jewish businessmen from Massachusetts, held out the prospect of employing hundreds of workers and giving the city a major industrial boost.

From the mid to late thirties, the city's social and economic life slowly came free of the grinding despair of the Depression, although the mobility of Jewish merchants, so evident in the 1920's, slowed down. With great effort, traditional activities were sustained. The Bangor Fair was held every year. The Bangor Symphony Orchestra played its annual series of concerts. Conventions still came to Bangor and outside speakers were brought in. On one such occasion, the well-known Zionist rabbi, Stephen S. Wise, addressed the Maine teachers convention. The clubs, such as the Athene, Shakespeare and Twentieth Century Club, continued to meet.

All of the voluntary philanthropic and religious organizations endured financial difficulties. Memberships lagged. Contributions were steeply below needs. Individual benefactors gave fewer and smaller gifts. To make their fund-raising campaigns more efficient and successful, many of the city's major philanthropic groups organized a community chest in 1938 with the goal of raising $55,000. The Hebrew Ladies Aid Society was the only Jewish group included, along with organizations such as the Salvation Army, the Boy Scouts, Traveler's Aid and the TB association.

In 1937, the Jewish community found an unexpected benefactor. Nathan Liss, a shopkeeper in Millinocket, provided funds to purchase the Somerset Private School, which had previously served the children of some of Bangor's wealthiest families. Liss, a quiet, unassuming man, and his hardworking wife, Dora, had no children and had saved all their earnings from their small clothing store in the mill town. After Dora's death, Liss arrived in Bangor with thousands of dollars in cash. He was pursued by the Braidys, Dora's family in Bangor, and Abraham Rudman, Liss's lawyer, to donate the money for a Jewish community center.

For the first time, Bangor Jewry had a proper facility for secular activities. The center became the energetic focal point for educational, social and philanthropic programs, while providing the still tightly knit Jewish community with a setting where it could educate and entertain itself. (The Hebrew school moved into the Liss building and sold the building on State Street.) The Jewish community could now define its collective nonreligious needs and measure its place in the city as a whole.

The gift that elated the Jewish community must have caused dismay and regret among some of Bangor's upper class. In the middle of one of the finest residential areas, just a block from Broadway, the "Jew trader," as Mildred Wasson had dubbed him, had found a place for himself and his community to work together. Among the immigrant groups, Bangor's Jews were not alone. In 1926, John Bapst Catholic High School was built on Broadway. Eighty years before, the Catholic church had tried to build in the same area, but anti-Catholic hostility was too great. There was no protest in the 1920's when the Catholic church built an edifice for $250,000 in the monumental style of Bangor's library and high school.

Inevitably, there were people in Bangor who gave in to the temptation to mourn the legendary past and to revile the threats to an insular, settled way of life. Mildred Wasson was certainly one of them when she wrote an article for the *News* in 1939. An influx of automobile-driving tourists roamed through her city in which fine old homes were converted to boardinghouses or pulled down for garages and gas stations. She recalled the words of a friend who perceived the spirit of "a presiding genius of demolition" hanging over Bangor, waiting to "destroy what the gods of beauty had provided . . . a stream with a park, a river-front that might suggest Venice, a river luxuriantly curling in its own beauty."

Unquestionably, nostalgia mixed with intolerance and prejudice in Bangor, as they did all over the United States. These were realities that Bangor's Jewish immigrants and their children could hardly ignore. But they were mildly harmful forces compared to the demonic spirits at work in Europe. For many years, those spirits remained of distant concern to people in Bangor and all over America. Entering the 1940's, the city continued to immerse itself in mild economic recovery and peaceful isolation from events abroad.

# CHAPTER 6

# *Sore Problems of Social Prejudice*

FOR THE JEWS of Bangor, May 20, 1941, was a moment of triumph. At the invitation of the Jewish Community Center, Eleanor Roosevelt arrived in the city to speak on "Peace and the World Today." The President's wife had long made tours on FDR's behalf, carrying his artful construction of mixed messages: preparedness for the possibility of war against fascism; support for Great Britain and mutually shared democratic values; yearnings for peace.

Accompanied by Governor Sumner Sewall, the First Lady toured the local air force base and city monuments and attended a festive formal dinner for 250 people. That evening she gave a speech from the flower-filled stage of the old wooden auditorium, visited in the past by musical grandees such as Nordica, Calvé and Carmela Ponselle. Mrs. Roosevelt's voice, high pitched and thin, carried through the auditorium filled with 2,500 people. Familiar to her audience by way of radio, her aristocratic cadence had an oddly reassuring musical lilt.

Her appearance provided a unique opportunity for Bangor's Jews to work with the city's civic and social leaders. To prepare properly for the event, Abraham Rudman, president of the Jewish Community Center, and Dr. H. O. H. Levine, its director, turned to the traditional non-Jewish leadership. Led by Dr. Harry Trust of the Bangor Theological Seminary, nineteen of Bangor's organizations joined the center in promoting Mrs. Roosevelt's visit. Several committees, with all but two filled exclusively by Jews, made the arrangements.

Jewish self-effacement and caution were evident in the souvenir program, a handsome compendium of information about the First Lady and the host city. The program's sociological profile of Bangor stated that the English, Irish, Scotch and French Canadians were the leading nationalities. While it even referred to the city's small black population, surprisingly, no acknowledgment was made of the 1,200 Bangor Jews.

Nevertheless, for the first time, Jewish leaders sat at the head table during a formal city dinner; and for the first time the *News* and *Commercial* identified the Jews as distinguished people at a citywide event. The "affair was one of the most important events of its kind ever held in the city and the occasion was attended by men and women prominent in the civic, educational and cultural life of the community." But on behalf of the Jewish Community Center, Dr. Trust, not Abraham Rudman or Dr. Levine, conspicuously represented the city in the ceremonial affair.

Omission, a subtle order of the day, reinforced the inferior position of the Jews. In the past, the press had simply identified the Hebrew Community Center or Jewish Community Center. For the First Lady's visit, the papers switched to the "sponsoring organization" or the "Bangor community center"—but not the *Jewish* Community Center. "Albert Schiro, representing the group sponsoring Mrs. Roosevelt's appearance" was the way one center member was identified. If the YMCA, Rotary or the Zonta Club, for example, had invited Mrs. Roosevelt, would any Jewish leaders have sat at the head table, served on committees, or been recognized in the press? In retrospect, one center member commented, "A Jew might have been included if the American Association of University Women had sponsored the event. But no other organization would have invited the Jews."

It was evident to many Bangor Jews that they measured themselves against the larger Christian community. With unusual candor, the 1940 annual report of the Jewish Community Center stated that Bangor Jewry engaged in "indiscriminate

self deprecation, awkward attempts at escape, and finally the
worst phenomenon that plagued any self-conscious minority,
namely, self-hate." Wanting to end its self-denigration, the center's board announced: "We are determined that our children,
and we, to the extent that we can overcome the unhappy results
of past maladjustments, shall not be burdened with those impediments. The Community Center is the approach of American Jewry towards the harmonious integration of their Judaism
in the general American pattern."

In 1941, that pattern was irrevocably changed. FDR's
strong hopes for peace were not realized. Within seven months
of Eleanor Roosevelt's visit to Bangor, America was attacked at
Pearl Harbor. By December 11, the United States was at war
against Germany, Italy and Japan. Nearly 4,400 men from
Bangor and its environs joined the service, including over 130
Jewish men.

At the same time, the war brought thousands of soldiers,
airmen and aviation engineers to the city to train at the Bangor
Air Base, renamed in 1942 for James P. Dow, a deceased soldier from Houlton. The field had grown slowly out of Edward
R. Godfrey's passion for aviation. He was a gentleman lawyer in
the city, who, starting in the 1920's, accumulated over a thousand acres of farmland to form an airfield. Right before the
war, after many years of negotiations, Godfrey sold all of his
holdings to the city and federal government.

Bangor's location on the northern route to Europe made
Dow Field an important point in the Air Transport Command.
Over 6,500 planes were prepared there for bombing and re-
connaissance missions in Europe. Wounded soldiers returned
to the base on their way to rehabilitation in the States. Eventually, six thousand officers and enlisted men worked at Dow. By
the end of the war, the federal government had invested over
$11,000,000.

For those who stayed behind in Bangor, the war provided
prosperous times. High employment and vigorous markets—
from lumber to dry goods to meat—helped to make new fortunes. For Bangor's Jews, the war was a break between a past of
modest economic success before the Depression and a present
that made many comfortable and a few affluent. The city's
Jewish industrialists thrived from manufacturing textiles, shoes,
army cots and woolen goods. The Viners, Medweds, Byers,

Emples and Striars filled orders for the United States Army and its allies. Their successes enriched their families and made Bangor a small but recognized center of Jewish philanthropy.

For many who left Bangor as well as for those who stayed at home, the war often caused painful change and loss. Dislocation was just the beginning. Bangor soldiers lived and fought in unfamiliar places next to men from disparate backgrounds. Sadly, for many there were injuries, stress, sacrifice and, for some, even death. By the end of the war, 112 Bangor men had died in service.

The Jews in Bangor experienced heartbreak that went beyond the trials of family and friends in active service. Slowly, the community learned of the destruction of Jewish life in Nazi-dominated Europe. By 1945, American Jews confronted the inescapable knowledge of the chain of camps in Germany and Poland where Jews died in the macabre machines of mass murder. At the end of the war, there was a reckoning and collective despair: the Russian and Polish villages where Bangor's Jewish immigrants had once lived were now devoid of Jewish life; their families were gone; their histories were irretrievably lost, as were the roots of Yiddish culture and religious piety.

Unquestionably, the destruction in Europe reinforced a sense of gratitude among the Bangor Jews for their lives in America—for security, freedom and abundant educational and economic opportunities. But many Jews came out of the war with a new sensitivity to the sharp edges of intolerance. American anti-Semitism survived through the war and into the post-war years. In general, college and university faculties remained closed to Jewish professors; hospitals often rejected Jewish doctors for staff positions; many businesses refused to hire Jewish workers; and within New England, and Maine in particular, hotels and resorts uniformly advertised that Jews were not welcome.

A new impatience and assertiveness grew in the face of this prejudice. With unexpected frankness in 1945, one Bangor Jew, in an unsigned article, wrote in the Jewish Community Center's newsletter about Jewish hopes and fears:

> There are too many frightened Jews among us. We are afraid of what our neighbors will say or think if we talk too loudly, grow a beard, or buy a new car. . . . It

is time for us to know that we are disliked *only because we exist.* And as long as we do exist, there will always be among us a few ill-mannered or ostentatious Jews. We are entitled to a few—our neighbors have them in their midst, too.

But the positive and dynamic attributes of the Jewish people have never been properly presented to our nation. It is time that our neighbors knew that living the good Jewish life is synonymous with living democratically, fairly and with respect for the rights of others. Basically our contribution has been a Code of Morals unimproved upon by man since it was conceived in the dim, forgotten past. Heretofore the word "Jew" has been synonymous, in the Christian world, with things debased. . . . We Jews cannot live sanely or importantly as a frightened people. We must walk unafraid, secure in the knowledge that we have a right to live. We are privileged to live in a democracy whose very cornerstone was laid on the Jewish concept of justice.

In fact, it was the triumph of those democratic values that led some people to believe that a new spirit of tolerance might grow in Bangor's calm postwar life. Unlike the immediate aftermath of the First World War, in 1945, there was no frenzy of reaction rooted in fears of radicals, unions or foreigners. There were no food and fuel shortages, no frigid, paralyzing winters and no influenza epidemics such as the one that killed hundreds of Bangor residents in the fall of 1918. Nor did America suffer again from massive disappointment over failed idealism. Indisputably, her democratic credo and economic and industrial force dominated the Western and Pacific worlds.

After the war, Bangor men rushed back to the business of living in their small New England city. More than ever, and paradoxically as well, postwar Bangor, a city of twenty-nine thousand people, seemed both closer and farther away from the rest of America. Distances were deceptive. The ease of congenial travel on an overnight Pullman train gave many people, including a first-time visitor to Bangor, the illusion of proximity. Approaching the city by train, arriving at the stately Maine

Central terminal, one might have thought that it was just "over the hill from Boston"—both in miles and culture.

In truth, Bangor was far—very far—over the hill from Boston and New York. Car travel, ever more popular, made Bangor seem harder to get to and farther away from Boston and New York. More and more, people drove by themselves, on a long, exhausting journey traveling through small towns, before the Maine Turnpike was built as far as Augusta in 1955.

The returning soldiers found a city little changed in its physical appearance, daily routines and social order. Unostentatious living was the growing credo for the wealthy and the middle class alike. The Wing sisters and Sylvia Ross were perhaps the last people in Bangor to enjoy lavish living, including the use of uniformed chauffeurs. Sylvia Ross, the daughter of William Engel, the only Jewish lumber magnate in Bangor's history, had become a Unitarian. Long accepted into the social circles of the Protestant elite, she was nevertheless considered to be Jewish by all who knew her. Every year, Helen Golden, as head of Hadassah, asked Ross for a contribution. Every year she sent her chauffeur to deliver her $25 check.

Postwar Bangor did little to adorn itself. In a daily ritual of sociability, women went downtown to shop, carefully dressed in suits or dresses, gloves and hats. On Main Street, which had changed little, there was no place for anonymity as friends met at Freese's and other fine local stores. Bangor was still a highly personalized society at all levels, where families, merchants and professionals honored the hierarchy of personal status and service.

At the end of the war, a few individuals in Bangor probed deeply into the meaning of America's democratic ideals and searched for tolerance. Two years into his ministry at All Souls Congregational Church, Rev. Arlan Andrew Baillie was one of those who called upon his congregation to intensify its quest for brotherly harmony. A tall, imposing man with a smooth, resonant voice, the thirty-three-year-old Baillie moved with assurance and grace, reflecting, in part, the stature of All Souls. His pink granite Gothic church stood at the pinnacle of Bangor's ecclesiastical world. Strong in number, with a membership of nearly five hundred (which swelled to eight hundred by the time Baillie departed in the early 1950's), the congregation included most of the most respected and richest families in the city—the Godfreys, Ranletts, Crosbys, Edwardses, Webbers, Hutchinses, Braggs, Jordans, Whittiers and Stetsons.

"Our task right now," Baillie told his congregation in February 1946, is "to consider the sore problems of the social prejudices that we display against Negroes, for instance, or against our Jewish neighbors, for another instance." America could not remain strong in the shadows of prejudice. It is to America that the rest of the world looks for its "ideals of justice and fair-play and democracy for which we took to the field and fought in a victorious cause." (That message, however, was somewhat ambiguous. The minister cited the disconcerting results of a poll among American soldiers: "fifty-one percent of them believed that Hitler had done Germany a great deal of good between 1933, when he came to power, and 1939, when the war started; . . . and twenty-two percent believed that the Germans had 'good reason' for persecuting the Jews!")

Although America had rid itself of slavery in the nineteenth century, Baillie declared there were new slaves: the "minority peoples who are chained and bound by the social prejudices held fast by the rest of us." Such feelings compel people "to single out the worst or the lowest or the meanest aspect of some minority people, like our Jewish neighbors, and jump to the unwarranted conclusion that the same particular aspect applies to all."

Baillie's message never entered the hearts of his congregation. His hopes ran into the resistant patterns of an entrenched social order that changed very slowly from its prewar configurations. Bangor in the late 1940's and early 1950's was still divided firmly into a tripartite network of Protestants, Catholics and Jews. The groups *qua* groups did not socialize with ease, although a few individuals mixed socially.

A small group of Protestant timberland owners, bank presidents, lawyers, doctors, and utility and railroad executives maintained their power on the nonpartisan city council and self-perpetuating school board. Through interlocking boards of trustees, Protestant leaders remained the stewards of the social and welfare agencies, the hospital, and the private educational institutions. Although their families were divided among All Souls, the Hammond Street Congregational Church and the Unitarian church, they mingled in the Shakespeare

and Athene clubs, the Tarratine Club, Rotary, and the Penobscot Valley Country Club.

In the late 1940's and early 1950's, however, the group's
influence was reflected in only one, albeit the more important,
of the two city newspapers. The morning *Bangor Daily News*,
with a circulation of approximately 65,000 readers, covered the
city and entire region. Since the 1890's, the Republican paper
had belonged to the long-established Edward H. Blake and the
Towle-Jordan families. Its fortunes climbed steadily until it
overwhelmed its traditional competitor, the *Bangor Daily Commercial*. In 1946, James D. Ewing and Russell H. Peters bought
the ailing paper and moved to Bangor for the sole purpose of
running a small-city newspaper.

Enthusiastic and somewhat naive, Ewing and Peters struggled against the harsh realities of escalating costs and the fierce
competition of the *News*. Reluctantly, Ewing terminated the paper in 1954 only two years after a sensational and bitter struggle with Maine's powerful Senator Owen Brewster. The
*Commercial*, the only paper in the state to oppose Brewster,
caused his stunning and unexpected defeat in the Republican
primary. The paper also exerted pressure on local issues, forcing the city government to open school-board, water-board and
budget-committee meetings to the public.

While the *Commercial* nibbled at the tightly controlled, secret workings of the city, actual power in Bangor was held by a
very few people. The city's inner circle, visibly concentrated in
All Souls, led to another inner circle where Henry Wheelwright
reigned from the 1930's until his death in 1956. Wheelwright
ran the Merchants National Bank as well as his small brokerage
firm, which invested the endowment funds of nearly all of
Bangor's charities, social organizations and private educational
organizations: the Eastern Maine General Hospital, the Bangor
Theological Seminary, Mount Hope Cemetery, the public
library—everything except the YMCA and the Family Services
Agency. Legacies and donations accumulated into substantial
funds, as in the case of the library, where Wheelwright had
more than $5,000,000 to invest.

Charities meant money and money meant power. Power
once concentrated had to be reinforced and secured. To maintain his control, Wheelwright single-handedly chose officers
and members on his boards. He operated like a big-city boss:

controlling the city council, school board and Republican appointments on the state and local level. But unlike Mayor Flavius O. Beal or Joseph Bass, the former publisher of the
*Commercial,* Wheelwright used his power beyond the public eye.
Even after his death, protective understatement prevailed in
the obituary in the *News*: "For many years Mr. Wheelwright
identified with the successful administration of the finances of
the Bangor Public Library and other organizations of Bangor."

His actions appeared imperious to some and autocratic to
others, but nobody accused Wheelwright of investing poorly or
profiting unduly from his monopoly over endowment funds.
Few, however, dared to defy him—fearing his power or the
illusion of power which he skillfully projected. Patiently, rival
brokers in Bangor waited year after year to chip away at Wheelwright's power and commissions.

Bangor Jewry had nothing to do with the public and private dramas revolving around Wheelwright and the struggles
for power in the city. The Protestants ran the city and the Jews
ran their businesses. They prospered in their own place in
Bangor's life. While only a quarter of Bangor's 1,200 Jews still
lived in the poorer areas around Hancock and York streets,
they remained a self-contained group. A census taken by the
Jewish Community Council in 1951 established that Jews owned
or worked in over two hundred shoe, clothing and dry-goods
stores; more than three hundred were self-employed; and fifty-
one men and women, such as the lawyer Ada Gleszer, were
professionals, mainly in medicine and law.

Bangor's Jews were fulfilling many of their individual and
communal goals. The census revealed that 272 men and women
were college educated and 26 went on to graduate schools.
Sixty-five percent of the Jewish community owned their own
homes. The average family size had dropped to only 2.9, which
was below the national average for both Jews and Gentiles.
Nearly half of the Jewish population in Bangor had been born
in the city, a quarter in New England, while the rest were
foreign-born.

Closed off from participating in the larger Bangor world,
except in business contacts and a few fraternal organizations,
Bangor's Jews remained exclusively involved with their sectarian organizations and institutions: the Jewish Community Center, the Hebrew school, which had over one hundred students,

and the Jewish Community Council. Organized in 1948, the Jewish Community Council sought to unify fund raising and coordinate policy for the center, the Hebrew school and the Bangor Jewish Federation. A number of Jewish leaders— Joseph Emple, Myer Minsky, Shirley Berger, Myer Segal, Henry Segal, Sidney Schiro, William Viner, Max Kominsky and George Ginsberg—rotated positions of leadership in the synagogues, local Bangor philanthropies and Zionist organizations.

Bangor's Jews greeted the creation of the state of Israel in May 1948 with relief and celebration. More than ever, support for Israel's welfare became their overriding mission. In this regard, they were similar to Jews throughout the country. Two people in particular best exemplified Bangor's Zionist fervor: Myer Minsky and Bessie Motiuk.

A Zionist for over forty years, Minsky was indefatigable in raising money for the Zionist cause by cajoling Jews in and around Bangor. In the 1920's and 1930's, he drove to Aroostook County each spring to get money from the Jewish potato farmers. He used to say that he spent one day raising $200 to $300 and three days with his car in the mud.

Bessie Motiuk, barely able to speak English and supported financially by her family, incessantly called upon Bangor Jews to contribute to Israel. In $10 and $15 contributions, she raised over $1,500 a year for her special Israeli fund. Each year she conveyed the money to the President of Israel: "My dear President of Israel and for all Israel," she proudly wrote and listed each one of her Bangor contributors.

The constituency that supported Myer Minsky and Bessie Motiuk gathered at the Jewish Community Center, the "common meeting ground for all Jews." Under the direction of professional administrators, the center successfully sponsored a rich mix of lectures, classes, cultural and social programs, a day camp and a nursery school. Beyond these activities, the center's mission was to promote "the appreciation of and cooperation with other religious, racial and cultural groups."

By reaching out to the Gentile community in the late 1940's and 1950's, Bangor's Jews looked for reciprocal overtures to fill in some of the broad spaces of social distance and ethnic segregation. From All Souls, Rev. Arlan A. Baillie, acting upon his vision of tolerance, made one of the first moves. After the arrival of Rabbi Avraham Freedman at Beth Israel in 1949, Bail-

lie proposed an exchange of pulpits. Baillie was encouraged by
the friendships that had already developed between a few of his
members and Jewish families who were well educated and eager for contacts with Gentiles.

Baillie regarded the interfaith program, which began in
1951, as a breakthrough and something that "had to be done."
Annually, Rabbi Freedman spoke at All Souls one Sunday
morning and Baillie went to York Street to preach at Beth
Israel on a Friday evening. Neither service was modified to
accommodate the gathering of Protestants and Jews. Baillie did
not intend to "leave Jesus out because the Jewish people were
sitting there." Many at All Souls may not have known exactly
what their minister was trying to accomplish. According to one
member of the congregation, there were people who said to
themselves, "Of course we don't like these Jewish people but we
ought to." Dutifully they followed their minister.

In time, people at All Souls appreciated the rabbi's fine
sermons and accessibility. Baillie and Freedman developed a
rapport and respect for each other as they led their congregations in the annual series of spiritual courtesy calls. The young
Freedman was distinguished-looking, calm, well educated and
articulate. His speech was eloquently tinged with a British-
sounding accent gained from four years of service in Canada
and twelve years in a synagogue in South Africa.

For the more affluent and educated, Freedman sought to
break through the isolated and subservient status of Bangor's
Jews. He actively engaged in pulpit exchanges with several
other churches, including St. John's Episcopal; he gave talks to
church youth groups; he lectured at the University of Maine
and the Bangor Theological Seminary; and he participated in
Rotary, mixing easily with the leaders of Bangor's business,
religious, professional and educational establishments, especially those from the University of Maine.

Beth Israel gained confidence from the rabbi's respected
position in the Bangor community. Henry Segal, the synagogue's fine historian, praised Freedman's contributions. The
rabbi was "especially effective as an interpreter of Judaism to
Christian ministers and teachers. His profound, philosophic
knowledge, his deep rabbinic scholarship, and his eloquent or-
atory have made him a favored spokesman." Another Bangor
Jew thought that the rabbi fitted the needs of Beth Israel "just

like a velvet glove." During Freedman's tenure, the synagogue prospered and was able to pay off its debts and grandly celebrate its diamond jubilee.

Over the twenty years that Freedman stayed in Bangor, the rabbi tried to stabilize the generational conflicts between the reform-oriented and Orthodox forces within Beth Israel. He was a pivotal figure, sympathetic to both the immigrants and their children. (Freedman unilaterally gave up some connections to the past. After forty years of remembering the name of the donor Jacob H. Schiff upon the anniversary of his death, Freedman discontinued the practice.) He respected the achievements and courageous sacrifices of the immigrants who strove to educate their children and improve their lives while remaining attached to their Jewish traditions. Freedman also understood the discomfort of the secularly educated and increasingly assimilated second generation that moved beyond the traditions and uneducated ways of their immigrant fathers.

Although trained as an Orthodox rabbi at Yeshiva University, Freedman came to a congregation that was already in transition. Beth Israel's three hundred members mainly followed Orthodox practices. They had, however, already made one major departure from traditional practice: men and women were allowed to sit together. This and other less significant changes enabled Beth El's Conservative members to reunite with Beth Israel.

In theory and commitment, Beth Israel, Beth Abraham and Toldoth Yitzchak all followed Orthodox practices. It was expected that every boy had to go to Hebrew school and have a bar mitzvah. But synagogue observance in all three shuls was generally devoid of fundamental training and knowledge of religious texts and laws. Synagogue ritual often seemed brittle and incomprehensible to the second and third generations. There were few families who did not suffer from being cut off, by geographic location and intellectual inclination, from Orthodox, Conservative and Reform practices and thoughts in other parts of the country.

Despite the general commitment to Orthodoxy in the 1950's, only a few families in Bangor's three synagogues, including the eighty families in Beth Abraham and thirty-five in Toldoth Yitzchak, were strictly observant. Many no longer followed the rules of kashrut or adhered to Sabbath laws. The observant Jews, particularly the immigrants, turned their heads when their children ate lobster on glass plates or had buttered potatoes with meat. Even one of the two kosher butcher shops in the city sold nonkosher meat on the side. Eventually, in the 1950's, Gotlieb and Rolnick gave up selling kosher food and became the largest meat market in Bangor.

Many of Bangor's Jewish immigrants accepted these changes as part of the price of being Americanized. Others would not change their own traditional forms of observance—especially on the Sabbath. They adhered to their own particular ways of maintaining piety and familiar rituals. When it rained on the Sabbath, Bessie Rosen asked one of her grandchildren to hold her umbrella. One Friday evening she walked many miles to her granddaughter's graduation, stopping at a friend's house along the way at sundown to light the Sabbath candles. Despite the competitive pressure to work all day Saturday, Abraham Berg closed his shop in the morning so he could go to shul. "I'll be a millionaire a day later," he would say. And Oscar Rolnick, a compulsive smoker, unable to puff on a cigarette during the Sabbath, would bottle smoke and inhale it in the synagogue.

Bangor's Jews went their own way, differing in tone and thought from the self-conscious and outspoken Jews in the urban ghettos of New York and Boston. In fact, Bangor Jews were proud that they were not like New York Jews. The Bangor style of being Jewish was to act and look like a Gentile. Christians were quiet. They did not talk with their hands. They did not call attention to themselves. Jews should not be outwardly emotional. Do not talk too loud! Do not make yourself known! Try to be inconspicuous! No "oy veys," shrugs, inflections, loud voices, no wailing at death vigils, no beating of breasts! Like the Yankees, keep a stiff upper lip and a quiet voice. Be honest, value your name, live up to your word. (There were some exceptions within the Jewish community who had questionable business practices and cut corners. One Bangor Jew had been barred from practicing law, another had been driven out of town for bootlegging.) Jews emulated the behavior of Gentile clients, customers or associates. Jewish children, only a few in each class, easily imitated their Gentile classmates.

The common mannerisms and values were binding, but the Jewish community was held together, inextricably, by one dominant taboo: the proscription against intermarriage. Fear and abhorrence circulated through the Jewish community; shame worked in the shuls to keep most people from marrying non-Jews. Some sat shivah or mourned if a family member married a non-Jew; some sought to ostracize those who broke away; most simply dreaded the possibility that their children would marry out of the religion. The taboo was equally strong and compelling among the observant and nonreligious Jews. "You did not do *that*" was the collective expression of the rule. Jews could abandon other aspects of Jewish observance—the Sabbath, kosher rules, wearing a hat or yarmulke all the time— but never intermarriage. Or almost never. In the early 1950's, 11 out of 322 married Jews had mixed marriages.

William Cohen grew up in the no-man's land of a Bangor mixed marriage: his father was Jewish, his mother Irish. The family lived on Hancock Street in the 1950's, surrounded by poor immigrants, meat markets, drunkards and brothels. Ruby Cohen, a baker, wanted his son to celebrate his bar mitzvah at Beth Israel, even though William's mother had not become a Jew. Cohen went to Hebrew school until several weeks before his thirteenth birthday, when the issue of bar mitzvah surfaced, this time for final consideration. Without proof of his mother's conversion, the synagogue refused to allow the ceremony to take place. Many years later, when he was a United States senator, Cohen wrote "Clara's Eyes" about the pain of exclusion that trapped his mother and him between two worlds:

> What passions are aroused
> when bloodlines are crossed
> and run into veins
> that cannot account
> for the loss
> of innocence?
>
> How many years
> you held your golden head
> high in silence,
>
> Amid those whispers
> and jaundiced looks,
> the epithets hurled
> at the flesh of your flesh
> that struck like stones.

There was no harbor,
no sanctuary, not
in the ranks of Christ or
Maccabee
for being half of each
they fell beyond
the reach of conformity.

Did you weaken ever once?
Did you ever wonder whether
it was worth it all
to be neither Jew nor Gentile? . . .

The strictures against intermarriage enclosed the community in a powerful web of Jewish associations. Gentile rules of economic and social separation were equally potent in reinforcing the social isolation of the Bangor Jews. "They won't take you in and neither will we," the Jews said to themselves from the time they arrived in Bangor in the 1890's through the 1950's. Slowly, however, Bangor was preparing to change by dismantling barriers of separation—from the subtle ones in evidence during Eleanor Roosevelt's visit in 1941 to the rigid taboos against intermarriage.

# CHAPTER 7

# *Breaking Through*

THE RIGID RULES that separated Russian Jews from Bangor's Protestant middle and upper classes gave way first to tokenism or tripartite representation. The system of accommodation permitted one to three Jews to serve on Bangor's most distinguished service associations and civic and charity boards. In 1951, only three Jews belonged to the Rotary, thirty-four to the Masons and forty-eight to the Elks. The Jewish Community Council census of Jews in Bangor and the surrounding towns stated succinctly: "a considerable number of people do not participate in general community organizations."

In the innumerable associations of a small city, contacts turned into trusted connections. Gentile clients utilized fine doctors and lawyers irrespective of their immigrant backgrounds. To build successful practices, Jewish professionals wanted and needed Gentile clients. Business relationships evolved among Bangor's Jews and Gentiles who had known each other from elementary school through high school and, for many, during four years at the University of Maine at Orono.

Three brothers, Abraham, Edward and Harry Stern, were among the outstanding lawyers in the city. Two were Harvard trained: Abraham Stern became the city solicitor for thirteen years and Harry Stern wrote a major treatise on Maine law. Edward Stern became a state senator and judge on the superior court. It was in 1966 that Ed ran as the Democratic candidate for the Maine state senate against Robert N. Haskell, chairman of Bangor Hydro-Electric. Having lost to a Republican in every other election bid as a Democratic sacrificial lamb, Stern had no desire to break tradition and win. When he beat Haskell, Stern demanded a recount to avoid going to Augusta. The victory was his anyway and he served in the senate.

There were also special ties and working relationships in the city that developed unobtrusively over many years. Mrs. Berger, or Mother Berger as she was affectionately called, was befriended by Jews and Gentiles alike. A pious, illiterate and struggling widow with seven living children, she had a store in one of the toughest parts of the city. She sold inexpensive items, often on credit, to the lumbermen and mill workers. She turned to lumber employers such as George Carlisle to collect for her. He considered her a good woman who always helped the woodsmen out when they needed it. He, in turn, always collected on her loans.

A few men and women in the city moved slowly ahead in the drama of new associations and quiet confrontations over prejudice. Dr. Lawrence Cutler was one of those who, with persistence and grace, broke through traditional barriers in his professional and public work. A soft-spoken man, handsome and appealing, he was revered and trusted for his concern and compassionate care. His patients were to be found all over the city: in All Souls, as well as Beth Israel and Beth Abraham. "He earned his way," said one of the prominent Gentiles in Bangor, in understated respect for his doctor.

That "way" was a long one for the son of a Russian Jewish immigrant who started as a peddler and eventually owned a small clothing store in Old Town. Lawrence Cutler studied at the University of Maine and Tufts Medical School. He trained in Boston and Portland hospitals before opening his practice in Bangor in 1934. Systematically, Cutler introduced himself to every trustee at the Eastern Maine General Hospital and many of Bangor's leading doctors, such as Alan Woodcock, Henry Knowlton and Albert Fellows. Cutler's abilities and modest manner brought him to the staff in the late thirties as the hospital's first Jewish doctor. For many years, however, it was a narrow track to be used by only one Jewish doctor. When he sought to obtain an internship for his brother at the hospital, Cutler was rebuffed: "We already have one Jew," he was told.

After serving for five years in the U.S. Army Medical Corps during the war, Cutler returned to Bangor. By then there were four other Jewish doctors in the city, not one of whom was able to care for his patients in the hospital. The closed system prevailed until the hospital experienced a crisis within its staff and Henry Wheelwright asked Cutler to fill the newly created position of chief of medicine. He accepted on the condition that Wheelwright and the board of trustees accept the principle of an "open staff," which would allow any qualified doctor to practice at the hospital. With Wheelwright's agreement, other Jewish doctors were finally permitted to tend to their patients at the hospital.

Inadvertently, Cutler broke another barrier as part of the first challenge to Henry Wheelwright's reign. In the 1950's, there were still no Jews and no Catholics in the Mechanic Association, which appointed trustees to run the Bangor Public Library. Wheelwright directed his nominating committee to recommend John O'Connell, the Catholic editor of the *News*. Unbeknownst to Wheelwright, the committee also nominated James Ewing, the publisher of the *Commercial*—hardly a Wheelwright choice. In the spirit of tokenism, the committee went even further and elected Cutler. Not long afterward, Wheelwright's monopoly over charitable investments was broken as others in the city were selected to invest some of the funds. He died in 1956, leaving no monuments to his control except the declining memories of his longtime rule. The mantle of leadership—but not unilateral power—passed to the gregarious Robert N. Haskell, chairman of the Bangor Hydro-Electric Company, who ran the hospital board for many years.

It was not just men who were called on to make tokenism work in the city. After the war, a few Jewish women were tapped to enter the field of ethnic representation on voluntary social and welfare boards that had never had Jews before. Two of the leading women were Mimi Stern and Catherine Cutler. Mimi Stern, the granddaughter of Bangor's first religious leader and wife of the prominent lawyer Harry Stern, joined the board of the YWCA. Catherine Cutler, Lawrence's wife, served on several boards, including those of the Family Welfare Society, the Community Chest and the Maternal Health League.

A member of the large Epstein family in Bangor, Catherine grew up in the confined and secure world of Bangor's Jews. Her father, Harry, who came to Bangor at thirteen, went from peddling into the wholesale dry-goods business. With a passionate belief in the promise of education, he sent his three daughters to college, after which all three married doctors from Bangor and Old Town. Catherine returned to Bangor from Wellesley, married Lawrence and built an outstanding career of volunteer work in Jewish and non-Jewish causes, particularly in the field of counseling for children. In the postwar period, Catherine and her husband were the first Jewish family to establish comfortable social relationships with many of Bangor's non-Jewish families.

Lawrence Cutler established new possibilities for the Jewish community, although he never considered himself as one of its leaders, nor did he actively participate in Jewish organizations. He was a distinguished figure in educational endeavors, serving on the Bangor school board for ten years and then as the first Jewish member of the Board of Trustees of the University of Maine. He remained on the board for twenty years as an active leader, including ten years as its chairman.

Equally respected was Cutler's counterpart in the legal world, Abraham Rudman. Patiently, Rudman built a large practice with Gentile and Jewish clients spread over a large area from Bangor to the outlying counties. All were attracted to his talents, diligence, honesty and modest demeanor. He was the Yiddish-speaking lawyer of choice for the Jewish farmers and businessmen in Aroostook County, including the Etscovitzes and Adelmans, small-town merchants such as the Unobskeys in Calais, and many retailers and businessmen in Bangor.

Rudman's father, a Russian immigrant, had started out as a peddler and eventually ran a clothing store on Pickering Square. His son graduated from Bangor High School, attended the University of Maine Law School in Bangor and then opened his practice in 1915 in the Kirstein Building. Abram Kirstein, the last of Bangor's prominent German Jews, owned the leading real estate and insurance firm in the city. As Rudman's mentor, Kirstein directed clients to the young lawyer in his building, eventually sponsored Rudman for membership in the Tarratine Club and facilitated his beneficial connection to Henry Wheelwright. Kirstein also encouraged many other Jews in Bangor when he established a fund for giving financial aid to college students from Bangor.

Rudman's career was marked by a series of prestigious appointments. In 1954, Wheelwright named him to the board of the Merchants National Bank. Rudman became the first Russian Jew to hold such a position. In the same year, he became the first Jew appointed to the state superior court. And in 1970, he moved up to the supreme court, the first Jew to sit on the highest court in the state. An honorary degree from the University of Maine in 1961 cited Rudman as "quiet, unassuming and unusually diligent," and "a distinguished attorney and modest civic leader." When he died in 1970, his obituary in the *News* stated: "He was the first jurist of the Jewish faith in the history of Maine to serve on both the Supreme and Superior Courts."

Rudman was active in the Penobscot County Bar Association and served on the Bangor school board for fifteen years. For many years, Rudman also served as president of the Jewish Community Center. He was proud of its programs and communal accomplishments. More than many Jews in the city, Rudman was exposed to social slights and restrictive practices. Among his clients were many Gentiles who treated Jews as "five o'clock friends." They were happy to have Jewish lawyers but disappeared after business hours, unwilling to establish any social relationships with them.

More serious than social slights, however, were practices that prevented Jews from staying at numerous hotels and resorts throughout the state. As a traveling judge on the state superior court, Rudman had to avoid hotels that refused to accept Jews. On occasion, he even found that a hotel reservation might not be honored. "We were very selective," one Bangor Jew said in reflecting on the prevalence of statewide prejudice. "We never tried to go to anyplace where there was any doubt whatsoever." With resignation, another Bangor Jew said, "That's the way it was."

Vacationing Jews from out of state, however, were indignant over their treatment. They flooded the offices of the Anti-Defamation League of B'nai B'rith with complaints and tales of insults. In the 1950's, in response to pressures both from with-out and within the state, the Maine B'nai B'rith, centered in Portland and actively supported by a local dentist, Dr. Ben Zolov, campaigned to end the bigoted practices. Rudman and the head of the Bangor City Council were part of a large group of Maine citizens who formed the Maine Equal Opportunity Committee to make such discrimination illegal. Finally, in 1959, the Maine legislature responded to the lobbying efforts by mak-ing it a crime, subject to financial penalties, to deny accommo-dations based on "race, color, religion, creed, ancestry or national origin."

The assault on the statewide systems of exclusion affected Bangor's clubs and organizations too. In the early 1960's, Lloyd Elliott, president of the University of Maine, declared the Pe-nobscot Valley Country Club off-limits for all University meet-ings and social events. The University would not condone the exclusion of Jews and other minority groups. Just a few miles from the campus, the club had long been an attractive place for University events. The ban was a serious blow to the club, which needed financial support and members. Under clear pressure from the University to alter its policy, the club invited Abraham Rudman and Lawrence Cutler to join. Both declined to become members, reflecting their sensitivity to the embarrassment and humiliation of the long-time restrictive practices. With time, however, other Jews joined the club as the memories of exclu-sion dimmed.

For almost ten years before the Penobscot Valley Country Club converted to an open membership, Bangor's Jewish golf-ers belonged to the Lucerne Club. The Lucerne-in-Maine re-sort had started with great hopes and large investments in the mid-1920's. The Depression and war years discouraged ade-quate membership and further development of the facilities. In the 1950's, a number of Bangor's Jews bought parts of the once-restricted resort: the golf course, main clubhouse and a section of beachfront on the lake. Once the Penobscot Valley Country Club opened its membership to Jews, the all-Jewish Lucerne club lost many members and was sold.

The changes in Bangor's social and economic attitudes toward Jews were part of a nationwide transformation in the tumultuous decade of the 1960's. As part of the civil rights movement, ethnic and racial groups found enlarged opportunities in colleges and universities, businesses and community affairs. For many in Bangor, the changes loosened religious bonds and obligations and ended the forced habit of looking exclusively to the welfare of its Jewish population. For others, however, acceptance led toward greater freedom to tend to the religious needs of the Orthodox community and decreasing apprehension over ethnic isolation and vulnerability.

The split in direction among Bangor's twelve hundred Jews occurred at a time when the community was, in many ways, at its strongest. The list of communal services was impressive. The thriving Jewish Community Center built an addition to the Liss building to accommodate new programs and services for the Hebrew school, with over one hundred children, for senior citizens, a nursery school, lecture series and art programs. In 1954, the Jewish community established a funeral chapel so that funeral services no longer needed to be held in private homes.

The community was still divided into three synagogues on York Street: the Litvishe, "the big shul;" the Russishe, "the shul across the street;" and Toldoth Yitzchak, "the shul on the corner." But in the early sixties, Bangor's Jews found themselves in a novel situation: Beth Israel and Beth Abraham each had a strong rabbi who revitalized his respective synagogue. Beth Israel's three hundred families, with their prestigious Jewish doctors, lawyers and leading businessmen, still dominated Bangor Jewry. They prided themselves on their improved social standing vis-à-vis the Gentiles and continued to speak for the Jews to the community at large.

Under a new rabbi, Beth Abraham, however, was ready to assert itself as the center of Orthodoxy. Fresh from serving as a chaplain at the Loring Air Force Base in northern Maine in 1961, Rabbi Henry Isaacs accepted the offer to lead Beth Abraham. Only the second yeshiva-trained rabbi that the synagogue ever had, he was the first to give sermons in English to the small congregation of approximately fifty families. Born in New York and trained at Yeshiva University, he was an energetic, assertive—even confrontational—Orthodox rabbi.

Isaacs had little to work with and much to hope for from his vision of building a new kind of Orthodoxy in the city. Certain requirements were in place: Bangor maintained a mikveh and also had one kosher butcher acceptable to the new rabbi. When Isaacs arrived in Bangor, he found a shul that continued its tradition of uncompromising Orthodoxy. There had been no changes in ritual: no mixed seating, no concessions to modernity such as a piano or clock in the simple, utilitarian, wooden synagogue.

But there was much in Beth Abraham that caused dismay for the rabbi. The liturgy was read but little understood. There was no talmudic study, no learning or instruction that led to informed religious concepts and a knowledge of tradition. To the rabbi, the values scale was distorted: "the important became unimportant and unimportant became important." And the children, the second and third generations, stayed away, impatient with ritual by rote, the squabbling and fistfights that occasionally broke out among the congregants. Few young people ever came to shul except sporadically to say Kaddish and other prayers for a dead parent or close relative.

Impatient and assertive—even charismatic—Isaacs reshaped the Orthodox commitment and definition of what it meant to be an Orthodox Jew in Bangor. He rejected the traditional two-dimensional definition: a Hebrew school training for bar mitzvah and a Jewish marriage for sons and daughters. The "rabbi militant" set out to nurture the first generation, restore the interest of the second, and educate and excite the third. He blew the strong winds of religious assertion—stirring in urban areas such as New York and Boston—by elevating the synagogue and downgrading the integrationist tendencies of the Jewish Community Center. He insisted that Jews could be particularist and observant, English-speaking and American. He made no apologies for his parochial concerns.

To educate his own children and those in his synagogue, he insisted upon establishing a religious or day school. He gave little weight to Gentile reactions or to the argument that Jewish children should be integrated into the Gentile world at an early age. If the Catholics had their schools, the Jews could have theirs too. Did the parents want their children to be religious? If so, according to the rabbi, they had to go to the day school, since the customary Hebrew school education—with a combination of after-school and Sunday classes—was inadequate for a proper religious upbringing.

The rabbi made the establishment of a day school a condition for his remaining in Bangor. The strong financial support of Max Striar and his family, drawing upon the resources of the James Striar Family Foundation, permitted the rabbi to maintain a day school for twenty years. Isaacs gathered—though not without controversy and dissension—students from Beth Abraham and Beth Israel. Starting with the first grade, year by year, he added children who were taught both secular and religious subjects until the school grew to over seventy students. (Rabbi Freedman, whose wife, Hannah, taught in the day school, gave his tacit approval.) Proudly, Isaacs proclaimed that Bangor was the smallest city in America with a thriving day school. He left the nurturing of an improved Jewish image and interfaith relationships to the congregation and rabbi at Beth Israel.

Those changes in the economic and social relationships between Jews and Gentiles in the 1960's reflected a broad transformation of Bangor's economic, political and social outlook. Bangor looked at its past and found a torrent of depressing statistics and analyses which supported what an untrained eye could see: the core of historic downtown was pressed under the weight of decaying residential and commercial structures.

For solutions Bangor looked south to Augusta and all the way to Washington, D.C. Bangor sought new ideas, strategies and money to arrest its urban decay. In the process, the Maine city adopted the national vocabulary of urban renewal, rehabilitation, removal, model cities. Social scientists, planners and engineers developed a new language of eradication, one that was indexed to qualify its users for federal and state money. A new cadre of professional city planners and consultants became the collective undertakers of the past.

Urban renewal was the flipside of America's traditional boosterism: in pursuit of funds, cities such as Bangor rushed to expose their blighted areas to state and national scrutiny. At their best, the new reformers sought to improve the quality of city life and lives of the poor, ill and destitute; at worst, they sought only to sweep the poor and their wretched housing out of sight. Directed by city committees, bureaucrats and consultants, demolition crews spread like massive armies over the layered history of used-up sections of American cities.

Bangor, whose population fluctuated between thirty-one thousand and thirty-eight thousand in the 1950's and 1960's, was ripe to proceed with surgery. The 1950's were unusually prosperous years with expanding consumer markets. The legendary connections to lumber and shipping were buried deep in the worn heart of downtown. Clustered around the Kenduskeag Stream, old warehouses, wharfs and the once-vibrant lumber and shipping offices were run-down and often unused. Unquestionably, lumber still counted in Bangor. Although the Great Northern Paper Company was no longer headquartered in the city, many of Bangor's largest landowners, such as the Webbers, the Hutchinses and the Wheatlands, continued to hold vast acreage in Maine's timberlands. Ownership, as well as management of the forests for commercial purposes, was centered in Bangor firms such as Prentice and Carlisle.

But supplies for the timber industry, once essential to Bangor's economy, could be found just as easily in national markets. In the 1950's, only small numbers of Canadians from Quebec—a few hundred at most—still gathered in Bangor to find work in the woods. The port was moribund: logs moved by train or truck; oil was brought in by barges and trucks. The interstate, pushing north from Augusta, connected Bangor to the capital in 1963. Heavy automobile and truck traffic moved a few miles west of the Penobscot River, shifting transportation routes near to Dow Field, currently used for both military and commercial aviation.

Bangor's process of self-scrutiny began in earnest in 1951 with the publication of a master plan. Echoing past plaints, there were calls for new industry to buttress the city's position as a retail and wholesale center. The plan documented the inadequacies of the downtown area. Oriented originally toward waterfront traffic, the area had no loading ramps, no spaces for large trucks, and few parking places for cars. Some practices had not improved. The whole city still dumped its sewage directly into the Kenduskeag Stream and Penobscot River, and the city's drinking water was still drawn from the same polluted river source. In 1954, Bangor finally established a new supply system by using water from Flood Pond, fifteen miles away from the city.

The planning board's series of reports on the city's economy and social ills made for dreary reading, especially the housing report issued in 1955. It presented an inventory of statistics that placed many of Bangor's eight thousand dwelling units below national and state standards. The language ran to the apocalyptic: "Poverty, crime, war, juvenile delinquency, racial discrimination, family disintegration, mental illness, dishonesty in government—as social ills—are all weak links of their respective fields, and although each has its own causes, they are all related to the housing problem, as well as to each other."

Faced with residential, commercial and vehicular inadequacies, the city's planning department and city council set up the mechanism for obtaining federal renewal funds. The council created a rotating Urban Renewal Authority, consisting of lawyers and businessmen, one woman, Mabel Wadsworth, and the city manager as an ex officio member. It was a careful balance of Catholics, Protestants and Jews and of representative forces in the community.

In the early 1960's, the Authority presented two major plans for clearance and redevelopment. The first was for the Stillwater Park area that became the first federally funded residential renewal project in the country. After the dilapidated housing was wiped out, the Urban Renewal Authority successfully sold land to private developers, who built over a hundred single-family houses.

The second plan focused on the Kenduskeag Stream area: the core of historic downtown that mainly seemed beyond restoration. According to a subsequent proposal, the Kenduskeag plan attempted to "tear out and replace the heart of the city." The Authority estimated the cost at $7,000,000 with the federal government paying 75 percent of the costs and the city the remaining 25 percent.

As proposed, federal money would be used for new streets, sidewalks, parks, parking, and sewers. Furthermore, it would pay for condemned properties and relocation grants for businesses to move to industrial parks on the edge of the city. The Authority would assemble properties, clear them of all previous obligations and encumbrances and sell them to local and outside developers.

With the backing of the city planning department, the Authority engaged in a heated and successful campaign for voter approval. The renewal vision was imprecise, but hope was ever present: Bangor would look more handsome, cleaner and modern. Downtown might even have the ambience of San Francisco's Ghiardelli Square. Hopes ran high—except among several merchants and businessmen who resisted moving to new offices and stores.

As the Authority proceeded with demolition and relocation, Bangor lost few of its vigorous businesses. Most moved to larger, modern buildings on the outskirts of the city. But everything—good, bad and in between—was razed in order to make clear, unencumbered space downtown. Bangor's preservationists had not begun to mobilize to form historic commissions and districts. National and local incentives for historic preservation, including tax advantages and special funds, were not yet in place. Even before the renewal project got started, the first building to expire in 1961 was the gracious, towered Maine Central Railroad station built in 1906. Next, in 1963, went the acoustically renowned Bangor auditorium, which had already been superseded by a new municipal building, designed primarily for sports events.

In 1969, the urban-renewal project targeted the legendary Mercantile Bank building on Broad Street and its seven adjoining brick buildings. Designed in 1833 by Charles G. Bryant, Bangor's most famous architect, the buildings constituted a landmark known as the Flatiron Block. In the same year, the city hall on Columbia and Hammond Streets was torn down. Like the train station, it was seen as too costly to rehabilitate with too little interior space suitable for the needs of modern businessmen and bureaucrats. The federal government paid $150,000 for the building, a sum that barely exceeded the cost of building Beal's monument in 1894. The money was added to other funds used to convert the old federal office building on Harlow Street into the new city hall. A new federal office building was built a few blocks to the west on Harlow Street.

Along with Bangor's lofty civic and commercial towers, the city excised the quarters inhabited around the turn of the century by the immigrants and lumbermen. This was the area where the Jews had started building their new lives in Bangor with small groceries, cheap clothing stores and kosher meat markets. Beyond the relics of buildings and shops, renewal left few traces of the seedy life in run-down apartment houses on Hancock Street. "It was a street littered with men who had failed, never got started, who sat on doorsteps and let the sun sink into their haggard faces flushed red with wine," William Cohen wrote.

The demolition project was scheduled to take five years. It lasted ten. It was projected to cost $7,000,000, but cost $12,000,000. One hundred and fifty-two buildings were cleared to make way for the invasion of developers. They, however, were slow to show up. When they looked at the bare land, the topography of downtown Bangor worked against their needs. Between river, stream and steep hills, Bangor had no open spaces for shopping malls and parking to attract a mass regional market of hundreds of thousands of people from the surrounding counties. Only banks were willing to build in the streamlined, flattened area next to the river.

Downtown was superseded by factories, offices, shopping malls and motels, which covered old farms and stretched around the borders of the interstate and Dow Air Force Base. Closed down once in 1948, Dow had been reopened as a strategic air base in 1950 after the outbreak of the Korean War. Forty-five hundred people, including nearly two thousand civilians, worked at the base. Approximately $8,000,000 of the $20,000,000 of the Dow budget circulated through Bangor's economy. In 1968, however, Dow was once again deactivated and transferred to the city, which became the sole custodian of the multimillion-dollar facility with its tower, sophisticated equipment, extensive runways and multiple structures. Bangor International Airport became one of Bangor's chief transportation and real estate assets.

In the 1970's, Bangor's soft economy, plodding demographics and taste for the conveniences of the national mall culture severed the currents of hope for downtown. As promised, the historic and commercial heart was torn out of the city—but it was never replaced. Even Bangor's ubiquitous and beautiful elms succumbed to blight and exposed the old streets and homes to painful scrutiny.

As the downtown was torn apart, the air was heavy with myths. Once the city, on the edge of a vast forest, was churchgoing and cultured; once, Bangor had been a center of lumber for the world; once, the port was jammed with boats and men; and once, Bangor was the wealthy, proud home for ship owners, lumber lords and officers of the Bangor and Aroostook

Railroad. Driving down Broadway or West Broadway, a resident might point contentedly to the homes of those who had
dominated Bangor's society. Inside their eye-catching facades,
the houses were thought to hold rich family histories: ones that
spoke of wily lumber traders, bankers, merchants, doctors and
lawyers, their children who went to Harvard and Bowdoin, and
those who returned to settle into ruling the city. "This family is
worth millions of dollars," a Bangor resident would proudly say
in pointing to a large old house. But the wealth and historical
residue were not as visible as Bangor residents thought. The
houses were no longer mansions, the gardens were no longer
well tended, and the better residential streets could not com-
pare with those in Portland, Portsmouth or Boston.

The rich Bangor past was well hidden. From the late nineteenth century on, the comfortable society did not write its
history, keep journals or paint pictures of its city. Even Waldo
Peirce, the Bangor-born artist who came back to live and paint
in the city after many adventurous years in Europe, was no
exception. The son of one of Bangor's most highly respected
and wealthy families, Peirce was a prolific artist who frequently
exhibited in New York galleries, but his work rarely depicted
the city he lived in. He generously donated paintings to institutions such as the Bangor Public Library and Jewish Community Center in the 1940's. Peirce also encouraged other painters
to come to Bangor. In 1940, Peirce invited his friend Marsden
Hartley to teach at the Bangor Art Institute. For $12 a week,
one of America's greatest painters of the twentieth century lived
in near penury and despair in the city, trying unsuccessfully to
sell his paintings and teach Bangor women to paint.

Little bits of Bangor's history reposed in the fine public library and struggling Bangor Historical Society. But overall,
there was a difference between extolling the myths and knowing
and valuing the history. Engaging in the former at the expense
of the latter was a Bangor habit. The authors of Bangor's 1970
comprehensive plan, endorsing and incorporating the Kenduskeag renewal project, assessed Bangor's historical sensibil-
ity: "Bangor's historical background, while not deeply
significant in its relationship to the nation's growth, is nevertheless interesting enough to warrant some degree of civic
pride." The harshest words were addressed to Bangor's con-

nection to the past: "Bangor has displayed an almost total lack of sentiment or regard for the past which has had a profound influence on the character of the present City."

That disregard was as true for the Protestant elite as for the Jews, whose separate historical lines did not mesh until the late 1960's and 1970's. By then, Jews were breaking through the confines of their strong ethnic bonds, Protestant restrictive practices and token representation. The second generation of accomplished professionals and businessmen participated in Bangor's biggest growth industries: the expanded retail shopping centers, the Eastern Maine Medical Center and the University of Maine at Orono. Sidney Epstein, for example, who was born in the city, became Bangor's largest developer and one of the most successful in the entire state. For many years, he ran a statewide chain of movie theaters started by his father in 1912. When television challenged the movie business in the 1950's, Epstein and his partners, the Boston-based, Bangor-born Kurson brothers (Newell, Kenneth and Robert), turned to real estate.

Finally, Jews not only joined important business and civic organizations—the Bangor Symphony Orchestra, Bangor Historical Society and Penobscot Valley Country Club—they also were welcome to buy homes on the coast in summer colonies long favored by Bangor's upper class. Bangor Jewry gladly raised money for civic needs, the hospitals and Christian institutions, such as the Bangor Theological Seminary, which faced severe financial pressures.

From within, the Jewish community was losing its self-binding force. Sons and daughters went off to college and never came back to live in the city. Intermarriage gained reluctant acceptance. The Jewish Community Center, which had united the Jewish community for so many years, yielded its dynamic place and professional leadership as members were pulled in two different directions. One route went outward toward Bangor's secular, civic organizations; the other route went back into the two highly differentiated synagogues. While most people still seemed to be related to everyone else—except for the two rabbis—families split willy-nilly between Beth Israel and Beth Abraham. The differences between them were no longer based on social and professional differences or minor matters of ritual. Beth Israel drifted toward the Conservative movement after Rabbi Freedman left in 1969; Beth Abraham, led by Rabbi Isaacs, became the assertive center of Orthodoxy.

In the 1970's, the Jews developed nostalgic myths about the cohesiveness and dedication of earlier generations. But the children of the immigrants retained little of the history and traditions of their parents. Was this because of the poignant tension that Catherine Cutler described in her history of the Bangor Hebrew School? As she explained, the school, or cheder, triggered a profound resistance to ritual and Jewish learning:

> The ancient laws of the rabbis, the Talmud and the ritual that were stressed in the school, not only represented typical medieval learning, but tended also to stress the rigidity and orthodoxy of the life of a pious Jew. The young students found frequent necessity to revolt against this rigidity because they could not bridge the gap between the life and thinking represented by the Hebrew School and public school in America. Crossing the ocean and settling in the United States represented a matter of a few years in the lives of the immigrant parents of these children, but centuries of progress in many ways separated the eastern European village of the late nineteenth century and Bangor, Maine, in the first two decades of the twentieth century.

In America's fluid, mobile society the immigrants could not force their children to be religious. Possibly, in some confused way, parents did not want their children to be truly observant if it meant postponing Americanization. In their new American setting, without wealth, businesses or social standing, Bangor's poor immigrants thought they had little to give their children— except an education in high school, college or university.

From the 1890's through the first world war, the immigrant generation forged a stable community through hard work and the slow, haphazard addition of family members and friends. But in their new lives, they lived in a plethora of contradictions: they were cohesive and schismatic, generous and callous, religious and unlearned, adventurous and rigid. At heart, they were pioneers who were tied to the past.

Encouraged by their parents' sanctification of American education, the second generation confronted the rigorous and complex demands of assimilation. In Bangor style, they did it with reticence and quiet voices. They remained Jews—almost always marrying Jews—but looked and acted like Gentiles. They grew up to be the taciturn generation that did not talk about being put on the fringes of Protestant society. They looked askance at the blustery, outspoken, self-conscious Jewish culture of the big cities. It was left to Bangor's Jews to make their own uneasy escape—as Americans and Jews—from the unwritten laws of exclusion. Through the Depression, two wars and finally the prosperity and tolerance of the postwar world, they moved slowly, patiently and successfully into the mainstream of Bangor life.

# II

---

# MOUNT DESERT
## ISLAND

# CHAPTER 8

# *A Summer Empire*

ONLY FORTY-FIVE MILES from Bangor, the coastal resort of Mount Desert Island flourished in summer splendor. Despite the short distance, the inland lumber city and the remote vacation land occupied vastly different worlds. In the late nineteenth century, when Bangor lost its grip on stardom and prosperity, the island—especially Bar Harbor—blazed forth to fame. Capital and native-born men and women flowed out of Bangor. Famous magnates and money poured onto Mount Desert. Alas, Bangor no longer represented the American dream come true. But Bar Harbor, separated in idyllic seclusion, represented an American dream that was still coming alive.

Bangor cast a jealous eye and sought to make connections. The *Bangor Daily Commercial* led the way: "An erroneous idea prevails with many in regard to Bar Harbor that should be corrected. Many think that Bar Harbor, with its beautiful scenery, its wonderfully invigorating air and all its natural advantages, is a place where only the very rich can afford to spend the summer." The paper reassured its readers: "There is room enough for all classes of people and they all can enjoy themselves in their way." And yet a caveat was in order. "To be sure, it might be difficult for a man of moderate means, but who had aspirations to social life, to come to Bar Harbor and have entree to the old aristocratic families of the country, but he could have thorough enjoyment in his own sphere and hearty enjoyment at that."

The warning was disingenuous but important. "Aspirations to social life" was what Bar Harbor was all about. The resort gave and withheld entrée to its rich new society for all to see. Gleefully, William Pattangall measured the summer social yearnings of Joseph Bass, owner of the *Commercial* and one of the few Bangor men who owned a cottage in Bar Harbor. "He longs for a position in society. Longs for it! Rather does he hunger for it, thirst for it, crave it as the opium fiend craves the drug, or the degenerate craves the exaltation of passion. . . ."

Gaining acceptance was a serious business from the late nineteenth century on. Mount Desert Island was a social frontier as well as Maine's most conspicuous connection to the Gilded Age. Along with other new resorts, Mount Desert provided a geographical escape from the cities and a social release from deep conflicts in American life: Christian superiority and homogeneity versus a pluralistic creed; exclusivity versus equality of opportunity; and prejudice versus acceptance of Jews.

Before the summer folk arrived, there had been peace and tranquillity in the stunning landscape of mountains, seas, lakes, cliffs and forests. The derisive poetry of Henry Walton Swift and Dacre Bush in 1873 recalled the pristine days of untouched nature:

> Thou favored isle, from busy haunts afar,
> Whose wildness mocks at man's destroying hand,
> No smoky industries thy beauty mar,
> No envious spires, no swelling domes, expand
> In insolence their petty forms, where stand
> With shadows creeping o'er their changing green,
> Thy mountains, solemn, beautiful, and grand;
> Yet has thy loveliness a softer mien:
> That sun in all its course gilds not more fair a scene.

Alas, before the tourists and cottage owners had appeared, Bar Harbor, Northeast Harbor, Southwest Harbor, Seal Harbor and Somesville had been little fishing and farming hamlets.

Though fresh as ever Nature's beauties smile,
How changed thy people since that former day,
When, dwelling lonely in their peaceful isle,
They cast their nets, or raked the fragrant hay!
Thy fishermen, thy farmers, where are they?
No in their stead are monied landlords found;
Thy sons as drivers win the stranger's pay;
Thy daughters, where the swarming flies abound,
On clamoring boarders tend and pass the chowder round.

By the mid-1870's, Mount Desert had been discovered. Not yet a stylish place, Mount Desert already had a stylish name. The brilliant mountain scenery, good air, and summer fun kept the "clamoring boarders" coming, especially to Bar Harbor. Steamships and trains broke the isolation of the island. Boats from Rockland and Portland increased their runs. The railroad, in 1884, finally made its way east from Bangor, opening up the Coastal Line, which stopped at Mount Desert Ferry, at Hancock, before going downeast to Calais. The Maine Central ferried train passengers eight miles across Frenchman Bay from Mount Desert Ferry to Bar Harbor, and then farther on to Northeast Harbor and Southwest Harbor. By the mid-nineties, over twenty-five thousand people were vacationing on the island.

Developers—the native-born, along with those from Bangor south to Philadelphia—bought properties, built houses and opened up roads into the hills behind the hamlets and along the water. Speculators, led by Francis H. Clergue of Bangor, put a scenic railroad up Green Mountain (called Cadillac Mountain in later days) with a $100,000 investment that failed after just a few years. Enterprising natives and others from around the state speedily brought a service industry to life. In the frantic crush to turn the coast into gold, they built a tawdry commercial waterfront at Bar Harbor. "To the lover of beauty," the writer Susan Coolidge, who vacationed in Northeast Harbor, observed, "it would be hard to find a more discouraging object of contemplation than the town proper, with its irregular huddle of shanty-like shops and ungainly tenements, painted in inharmonious colors and dominated over by monstrous hotels of the same flagrant architecture, whose every line seems an affront to the canons of taste." The ugliness mattered not at all to those seeking summer solace. By 1890, they poured in to fill Bar Harbor's nineteen hotels with four thousand rooms—those great "wooden barracks," including seven hundred at Rodick's alone.

But crudeness and crowding did not last for long. Instead, Bar Harbor would ensure its success by a spirited display of family wealth and position. As a resort, it would rank second only to Newport, Rhode Island. In a time of escalating fortunes, with the emergence of approximately four thousand American millionaires between the Civil War and the 1890's, legions of the rich, as well as well-established families, descended on Bar Harbor. Reaping wealth from running railroads, industry, utilities and investment banks, the nouveaux riches, or "squillionaires," mixed with the "old gentry" of good names and valued lineage: doctors, lawyers, small manufacturers and "civic leaders."

The railroads and steamers carried vacationers with cosmopolitan tastes, exacting standards of hygiene and the ambitious desire to replicate resplendent homes and institutions—churches, clubs and associations—of their native cities. Families staked their claims on Mount Desert—many with a tenacity and attachment that continues to this day. Prime parcels were bought up. Another great American land boom took off. Religion, philanthropy and culture took root. Bar Harbor's summer residents spawned an impressive set of institutions: their own Congregational, Catholic, Episcopal, Methodist, Baptist and Unitarian churches; a hospital, a YMCA, a YWCA, the Jesup Memorial Library and a Greek-like temple, the Building of Arts. Starting in the 1880's, the magnetic mix of land, money and the beau monde flourished in Bar Harbor.

By the late 1890's, summer residents, or rusticators as they were popularly called, had hurriedly built (or bought) 250 cottages. Spectacular homes and grandiose gardens, such as Blair Eyrie built by the New York investment banker Dewitt C. Blair and Kenarden Lodge owned by John S. Kennedy, a leading railroad financier, embellished Bar Harbor and spread its fame. The summer residents—the comfortable, the quietly rich and the extravagantly rich—formed complex strata of a beguiling new society. "The cottages, or villas which encircle the town," W. B. Lapham wrote in his laudable guide to the island, "represent the best society of New York, Baltimore, Newport and

Philadelphia from June to the middle of September, its streets and drives are thronged by the gaily dressed migratory butterflies of the world of fashion, airing their silken wings in the cool sunshine of the Maine coast, after comparative inactivity during the winter of the large cities."

There were Vanderbilts, Schiefflins, Opdyckes, Morrises, Ogdens, Bowens, Thorndikes, Amorys, Palmers, Jesups, Thayers, Lawrences, Dorrs, Fabbris, and Pulitzers. A host of advantageous marriages were carefully encouraged as old names crossed with new money. Eventually, it would seem, everyone who mattered became related to everyone else in labyrinthine connections that tied an emerging and aspiring intercity aristocracy tightly to each other.

A special mix of American improvisation and pride, social ambition and European taste flourished in the culture of outdoor life on Mount Desert. European travel was an active reference point for both the old gentry and the nouveaux riches. Returning to the island, they reassured themselves that the Mount Desert landscape was equal to the beauty of the Bay of Naples, the mountains of Switzerland, the lake country of Northern England and the fjords of Norway.

From Sea Urchins, her newly built cottage in 1889, the piquant writer Mrs. Burton Harrison exclaimed: "How astonishing are these Aladdin palaces at Bar Harbor! One year, one sees a barren height, with rocks & firs & junipers & bunch berries, its only inhabitants, the next season, one goes into a lighted portal, with flunkies right & left, across velvet carpeted steps with a hall where 'family' portraits are hanging—there is a dinner cooked by a chef, and after it, music by a secretary of the Russian Legation & a new baritone from Dayton, Ohioh [*sic*]!"

The commodious and richly furnished cottages were built to accommodate families of parents and children, aunts, uncles, in-laws, cousins and numerous guests. The sheer numbers required huge staffs of gardeners, drivers, stable hands—even footmen—along with maids who did endless cleaning, washing, ironing and cooking. Some homes were more formal than others. Louise de Koven Bowen from Chicago settled with her family in her palatial, manicured, French-colonial cottage in Hulls Cove, a few miles from Bar Harbor. Baymeath had eleven bedrooms and ten bathrooms, a room for arranging flowers with two hundred vases of every size, and a stable for twenty-two horses. In the splendor of her cottage at the edge of Frenchman Bay, Mrs. Bowen entertained thirty-five for lunch every afternoon.

Summer residents imported some of America's finest architects to design cottages, churches, clubs and libraries. Peabody and Sterns; Roche and Tilden; William R. Emerson; Bruce Price; Andrews, Jacques and Rantoul; McKim, Mead and White; and Frank Furness produced some of their best work on the island. Fred Savage, a gifted architect and native of Northeast Harbor, was the most prolific. By 1906, he had designed over three hundred buildings on the island. The architects built in a versatile array of imitative and innovative idioms: Italian, French, English, Swiss, Tudor, Queen Anne, Medieval, Renaissance and shingle styles. "It is the fashion to call these country houses cottages," the architect Bruce Price commented with judicious acumen, "but the cottages exist only in name. The cliffs of Newport, the rocks of Mt. Desert, the shores of Shrewsbury . . . have cottages that would be mansions in England, villas in Italy, or chateaus in France."

In the annals of American architectural history, Mount Desert claims a small but honorable place. It was on the island that the taste for Queen Anne structures evolved into the splendid shingle style to house the informal activities of large, vacationing families. William R. Emerson, a Boston architect, started the shingle tradition in 1879 with his design for Redwoods, owned by Charles J. Morrill. Shingles covered the cottage from top to bottom, blending harmoniously with the land and sea. The house captured the ocean breezes and the striking coastal light. With seeming abandon, Emerson and his fellow practitioners of the shingle style employed a varying range of forms: towers, bays, porches, piazzas, porticoes, loggias, leaded glass windows and gables.

The art of "floriculture" thrived on Mount Desert. The transformation of the physical landscape, through planting and replanting, was almost as stunning as the erection of the cottages. "It is a common sight to witness trees coming along through the village streets with their tops extending above the roofs of the houses on the side of the streets," the *Bangor Daily Commercial* stated. The magnitude of change led to exaggeration and awe. "The drives about the estate," the *Bar Harbor*

*Record* wrote of George Vanderbilt's Pointe d'Arcadie, "give promise of equaling the famous roads that were built by Caesar in the days of yore." Equally astounding was the landscape work of Beatrix Cadwalader Jones, the daughter of Mrs. Mary Cadwalader Jones of New York. "A young lady who moves in the upper circle of Bar Harbor society," the *Bangor Daily Commercial* noted, works in a "short skirt which comes to the top of a clumsy pair of rubber boots plodding about in the clayey soil directing the men how they shall wield their axes. . . . Miss Jones is a decidedly new woman."

The "season" throbbed to the invigorating beat of rigorous sports and entertainment: canoeing, sailing, hiking, climbing, biking, riding in horse shows and driving over the island in a full array of sporting carriages. Society gathered in their cottages and exclusive clubs: the Kebo Club for horse shows and golf, the Canoe Club, the Reading Club for the covert consumption of alcohol in a dry state, the Pot and Kettle Club for male comradeship and gastronomic pleasures, the Bar Harbor Swim Club and the Yacht Club. Picnics, teas, dinners, receptions, dances and fetes, along with exhilarating conversation, pleased residents and visitors alike. "Intelligent, lively and entertaining"—and far superior to that of Newport—was the way Edith Wharton responded to the conversation at Bar Harbor when she visited her sister-in-law, Mrs. Mary Cadwalader Jones.

The society of the rich attracted the society of the powerful. There were visits by Presidents, Vice-Presidents, ambassadors, consuls, cardinals and bishops. The appearance of the American and British squadrons further revved an already frenzied social life. It hardly seemed to matter that the American navy was barely a navy: according to one of its critics, the navy was too weak to fight and too slow to get away. No matter what, it had enough power to get to Newport and Bar Harbor, dazzle the summer population and stir the towns with receptions and romances.

Such a social life was prime material for boastful writers and residents in the 1880's. Mrs. Burton Harrison, ever the prominent and watchful figure in New York, Washington and Lenox society, observed the doings of Bar Harbor with both enthusiastic and ambivalent amusement. "It is *so* much nicer here," she wrote her son at Yale, "without the people! The houses are filling up, however, & the Philistines will soon be upon us. Already two or three stylish buckboards have dashed up, laden with frills & finery, to leave cards at the Sea Urchins, alas! If I *could* only live in a place where there was no necessity to 'make and [*sic*] effort'!" But efforts she made. She attended flower parades by day and boat parades by night.

Best of all was the visit of President Benjamin Harrison to the neighboring home of Secretary of State James G. Blaine. In the President's honor, Mrs. Harrison (no relation) organized a flower parade. "Many people familiar with those flower drives in Nice & elsewhere," she proudly wrote, "said the decorations of this were ahead of any they had ever seen." Another day, the President, in a flower-bedecked steamboat, went on a boat trip for several miles around the coast to Somes Sound. Filled with diplomats and high society, the boat hit fog and rough seas around Schooner Head, conditions which "had the effect of reducing many of our gay members to solemnity, not to say silence. . . . His Excellency, who retired to the pilot house, looked rather white, ditto Mr. Blaine. . . . Mavring Bey, the Turkish Minister, was first to succumb, and lay prone upon the cabin sofa, murmuring 'Mon Dieu, Mon Dieu, pourquoi-est-ce que je suis venu? [My God, my God, why did I come?]' "

As the boat entered Somes Sound, the fog lifted, the waters calmed, and the presidential party sailed gingerly around the island away from Bar Harbor. They saw a serene landscape: numerous small islands lying off of Mount Desert Island; vistas of cleared, vacant land; scattered, isolated farms and houses; a few modest summer cottages; and several medium-sized wooden hotels, which thrived with quietly contented summer boarders at Seal Harbor, Southwest Harbor and Northeast Harbor.

Did anyone inform President Harrison that Northeast Harbor possessed a different aura and mystique from other places on the island? Already, it was a summer enclave with its own carefully controlled dynamic: slow growth, a quiet commercial life, and a discrete, unpretentious appearance. The community grew serenely, seemingly from within. Centered around the founders of the community, Charles W. Eliot, president of Harvard, and the Episcopal bishop of Albany, William Croswell Doane, Northeast Harbor promoted itself through a network of relatives, friends and acceptable friends of friends from Boston, New York, Philadelphia and Albany. The summer residents took pride in the simplicity of their lives: their closeness and respect for the local population, the moral and spiritual cohesiveness of their community, and, above all, their harmonious, educated counterpoint to the brassy and irksome display of Bar Harbor.

In fact, approximately twelve miles—but many hours by carriage over bumpy dirt roads—from the muted life in Northeast Harbor, traffic in Bar Harbor was congested and the streets were far from clean. Conditions were so poor that an indignant Mary Cadwalader Jones appealed to the commissioner of sanitation in New York City to send some of his workers—the "white wings"—to clean up the mess in Bar Harbor. "Simply vile. . . . It interferes terribly with our summer enjoyments," she was quoted as telling a reporter from the *Bangor Daily Commercial*.

Yet, however much Bar Harbor and Northeast Harbor differed in taste and style, they still shared a set of underlying values and beliefs: a desire for exclusivity, social safety, and relief from congested cities and the problems of new immigrants. The social landscape changed quickly: Boarders at Bar Harbor's big hotels soon felt unwelcome; throughout the island, excursionists—and certainly lower-class immigrants—were discouraged; and the local population was transformed into a service class that tended the luxurious needs of summer residents.

In 1890, the ever-curious and analytic Charles W. Eliot wrote an essay that praised the simple life of the local population in the township of Mount Desert on Mount Desert Island. Men worked as farmers, fishermen, or shipbuilders; the women spun wool, made butter, and tended children and the home. The men were independent, self-sufficient and content. "One who engages a Mount Desert laborer or mechanic to do a piece of work," Eliot wryly commented, "will probably receive the impression that it is the employed who consents to do a favor to the employer."

Just fourteen years later, Eliot presented a markedly different picture. By this time, many local residents had sold much of their land to summer people. The men and many of the women worked for summer residents, tending shops, providing food, gardening, doing laundry, working in hotels and teaching the summer children how to sail. In return, the summer people benefited the town in innumerable ways: they built new houses, roads, schools, libraries and mountain trails. They established churches, which significantly improved the religious life of the local population: ministers now regularly performed christenings, marriages and burials.

In his typically confident manner, Eliot expressed no doubts about the contributions of the summer people to the year-round residents. Neither did George Street, a Congregational minister from Exeter, New Hampshire, and a summer resident in Southwest Harbor. In his history of Mount Desert, first published in 1903, Street lauded the improved standard of living for the local population. "If they [the summer residents] introduced some undesirable luxuries, emphasized some unfortunate class distinctions, and were responsible for some vices formerly unknown, yet on the whole their influence was healthy in matters sanitary and social and religious."

Class distinctions showed up in many ways. A native of Northeast Harbor, Emily Phillips Reynolds, remembered as a child saving a dollar to have her hair washed and combed at a beauty shop in Northeast Harbor. Happily she climbed the stairs to the second floor and asked Mrs. Coburn, a black lady from Philadelphia, to do her hair. "When I made my request she said she didn't *do* Natives. Crestfallen, I left and was very disappointed and perplexed for I had never been called a Native before." Emily Phillips Reynolds also learned that the summer people were not to be disturbed or annoyed. "Keep out of the face and eyes of the Rusticators was a common lesson we learned early."

In Northeast Harbor, they may have appeared for the first time in 1898 when membership in the newly built swim club was for summer residents only. At the Bar Harbor Swim Club, it was rumored that when, by chance, a local resident fell into the pool, the water was drained and the pool refilled. In Hulls Cove, Mrs. Bowen remembered a discomforting incident with Larson, whom she brought from Chicago to run her stable and oversee the liveries for all her drivers. The only time she ever saw Larson angry was when he wanted to purchase a stretcher for the men's breeches, which the Bowens required to be laundered regularly and which tended to shrink while drying. " 'Oh, Larson, that is so expensive! Can't you and the men put on the breeches and let them dry on you?' He really was quite annoyed and replied, 'I would not take cold even for Mrs. Bowen,' so the stretcher was bought and the breeches were frequently washed."

Yet the relationships with the service class and local population were more complicated than such incidents would suggest. Local residents were admired and often idealized for their skills, fortitude, traditions and uncomplicated ways. "Just as the white man," E. Digby Baltzell wrote, "symbolized by the British gentleman, was roaming round the world in search of raw materials for his factories at Manchester, Liverpool or Leeds, so America's urban gentry and capitalists, at the turn of the century, were imperialists seeking solace for their souls among the 'natives' of Lenox, Bar Harbor or Kennebunkport. . . ." Those natives had once owned all the land, they had a pride in their own culture and families, they were sturdy and competent, and they were Protestant.

Some of the natives, however, had surprising forebears, as Charles W. Eliot discovered. "John Gilley: Maine Farmer and Fisherman" was Eliot's homage to one Northeast Harbor family. Eliot called the Gilleys "the true American type." With deftness, Eliot traced their family history, through maternal and paternal lines, from their present home on Sutton Island off Northeast Harbor, back to Gloucester, Massachusetts. Interesting antecedents were found in the alliance of Hannah Lurvey and William Gilley, the parents of John Gilley and their eleven other children. As expected, Gilley was an English name. But the name Lurvey, Eliot wrote, was a corruption of the German Jewish name Loewe. The Lurveys acknowledged that the first Loewe who went to Massachusetts was of Jewish descent from Archangel, Russia. "It is noticeable that many of the Lurveys have Old Testament names, such as Reuben, Levi, Samuel, Isaac, and Jacob, and that their noses tend to be aquiline."

Bishop Doane, who was always interested in souls, pronounced a loving judgment on the natives of Northeast Harbor. They had known adventure at sea and bravery in the Civil War. "The competency on which they lived simple and unspoiled lives, of home comfort and neighborly companionship, was gained by honest toil and careful frugality." They were "fond of dwelling upon the old times, and full of reminiscences of the island in its early condition, intelligently interested in public questions of the time, and with a fresh and original way of putting things, which gave the zest of real raciness to their talk. And they were kind and cordial in all their attitudes to us who came from outside."

Men of religious and scholarly intent were not the only ones who valued and idealized the local population. In the realm of light fiction and romance after romance, Bar Harbor produced a popular and special genre: democratic regeneration through the local stock. Henrietta Rowe's *The Maid of Bar Harbor,* written in 1905, was a tale in two parts. One part presented the corrupting effects of summer wealth on a venal local family. The other part was a convoluted set of romances. One local family initially appeared to be poor, uneducated and of undistinguished lineage. As the plot evolved, however, they proved to be well-to-do survivors of sterling Nordic descent and the saviors of a summer family in decline.

Arthur Train, a popular writer in New York and Bar Harbor, worked on a similar theme in his short story *The Viking's Daughter.* Train's revered protagonist, the lawyer, Mr. Tutt, was hired to break up the impending marriage of the son of a rich industrialist and summer resident to Dizzy, a lobsterman's daughter. Obstacles were overcome, heroic rescues were performed. Dizzy was "strong, brave and resourceful, gentle and kind." She too came from fine stock, which the family Bible traced back to fourteenth-century England. As in Rowe's tale, morality won, caste was overcome, good Nordic and Anglo-Saxon roots held firm, and a loving marriage took place.

In the real world of Bar Harbor, however, the crossing of class line was rigidly shunned. But romance and freedom from Victorian social restrictions were crucial aspects within society itself. One giddy lady, Alick J. Grant, wrote of the gay Bar Harbor life:

> For I've danced and I've flirted and feted
> And turned night into day;
> And the wonder of all to me, dearest,
> Is why I've not fainted away,
> At the sight of such splendor and fashion—
> For you know, dear, it's not so at home.
> How I wish that the summer was longer,
> How jolly, forever, to roam
> In this island of lake and of mountain,
> Where life is one long pleasant dream
> And the shadows of life are forgotten
> Save to render the contrast supreme. . . .

\*    ·*    \*

I'm engaged to be married
To the youth whom I met on the rocks;
But until I shall give you permission,
Don't mention a word to our folks.
He has plenty of money, a steam yacht,
A rent roll exceedingly high,
And he says he will come to Bar Harbor
Every year for the summer. Good-bye.

For some, Bar Harbor was considered too gilded. Marion Lawrence Peabody, the daughter of Bishop William Lawrence of Massachusetts, recalled her mother's reluctance to accompany her husband to Bar Harbor. For years, she thought it a "wild place where girls from New York and Philadelphia walked up mountains 'swinging their arms'!" In Boston, her daughter wrote, you "kept your hands in a muff in winter and in summer clasped over a purse or card case at your waist."

In "A plea for Bar Harbor," published in *Outing* in 1885, Robert Grant wrote, "The intimacy established between marriageable young folk is the great feature of life at Bar Harbor." Women in Bar Harbor gained greater emancipation through relaxed social customs than they would have through political rights. Independent in action and thought, women learned to "discuss and to form opinions." But Grant was not sure how long these mores would prevail given the trend toward luxurious living and the influx of "much foreign blood."

As Grant well understood, romance was a delicate dance that set the stage for making important marital alliances. The infusion of foreign blood that Grant wrote about was one of the most serious threats. To reinforce upper-class Protestant culture, a robust Christianity flourished on Mount Desert. The religious spirit on the island, however, differed markedly from that of strict, observant Methodist communities such as Ocean Grove in New Jersey and Oak Bluffs in Martha's Vineyard. Nor did Mount Desert have anything in common with summer colonies such as Asbury Park, which attracted advocates of social reform, or mountain retreats like Lake Mohonk.

Although it was by no means the largest of the many denominations on the island, the Episcopal church dominated the upper echelon of the island's social life. Bishops and ministers presided at the pastoral courts of the wealthy and well-to-do. The roster of Episcopal clergymen was a Who's Who of the church: in addition to Bishop Doane and Bishop Lawrence, there were Rev. William Huntington of Grace Church in New York and Rev. Cornelius Smith of St. Thomas Church, also in New York. There were also many ministers—such as Rev. John Whiteman of Greenfield, Massachusetts—who lived in small towns in New England.

With the help of local families who contributed land and labor, the Episcopal leaders built churches such as St. Saviours in Bar Harbor, in the grand shingle-style tradition, St. Jude, a fine Emerson edifice at Seal Harbor, and several small chapels that dotted settlements throughout the island. St. Saviours, the largest and richest, was ever expanding. St. Mary's-by-the-Sea, in Northeast Harbor, replaced a simple twenty-year-old wooden-slab structure with a new stone church in 1902. These churches were filled with beautiful stained-glass windows, unusually fine ritual objects and stately commemorative plaques that testified to the dedication and wealth of the members.

Ministers officiated before full congregations at Sunday-morning services. In Northeast Harbor, in particular, the Sabbath observance continued throughout the day and ended with a sunset service of hymns and scriptural readings. The tradition was begun out of doors overlooking the water at Bishop Doane's home, Magnum Donum (Great Doane). In later years families gathered in a circular clearing in the woods, beyond the great lawn and splendid shingle cottage of Rev. Cornelius Smith on Somes Sound.

By far the most splendid moment of affirmation and recognition of Mount Desert Island's Episcopal community occurred in 1904. The archbishop of Canterbury visited the island and, for the first time, celebrated Holy Communion outside of England. The archbishop came at the behest of Bishops Doane and Lawrence and of J. Pierpont Morgan, who regularly visited the island on his yacht. Marion Lawrence Peabody remembered the excitement of setting out from Bar Harbor on Morgan's legendary yacht *Corsair* to hear the archbishop preach at St. Mary's-by-the-Sea. To the discomfort of all but himself, the august banker insisted that his guests consume a six-course breakfast. When they arrived, bishops, ministers and many summer residents filled the church. More attention, it seemed, was paid to the celebrated banker and benefactor of the church than to the archbishop himself. The Morgans were the "observed of all observers and there was an atmosphere more of the theatre than of church," Peabody recalled. Only when the archbishop spoke did the atmosphere become more spiritual.

If the archbishop's visit was a unique and imperial event, the presence of Rev. Endicott Peabody of Groton and Dr. Samuel Drury of St. Paul's School made equally deep, long-lasting impressions. Each summer in Northeast Harbor Dr. Drury conducted communion for the children and parents of his school. Peabody preached at St. Mary's-by-the-Sea. Their presence reinforced the significant connections between the boarding school and summer resort.

The summer was the only extended period of time that boarding-school boys spent with their parents. And it was active, robust families that Endicott Peabody was concerned about—the one large family he created at Groton, starting in 1884, as well as the individual ones from whom he received his boys. At Mount Desert, Peabody found many of them: the Lawrences, Moffats, Morrises, Fabbris, Sauterlees, Schiefflins and Auchinclosses among them. "No later than the age of twelve," the writer Louis Auchincloss recalled, "I was certain to come under the jurisdiction of this huge, magnificent old man whose cheerful greetings to my family when encountered during a Mt. Desert Island summer never fooled me for a minute about the ultimate hardships of his strict disciplinary academy in cold New England winters."

Peabody's mission was to train boys—never more than two hundred at any time—to achieve an active and civically responsible life and to "cultivate manly, Christian character." The quality of the Groton education, the associations with the best and richest families and the exposure to the forceful personality of the headmaster attracted many to the school. But only Christians were welcome. Groton, along with other boarding schools in New England, formed a formidable barricade to preserve the upper-class Protestant social order.

Peabody wrote about a "gentleman of the Jewish Faith" who contacted one of the church boarding schools, presumably Peabody's own. The unidentified gentleman may very well have been Jacob H. Schiff, the senior partner of Kuhn, Loeb and

Company, who was one of a few Jews who made inquiries about the school. The father wanted to know if his son could be excused from chapel if he went to Groton. Impossible, Peabody replied. "The boys all go to Chapel together. . . . It is an integral part of the life of the community. If a boy were to give up attendance at Chapel, he would still have evening prayers at the house; if he were absent from those there would still be Sacred Studies; there would remain a Christian atmosphere, which, we trust, pervades the place, and from this he would find no retreat." The father, concluding that his son would become a convert or an atheist, decided not to send his boy to Groton.

In Peabody's assertively Christian world, there was no place for prominent, wealthy Jews. None were at Groton and there were no more than one or two at the closely related, status-conscious summer resort of Mount Desert Island. Money could not buy their way in. Upper-class Protestant society, according to historian John Higham, had to "sharpen the informal lines of status." It did so by "grasping at distinctions that were more than pecuniary, through an elaborate formalization of etiquette, the compilation of social registers, the acquisition of aristocratic European culture, and the cult of genealogy. . . . Practically, anti-Semitic discrimination fostered another means of stabilizing the social ladder. . . ."

Of the double threats to the old elites—new industrial wealth and the disruption of traditional patterns of leadership in the immigrant-filled cities—the immigrants caused the greater dismay. The Jewish population in America grew from 250,000 in 1871 to 1,000,000 by 1900. H. G. Wells, visiting America in 1906, was startled at the impact of the new immigrants. "In the lower levels of the American community," he wrote, "there pours perpetually a vast torrent of strangers, speaking alien tongues inspired by alien traditions. . . . The older American population is being floated up on the top of this influx, a sterile aristocracy above a racially different and astonishingly fecund population."

The new system of social classification shut out the German Jewish immigrants just as they were gaining secure economic and professional positions. Suddenly, status was defined by interlocking associations: family connections, memberships in clubs, affiliations in schools, private organizations, and professional associations, especially in medicine and the law. The process involved, as Oscar Handlin has written, the privatization of social life, which was "devoid of public interest and not subject to governmental interference."

Clubs that had turned to Jews as founding members, such as the Union League Club in New York City, before and during the Civil War, now turned down their sons for membership. "There were moments," H. G. Wells wrote after visiting New York City, "when I could have imagined there were no immigrants at all. . . . In the clubs there are no immigrants. There are not even Jews, as there are in London clubs."

And the resorts, the most blatantly commercial and public forum of seeking status, joined in the exclusion. They became the most conspicuous of the social battlefields. Incidents of discrimination turned into public issues. Joseph Seligman, one of New York's most prominent investment bankers, was turned away from the Grand Union Hotel in Saratoga in 1877, a place where he had stayed on several occasions. The press reported that Seligman was told at the desk that the owner of the hotel, Mr. Hilton, would not allow him to register with his family. "I am required to inform you that Mr. Hilton has given instructions that no Israelite shall be permitted in the future to stop at this hotel." The new resort at Coney Island followed suit. The president of the Long Island Railroad and Manhattan Beach Company made a public statement that Jews would not be accepted at his resort. "We do not like Jews as a class. There are some well behaved people among them but as a rule they make themselves offensive to the kind of people who principally patronize our road and hotel, and I am satisfied we should be better off without than with their custom."

By the late 1880's, half of the hotels in the Catskills would not accept Jewish boarders. Land in the Adirondacks was not sold to Jews, except in isolated, undeveloped areas by maverick property owners. Lake associations and clubs barred Jews from membership.

The well-to-do German Jews were dismayed by the growing phenomena of prejudice and social discrimination in a country where they had thus far seen little of it. Some sought explanations and answers. Philip Cowan, the editor of the *American Hebrew*, a Jewish newspaper, wrote to prominent non-Jews asking for their frank opinions about prejudice. "In recent years and particularly during the summer season, there has been manifested in the country an antipathy towards persons of the Jewish faith strangely at variance with that liberality of spirit supposed to be inherent in the American character, and contrary to one of the great teachings of Christianity: 'on earth peace, good will toward men.' " Jews are refused admittance at summer resorts, clubs and some private schools. "No discrimination on account of character is ever made. The fact that one is of the Jewish faith seems sufficient to bar association with him." Cowan asked for answers on several questions: Was prejudice due to religious instruction? What could be done to alleviate it? Do Jews behave differently from others?

Rev. H. C. Potter, bishop of New York and minister at St. Bartholomew's Church, responded that "there are many people of all races who grow suddenly rich, and whose coarse, aggressive, ostentatious, and selfishly-inconsiderate bearing would be pretty sure to provoke resentment no matter what their lineage." Rev. Robert Collyer referred to some Jews at a hotel that he frequented who were "loud and pushing." He observed that "money had grown ahead of their manners."

Charles W. Eliot answered tersely that he was uncertain as to what could be done about "race prejudice." He suggested that Jews should aim for "education with Christians at such schools and colleges as receive both; association with Christians in good works for society at large; association with Christians in all clubs or associations of business men; the careful education of women, so that Jewish ladies may be inevitably recognized as attractive and cultivated women in any society; the taking part by young Jewish men in manly sports and in the militia organizations." Eliot conceded that these were slow-working remedies that would "hardly touch the evil for the present generation." W. M. Thornton, president of the University of Virginia, objected to the Jews because they were interested only in commercial matters. "I often talk with Jews," he wrote Cowan, "and I have never had one of them mention a book to me or speak of a magazine article or indicate in any way that their activities were engaged in aught but business."

Some of the more than twenty respondents suggested that Jews improve their manners and become less clannish. In general, the focus was on behavior and etiquette and not on the deeper issues of status, prestige and power. If there were Gentile leaders such as Rev. Henry Ward Beecher who, at the time of the Seligman affair, decried the prejudice and defended the Jews, there were even more who were actively anti-Semitic and wanted to have nothing to do with Jews. And there were many people—especially in resorts such as Mount Desert Island— who simply accepted and perpetuated the systems of exclusion.

For the Jews, however, indifference was not possible. Presented with the new barriers to acceptance, many fought back, especially in New York and along the New Jersey shore. Seligman built a hotel for Jews in Saratoga. By the turn of the century, half of the vacationers in the resort were Jewish. Nathan Straus built a hotel where Jews would be welcomed in Lakewood, New Jersey, after he had been rejected at one of the resort's renowned establishments. Atlantic City, exclusively Gentile and fashionable in the 1890's, started losing its traditional clientele after the turn of the century. Within a decade it became an overwhelmingly Jewish resort. In the Adirondacks, some of the richest and most prominent Jews in America—Otto Kahn, Julius Bache, Adolph Lewisohn, George Blumenthal and Louis Marshall—built their own camps and associations on Upper Saranac Lake, away from the restricted areas.

Mount Desert Island differed from the others. Isolation was the key. "To support a Coney Island," Charles W. Eliot observed in 1904, "a Brooklyn is necessary, and a Metropolitan Boston for a Revere Beach." Yet Eliot acknowledged the way of life at Mount Desert Island could not be taken for granted. "It is easy, with or without deliberate design, to change the nature of the resort." Already, he wrote, Newport, Saratoga and Bar Harbor served a different class of people than twenty years before. "There are several places within sight of Mount Desert," Eliot warned in his homily on the island, "and enjoying the same climate, which testify that it is hard to establish a successful summer resort, and easy to impair or degrade one already established."

# CHAPTER 9

# *Visionaries*

In 1907, ARTHUR TRAIN lamentingly called his beloved summer home "The Isle of Mt. Deserted." Writing for the *Bangor Daily Commercial,* Train imagined the worst on all fronts: autos on his island, farmers in the towns, Jewish hotel operators on the scene and low-class tourists all around. "It was on July 4, 1920, ten years after the evacuation of Bar Harbor by its summer residents, that I determined to revisit the scenes of my youth and observe what changes, if any, time had wrought there."

There were more than he could bear. Gasoline had ignited fires all over the island, charring the land and causing summer residents to flee. Bar Harbor was being forsaken even by the local people who had built hotels for the auto tourists. The fancy and rich did not drive over. But the farmers did. In the deserted town one reckless farmer ran his car over some dogs, hit the village clock, and rammed into horses and the post office. A day later "six hundred and ninety-seven old ladies who boarded at the hotels called for their time and left town. They took with them one thousand three hundred and twenty-nine maids and nieces. . . ."

Train spun out his calamitous tale. Hoards of excursionists came by railroad to the terminus at Bass Harbor, the new center of island life. It was a "thriving town with two large hotels (owned by Moe Levy of New York, one of them having a thousand fully furnished rooms), fourteen garages, two gasoline factories, car works and train sheds." One of Train's friends ran "Foley's Furious, Frantic, Frenzied Terrific Twenty-five Cent Tours Round the Island in Forty Minutes." The old carriage drivers waited on tables at Moe Levy's hotel. Mount Desert Island, Foley cried, was just like Coney Island.

If Train's prophecy was dire, the pressures for change were real. Disputes were erupting on Mount Desert Island: cars versus carriages; the clash between local businessmen and the summer residents; popular access to the island versus private exclusion. Nonetheless, the old ladies, their maids and their horses stayed around. The farmers did not come. Society did not leave the island. The Kebo, the Pot and Kettle, and the other clubs thrived. There were no fires and, for the moment, no autos. And, in Bass Harbor, there were no Jewish owners running their thousand-room hotels.

But there were, as Train well knew, a few acceptable exceptions. Already, a small number of Jewish summer residents and merchants were present on Mount Desert. The powerful, iconoclastic and eccentric owner of the New York *World* and St. Louis *Post-Dispatch*, Joseph Pulitzer, was one. The publisher of America's largest newspaper was an immigrant from Hungary whose parents were Jewish. He was married to Kate Davis, a non-Jewish woman in high standing in St. Louis society, who had learned to her dismay, only after their wedding, that her husband was Jewish. The rich Pulitzer brought his family to Bar Harbor in the 1890's and established them in Chatwood. When Pulitzer lavishly renovated the cottage to include a "tower of silence," as the locals called it, his family became one of the most conspicuous on the island. Walter Damrosch, the musician and conductor, was another Jew who settled in Bar Harbor. Married to the daughter of James G. Blaine, Maine's venerated senator and later U.S. secretary of state, Damrosch was easily accepted in Bar Harbor society. In both instances, Jewish men married Gentile women, and their children, who were Gentile, were accepted in society at the summer resort.

Neither Pulitzer nor Damrosch tested the boundaries of the liberality of Bar Harbor's society, but Jacob H. Schiff did. In terms of power and prestige in business and philanthropy, Schiff easily qualified for membership in the cottage community. Schiff had come to America in 1865 from a Frankfurt Jewish family, long distinguished by its prominent bankers and rabbis. In 1875, he was invited to join the firm of Kuhn, Loeb and Company, which had started a New York commercial bank a few years before. Ten years later he was its senior partner. "Aggressively ambitious, adventurous, opinionated, and strong-willed" was how his nephew James Warburg accounted for Schiff's impressive success. Short in size, imperious and formal, Schiff was a forbidding figure to many people.

From the 1880's through the second decade of the twentieth century, Schiff, as the head of Kuhn, Loeb and Company, was one of the most powerful investment bankers in the country. Schiff placed American railroad and government securities in foreign markets. Along with other bankers, railroad tycoons and industrialists, he rode the attendant wild waves of prosperity and panic. He advised the Pennsylvania Railroad, for which he raised more than a billion dollars in financing, and other railroads, including the Union Pacific and Northern Pacific. Schiff sat on the boards of the National City Bank, the Equitable Life Assurance Society and other large corporations, as well as political commissions and many philanthropic organizations.

Power, however, did not necessarily bring social prestige. Schiff was the only one of the elite group of financial magnates who was not listed in the *Social Register* at the turn of the century. (The key listing of prominent figures along with their professions, clubs and church associations was first published in 1887 in New York.) According to the historian Frederick Lewis Allen, the omission was due solely to the fact that Schiff was "a Jew, and the Jews constituted a group somewhat apart; the fashionable clubs were almost exclusively gentile; and the Social Register was virtually a gentile register."

Schiff was not only Jewish, but he was the leader of American Jewry in the realms of philanthropy, public policy and the growing fight against anti-Semitism—helping to establish the foundations of Jewish life in America in the twentieth century. His reputation for wealth and charity followed him wherever he went. In 1899, Bishop Potter of New York maintained that Schiff was the greatest philanthropist of his day in their city.

He was unique. Wherever he lived—in Maine, New Jersey or New York—Schiff considered himself to be a religious Jew.

He was married to a Jewish woman, Theresa Loeb Schiff, daughter of a founding partner of Kuhn, Loeb and Company. Compliant and respectful, she joined her husband in maintaining rituals of Jewish observance for their extended family of Schiffs, Warburgs and Loebs. According to his nephew Paul Warburg, Schiff's religion was "a strange mixture of orthodoxy and ritualistic liberalism he had concocted for himself. . . ." He said prayers after meals, observed all religious holidays, blessed his children and grandchildren each Friday evening, insisted that his two children marry Jews, attended Temple Emanu-El in New York each Saturday, and did no work on the Sabbath.

Within his own family, who regarded him as authoritarian and rigid, Schiff encountered mild tolerance and slight interest in religious observance. When his nephew James Warburg was engaged to a non-Jewish woman, his parents never expressed any objections. Schiff, however, was unable to contain his disappointment and concern and telegraphed Warburg: "I wish you joy . . . but cannot refrain from telling you that I am deeply disturbed by your action in marrying out of the faith in view of its probable effect upon my own progeny." Schiff's fears came true. Most of his many grandchildren married into upper-class Protestant families.

Regardless of his strong identification as a Jew, Schiff found respect and tolerance for himself and his family on Mount Desert Island. Starting in 1903, every other August, Schiff and his wife visited the island with their son Mortimer, their daughter Frieda, who was married to Felix Warburg, and the many Schiff grandchildren. They rented one large cottage after another until they finally settled on Farview on Bar Harbor's Eden Street, a house with elaborate pseudo-Italianate design: fine gardens, terraces and a flower-filled inner courtyard.

The entourage traveled with sixty pieces of luggage, a nurse, a valet, a maid and a governess in Edward Harriman's private railroad car, joining the many other private cars on the Bar Harbor Express, which went to Mount Desert Ferry. Edward M. M. Warburg, one of Schiff's grandsons, remembered the joy of the trip to Bar Harbor. "Each car was a house on wheels with brass beds in the master bedroom, sleeping accommodations for the whole family including upper and lower berths, which naturally we children adored. Each car also had its own kitchen and dining compartment from which one could gaze out with wonder as the New England coast sped by." (The horses and carriages came by boat from New Jersey and the Warburg yacht was brought by its crew to the small harbor.)

Schiff's presence in the community was duly noted by the *Bar Harbor Record,* in which he was identified as a person of importance and as a Jew. Detailed articles on Schiff's business undertakings were reprinted from national newspapers. When Schiff spoke at the local YMCA in 1908, the *Record* reported that "his address was practical and inspiring and by his simple yet eloquent manner held the undivided attention of the entire audience." With typical effusiveness, the paper stated that "the meeting will be one long remembered by those present." Schiff's philanthropy for non-Jewish and Jewish causes was followed in short reports: $500,000 to Barnard College for a building, $100,000 for a technical college in Palestine, donations to the Red Cross, Montefiore Hospital and to Beth Israel Synagogue in Bangor—the closest synagogue to Bar Harbor.

Schiff and his family led a quiet social life on the island. The grandchildren preferred tennis and swimming at the Bar Harbor Swimming Club to a regimen of mountain climbing with their grandfather. They endured the foggy days and thrived on the clear ones. "Echtes Bar Harbor wetter" ("typical Bar Harbor weather") was what the family exclaimed on the good ones. Since Schiff was hard of hearing, the family centered its entertaining at home with family and friends, mainly from New York. As an exception, once or twice a summer, Schiff and his wife, Theresa, visited with Charles W. Eliot in Northeast Harbor. Schiff, who spoke with a strong German accent, would report back to his children about his visit with the Harvard president. Frieda Warburg recalled with amusement that her father would pronounce at dinner: "Today I had the most interesting conversation with President Eliot. And he said to me, in that peculiar New England accent of his . . ."

Repeatedly, in their extensive correspondence, Eliot encouraged Schiff to split his summer vacation between Rumson on the Jersey shore and Mount Desert Island. The two areas differed significantly. The Jersey shore attracted large numbers of Jews, Mount Desert but a handful. In Rumson, where Schiff owned a fifty-acre estate, he twice encountered the bitter cross-currents of acceptance and exclusion in a summer colony. Although he had been a founder of the Rumson Country Club, when he sought to gain memberships for others in his family, he was turned down. On another occasion, Felix Warburg, Schiff's son-in-law, tried to bring family members into the Sea Bright Tennis Club, to which Warburg had donated some tennis courts. He was told that he was the only Jew whom the club would allow as a member. In both instances, the Schiffs and the Warburgs left the clubs that they had prominently supported.

In addition to Eliot's friendship, Schiff may also have appreciated the outpouring of indignation in Northeast Harbor over the Dreyfus Affair. In September 1899, twenty-seven residents in Northeast Harbor, including Rev. William Huntington, Ellen Vaughan, Andover Wheelwright, Mary Wheelwright, Eliza Gardiner and S. K. Doane, sent a letter of sympathy, in French, to Mme. Dreyfus in Rennes. "The heart of the entire world is turned toward you," it stated, as the retrial of Capt. Alfred Dreyfus took place over the anti-Semitic-inspired charges of espionage. "The trial has shown the innocence and noble character of your husband, and the large public that has followed this battle with anguish, has given to him and to his children, the honor for which he has fought until now and for which he is still fighting in France."

On Mount Desert Island, Schiff found many of the men with whom he dealt closely in his business and philanthropic worlds: J. Pierpont Morgan, Alexander Cassatt and John S. Kennedy, to name a few. But prejudice was capricious. Although Jews prospered in all-Jewish investment-banking houses, they were unable to achieve positions in the Protestant banking firms. Socially, Schiff and Kuhn, Loeb were distant from the three other great firms: J. P. Morgan and Company, First National Bank, and National City. Despite close business dealings, anti-Semitic comments and attitudes were evident in clubs, conversations, and private correspondence.

Even at Harvard, under Eliot's liberal and expansive regime, Schiff had encountered a painful incident of family humiliation. In 1902, Schiff wrote Eliot about James Loeb. It was through Loeb, Schiff's brother-in-law, that Schiff had taken an interest in Harvard. He had paid for the building of the Semitic Museum in 1902 and generously supported the research of members of the Semitic department. Loeb, who had attended Harvard, was the sponsor of the distinguished Loeb Classics, which offered new translations, along with the original texts, of major classical works.

"Some time ago," Schiff wrote Eliot, "my brother-in-law James Loeb, told me, it had been suggested by a number of his friends, that he become a candidate for Overseer [of Harvard], and that he had put himself into the hands of his friend Mr. Mott Hallowell." Bringing the matter up to date, Schiff continued: "Today I asked him how his canvas for the Overseer stood and he then told me, that he had last week received advice from Mr. Hallowell that the Nominating Committee had declined to put up his name, because it deemed it unwise to advocate the candidacy of a Hebrew." Schiff asked Eliot to look into the matter and give his "own version." His brother-in-law, Schiff wrote, "does not know I am writing you, nor do I do this for the purpose of bringing any pressure to bear to have the existing situation changed, of which he would not approve."

Eliot immediately contacted Hallowell, a Boston lawyer, who responded quickly to Eliot's concerned inquiry. Embarrassment and delicate evasions were threaded through Hallowell's response.

> By a misfortunate [*sic*] misunderstanding, I probably am the originator of a report which I hear has reached your ears, to the effect that the name of James Loeb was turned down by the committee on nominations for the board of overseers, on the ground of his nationality. I was under the impression myself, and repeated it to two different persons and probably it went further through their agency.
>
> Learning my error I have communicated the fact to them, with the request to deny it, and if I hear the report in any other quarter I shall most certainly take pains to correct the impression. I write to you as I can easily understand the annoyance it might cause you, and it seems best that you should know its origin.
>
> My original impression was obtained in a talk with one of the committee. The latter, whom I have known for a long time, I know from experience to be both conservative and accurate. At the time, I myself was in somewhat of a hurry. So although he is kind enough to

acquit me, I felt that a correct analysis of the facts must place the blame on my shoulders.

Other than contacting Hallowell, Eliot's response to Loeb's withdrawal is not known. Nevertheless, Eliot was able to mollify Schiff and to sustain his deep interest in Harvard. In Eliot, Schiff found a deeply sympathetic friend. When many in Boston and Cambridge were lobbying for restriction of immigration, Eliot lauded the aspirations of Jewish immigrants in America. His recognition of Jewish contributions to American society gave Schiff much comfort and hope. "I have only during the past few days found the opportunity to read the address you delivered upon the celebration of the settlement of the Jews in the United States," Schiff wrote to Eliot in 1906. "I would like to say to you how grateful I feel for this appreciation on your part, so publicly expressed, of what the Jew and his faith has meant and still means to mankind. At a time when, sad to say, race hatred and prejudice is rampant in the old world and has even in the new world not entirely disappeared, such words as you have spoken cannot but have their far-reaching value and influence."

Whenever possible, Schiff fought anti-Semitism, using his vast resources in America, Europe and Asia on behalf of Jews throughout the world. He rewarded friends and punished enemies, especially Russia, which persecuted its Jewish population. To weaken Russia during the Russo-Japanese War in 1904, Schiff became the principal financier of the Japanese. Ten years later, during World War I, Schiff barred Kuhn, Loeb and Company from aiding the British and French as long as they were allied militarily and financially with Russia. In New York, along with other Jewish leaders, he established institutions and organizations—both local and national—to meet the needs of German and eastern-European Jewish immigrants.

The summer resort of Bar Harbor, however, presented a totally different world. Maine did not foster the special ties to Jewish communal life that Schiff had established either in New York City or at the Jersey shore. Essentially, Schiff was the only prominent, practicing Jew who regularly returned to Mount Desert Island. A few others, such as Otto Kahn, Schiff's flamboyant partner at Kuhn, Loeb and Company, tried the island for a season or two. Like tasting a rich dessert, Kahn rented Pointe d'Arcadie from George Vanderbilt for two summers, and then moved on to other vacation spots.

Samuel Fels, the co-owner of Fels-Naphtha in Philadelphia, had a cottage in Seal Harbor. A small number of well-known Jewish musicians, such as Josef Hofmann and David Mannes, came to the island for several weeks to perform at the Building of Arts and add panache to the island's cultural life. There were other short-term visitors. The scientist Simon Flexner, director of the Rockefeller Institute of Medical Research, stayed in Seal Harbor for a few seasons. Lillian Wald, founder of the Henry Street Settlement House on the Lower East Side, was the guest of her close friend Jane Addams in Hulls Cove for many summers. But the Jews did not form a community—or challenge. They never congregated in a specific hotel, as was the case in Saratoga, or owned land in separate areas, as in the Adirondacks.

Although Schiff did not have a community of Jewish peers in Bar Harbor, he was well aware from walking on Main Street that a few Jewish merchants worked and lived in Bar Harbor. The dazzling wealth and fancy reputation of Bar Harbor were magnets for a handful of enterprising Jewish immigrants. They were never cohesive and they were not inclined to establish any Jewish institutions. Since the island had no synagogue, on several occasions Schiff actually called the Jewish men in Bar Harbor to come to Farview to form a minyan and pray with him.

The Jewish immigrants settled smoothly into the booming coastal town, trying, like their Gentile counterparts, to cash in on the prosperous summer trade, which sustained them for most of the year. They remained open all year, however, to serve a captive local population, since Bar Harbor was the only place on the island to shop for clothing and dry goods. The untidy aura of the town, with its erratically shaped wooden buildings thrown up quickly and cheaply, absorbed the Jewish immigrants' awkward ways as well as those of some Penobscot Indians who camped in town and sold baskets and canoes and the Japanese merchants who owned curio shops. There were also many peddlers, including a few Jews.

Success and recognition came quickly for the Jewish immigrants. Most sold clothing for summer needs. Since there was no ready-made sportswear, local tailors designed and fabricated

custom clothes for summer use, and shoe merchants sold special shoes for climbing. The *Bar Harbor Souvenir,* published in
1906, and *People and Places: Lubec—Jonesport—Ellsworth—
Machias and Bar Harbor,* issued in 1908, identified several Jewish
merchants. The promotional publications listed over sixty businessmen in Bar Harbor, including bankers, lawyers, real estate
agents, contractors, pharmacists and others who figured in the
town's commercial and professional life. Consistent with all of
the other descriptions, the Jews were praised for their stores,
good characters and fine backgrounds.

Max Franklin, a Jew who had arrived in the early 1880's
from Germany, claimed to have the largest "Dry and Fancy
Goods Store." He sold kitchenware, linens, dresses and sportswear in his own large building on Main Street. Much respected
in the town, he became a director of the Bar Harbor Banking
and Trust Company and belonged to the Masons, the Odd
Fellows and the Grange. His immigrant background was generously appreciated: "Mr. Franklin is entitled to a great amount
of credit for the success he has attained. Coming to a strange
country, with little or no capital and no experience of the manners and customs of the people, he has shown a rare business
capacity and power of adaptability that can be appreciated
freely only by those who have attempted their fortunes in
strange lands."

"Perlinsky's," a Jewish establishment owned by Mark Perlinsky, a Russian-born immigrant, called itself a small department store for women's clothes, trunks, lingerie and other
assorted items. The publication stated: "In his long residence
here, Mr. Perlinsky has won respect for personal as well as
industrial qualifications." He too belonged to several of the
local fraternal and commercial organizations. The tailor Abraham Simon made suits, riding breeches, yachting outfits and
uniforms of any kind. A picture of him was included in the
*Souvenir,* as well as the claim: "There is a nobbiness about the
clothes made here that is not surpassed in the most fashionable
centers."

Another tailor with a prosperous business was A. M. Schiro.
At times he employed as many as fifteen other tailors to produce uniforms for the liverymen who drove the fancy carriages.
He also designed women's clothing specially suited to the in-
formality of summer life. He started his store in 1902 soon after

he arrived in the United States, undoubtedly aided by his brothers and cousins in Bangor.

Nathan Hilson established his men's store in 1880. He was called "one of the oldest top-to-toe outfitters in this section." Eventually his store offered the finest-quality men's clothing in Bar Harbor. "He is numbered among Bar Harbor's progressive business men, being esteemed personally as well as commercially. . . ." Julius Kurson came from Russia in 1889. Only a year later he opened a men's clothing store on Cottage Street. By 1906 he had a store of two thousand square feet on Main Street and employed four people. "This store has two large plate glass windows and enables Mr. Kurson to display a great quantity of goods and the windows attract much attention." To add to Kurson's stature, the publication stated that his "Russian home was in the province of Courland, City of Litan. This is one of the Baltic provinces, where the highest grade of people live, and from whence the regeneration of that country is likely to come."

Other Jewish merchants included Morris Franklin, who owned a shoe store, and Nathan Edmur and Nathan Povich, who ran furniture stores. Povich, the father of five sons, was the most anxious to retain Jewish rituals and to train his sons for bar mitzvah. Frequently, he went to Boston to offer the job of Hebrew teacher to a greenhorn, fresh off a boat from Europe, and bring him back to Bar Harbor. A succession of them passed through his home. One, Sam Seplin, was lured by Povich to Bar Harbor after he read an ad for a Hebrew teacher and shohet in a New York Yiddish paper. When the job did not work out, Seplin went into the cattle business, selling cows to the dairy farmers on the island.

Unlike Jacob H. Schiff, who moved back to New York City after his month-long vacation, the Jews in Bar Harbor lived month after month and year after year with few Jewish associations and infrequent ritual observances. Their world was overwhelmingly dominated by the Christian culture of the summer residents and local population. Nevertheless, many of them sought to observe Jewish rites and holidays. "Mr. Nathan Povish [*sic*] is the happy father of 8 children, the latest a baby boy born last Saturday," the *Bar Harbor Record* announced. "The event of circumcision will be celebrated at 12:00 Saturday and all the many friends of Mr. and Mrs. Povish are cordially invited to attend the ceremony at which a well known Bangor rabbi will preside." Some families bought kosher meat from Bangor and rigorously maintained the dietary laws. In addition to Hebrew teachers to train the boys for bar mitzvah, rabbis and hazzanim were brought from Boston to lead the Rosh Hashanah and Yom Kippur services in a hired hall.

Although the number of Jewish merchants and tailors swelled in the summer, the year-round Jewish population remained small. Jewish children mixed freely with their Gentile friends in Bar Harbor. While some of the immigrants were unhappy with a sporadic religious life and the paucity of marriageable Jews, others were satisfied simply to join a synagogue in Bangor for holiday celebrations. Other people settled in for a few years and then restlessly moved away from the island. A few married non-Jews and drifted to the Congregational church. In the fortuitous mix of immigrant families, no forceful leaders emerged with a commitment to building an observant Jewish community.

Most of the shopkeepers, both Jewish and Gentile, knowing that they existed to serve the fancy trade, practiced the mores of deference. Sometimes, the immigrants did so with naive humor. One of Nathan's sons, the writer Shirley Povich, remembered a conversation between his mother and a "patriarch" of Bar Harbor. "Well, Mrs. Povich," Mr. Stafford said, "we have customs in Bar Harbor. . . . Here is what we expect from all of our people." In broken English Mrs. Povich said, " 'Have a chair, Mr. Stafford.' " And he began to say what an important man he was in town, and she said, " 'Well, Mr. Stafford, have two chairs.' " The merchants knew to step aside when summer people walked on the streets and that it was often necessary to show their goods to women as they sat in their carriages, because some customers did not wish to enter the shops.

After the turn of the century, however, some of the locals in Bar Harbor began to resent the domination of the summer colony. They objected to the antiquated taste of the rich as they tenaciously indulged in their pastoral summer setting. "It is to escape the sights and sounds of the city," Charles W. Eliot wrote in 1904, "that intelligent people come in summer to such a place as this rough and beautiful island; and the short-season populations do not wish to be reminded in summer of the scenes and noises amid which the greater part of their lives is inevitably passed." The signs of city life came most forcefully with the automobile. When year-round residents sought to bring them on the island, the struggle with the summer population was fierce.

In 1909, for the first time, clashing economic and class interests were explicitly exposed. John T. Hinch, a dentist in Bar Harbor and the head of the local automobile committee, accused the "city millionaires" of trying by "every means in their power to make Bar Harbor a quiet, exclusive resort where their little clique can have full sway and where no state of Maine man is welcome." The cottage people, he wrote, knew that autos would bring a different kind of visitor who would revitalize the hotel life. With a surge of defiance and independence, he wrote: "The businessmen of Bar Harbor are beginning to realize that what the millionaires want is unreasonable and unjust."

Another issue, one of enduring importance, was also coming to the fore. Preservation of the natural landscape was a matter of growing concern to many of the leaders of the summer community, especially Charles W. Eliot, whose call for action invoked the idealism of his son, Charles, who had died not long before. A visionary democrat and landscape architect, young Charles had organized the Trustees of Public Reservations for Massachusetts to preserve scenic and historic areas. He had been equally concerned with Maine's future. "Can nothing be done," he wrote in 1888, "to preserve for the use and enjoyment of the great unorganized body of the common people some fine parts, at least, of this seaside wilderness of Maine?"

In 1901, the father convened an illustrious group of ministers, scientists and summer residents including George B. Dorr, George Vanderbilt and Bishops William Lawrence and William Doane. "By what means," Eliot asked them, "can some public reservations of interesting scenery be secured for the perpetual use and enjoyment of all the inhabitants of Mount Desert, natives, cottagers and transient visitor alike?" Eliot explained that over the past twenty years, he had seen beautiful spots on the island become inaccessible. "Place after place where I was in the habit of walking or picnicking has been converted to private uses, and resort to it by other than the owner has become impossible."

Given his stature in the academic world and on the island, Eliot's wishes were hard to resist. As president of Harvard, he spent the last years of the nineteenth century building a great university through cultivating its graduate programs, improving the quality and diversity of the faculty and converting the undergraduate curriculum into a new system of elective studies. He was independent, deeply religious, outspoken and inveterately curious about matters great and small. (Mrs. Eliot once asked a neighbor in Northeast Harbor what he thought of a portrait of her husband. After looking at it for a while, the farmer commented: "Yaas, that's him sure, but he ain't asking no questions.")

Eliot also wrote and spoke prolifically about the great public-policy debates of his time: the Spanish-American War, the nature of wealth, the restriction of immigration, and World War I. Equally free with advice on minute matters of behavior, he once informed Bishop William Lawrence of Massachusetts that he should hire a secretary to answer his mail and telephone. "Of course," Eliot told the bishop, "you should never go to the telephone yourself, or be called upon to decide anything on only telephonic notice."

Eliot's meeting in 1901 was another triumph for him. He convinced his fellow residents on Mount Desert Island to establish the Hancock County Trustees of Public Reservations. Two years later, the association was incorporated by the Maine legislature "to acquire, by devise, gift or purchase, and to own, arrange, hold, maintain or improve for public use lands in Hancock County, Maine, which by reason of scenic beauty, historical interest, sanitary advantage or other like reasons may become available for such purpose."

The person whose life was most affected by the Mount Desert Island conservation movement was George Dorr, an important summer figure whose family had built Oldfarm in Bar Harbor in 1878. At the age of forty-nine, Dorr carried an air of formality and aloofness as well as evinced a strong physical vigor. He was a scholar, a professional horticulturist, an indefatigable trailblazer on the island and sole heir in a family of wealth and high social standing in Boston and Bar Harbor. In response to Eliot's campaign, Dorr donated a large portion of his own lands, aggressively bought additional properties for the trustees and pursued gifts of land and money from his peers. By 1913—just ten years later—Dorr's efforts had accumulated nearly five thousand acres, including some of the island's most scenic mountaintops.

Success on one front, however, produced difficulties on another. Southwest Harbor, with the smallest and least-powerful summer community, had voted in 1911 to allow cars. In 1913, pressure built up in the state legislature at Augusta to force all of the island's towns to allow automobiles. Within the year, Bar Harbor capitulated, while Northeast Harbor and Seal Harbor held firm for only two more years.

As a result of the introduction of the automobile and of conflicts between land speculators and the trustees, in January 1913 the state representative from Bar Harbor introduced a bill to revoke the charter and tax-exempt status of lands owned by the Hancock County Trustees of Public Reservations. Although Dorr was able to get the bill defeated, he realized that the trustees needed greater protection than they could find in Augusta.

With Eliot's backing, Dorr turned to the federal government and the national conservation movement, where he felt more at home in Washington than in Maine's state capital, Augusta. He had numerous friends—and friends of friends—in the small, elitist federal government. Bearing the grace and wealth of a Boston patrician, Dorr had immediate entrée to the highest officials in Woodrow Wilson's administration, including the President himself. Dorr embarked on a campaign to give the trustees' lands as a gift to the federal government in the form of a national monument or national park.

The process took two years of arduous work and increased financial commitments from the summer residents. While Dorr perfected the deeds and boundaries, Eliot solicited funds. He turned to John D. Rockefeller, Jr., with whom he served on three of the Rockefeller philanthropic boards, including the Rockefeller Foundation set up in 1913 with an endowment of $100,000,000. Ever ready to assess character, Eliot viewed Rockefeller—forty years his junior—as a serious, diligent, cautious and reserved man.

A relatively recent property owner in Seal Harbor, Rockefeller was perfectly suited in temperament and interests to join Dorr and Eliot's crusade. On his first extended stay in 1908, he had rented one of Bar Harbor's largest cottages. Then, following the advice of Dr. Simon Flexner and his wife, Helen, JDR, Jr., moved to the quieter and less pretentious town of Seal Harbor. Both he and his wife, Abby Aldrich Rockefeller, sought to connect their lives closely to simple New England virtues and the beauty of the island. In 1910, he purchased The Eyrie, a mock English cottage set on a high ridge overlooking the Eastern Way and the Cranberry Isles. Along with significantly enlarging The Eyrie, JDR, Jr., an amateur landscape architect, started to design and build carriage roads on his extensive property just as he had done at the family's Pocantico Hills estate near New York City.

In his earliest appeals to Rockefeller in 1914 and 1915, Dorr explained that the trustees could not afford to protect their land either from fire or from the threat of taxation. Eliot, on his part, informed Rockefeller that Dorr could not afford to finance additional land purchases and the verification of deeds on his own. In response to the joint appeals, Rockefeller agreed to contribute $17,500, his first substantial gift to the trustees.

It was the beginning of a close and fruitful relationship among Dorr, Eliot and Rockefeller. As they moved through intricate negotiations into the larger public domain of the federal government, the triumvirate took over the leadership of the island. Slowly, they stretched their concepts of public access to the island far beyond the privileged boundaries of the small Protestant summer colony. Rockefeller became the active but cautious patron of Dorr's preservation campaign. Eliot became the intermediary between the other two: while pressing Rockefeller for more and more generous contributions, Eliot had to justify Dorr's frenetic activities to the orderly and meticulous patron.

If Mount Desert Island and Bar Harbor were to be sold to the people of the United States, the island could not be promoted as an exclusive resort for the rich. Therefore, Dorr turned to ornithologists, geologists, botanists and historians to convince the public that the one hundred square miles of Mount Desert Island were unique. A flood of scientific detail was set loose, describing the island's thirteen granite peaks, nine clear freshwater lakes, many bays, the fjord at Somes Sound, the molten masses, glacial movements, ice sheets, forests, trees, cliffs, gorges, boulders, coves, harbors, meadowlands, marshes, aquatic life, migratory patterns of sea and shore

birds as well as vegetation that was uniquely situated at the
crossroads between the southernmost boundary of the Arctic
zone and the northernmost boundary of the more temperate
area to the south. A rich history was called forth to retrace the
exploits of the early explorers and settlers. The colonial struggles involving the French and English were retold through histories of Pierre deu Guast (Sieur de Monts), Samuel de
Champlain, Antoine de La Mothe (Sieur de Cadillac), the Jesuit
mission at St-Sauveur, Samuel Argall, Mme. de Gregoire, Mar-
quis de Lafayette, Sir Francis Bernard and Abraham Somes.

While Dorr was selling Mount Desert, a struggle was under
way in Washington to promote a national constituency for a
unified park system and to convince Congress to create a national park service under the jurisdiction of the Interior Department. Both Franklin K. Lane, secretary of the interior, and
his assistant, Steve Mather, became strong supporters of Eliot
and Dorr's efforts. The year 1916 turned out to be climactic:
Congress created the National Park Service; President Wilson
accepted from the trustees five thousand acres of land as a "free
gift" to the United States under the designation of the Sieur de
Monts National Monument.

For Dorr, the Sieur de Monts National Monument was only
the first step toward the proper maintenance and expansion of
the lands the trustees had brought together. More and more he
turned to Rockefeller, who wanted to extend his carriage paths
over lands owned by the trustees and federal government. Dorr
needed money to expand the holdings of the monument and
convert it into a federally supported national park. In 1916, the
trustees and federal government granted Rockefeller the permission he sought. At the same time, Rockefeller started to
fund the acquisition of lands on the western part of the island.

In pursuit of additional moneys, Dorr presented his case in
1918 before the appropriate committees of the House of Representatives. In a hearing before the Subcommittee on Public
Lands, Dorr tried to meet all the popular concerns of the congressmen. To counter any dubious objections, he twisted and
stretched his arguments. When asked about accommodations
around the park for the traveling public, the patrician Dorr
spoke of hotels and boardinghouses in Bar Harbor—but never
of the fancy cottage community whence he came. "Our idea as
to the park has been to develop it for the brain workers of the

country, people who would be responsive to the beauty and inspiration of its scenery, and can get away for a brief or longer holiday. They are going there now in numbers, but what we want to provide for specially is the need of people of moderate or narrow means who would appreciate what it has to give in beauty, interest, and climate."

Dorr submitted letters of endorsement from such distinguished summer residents as David B. Ogden, George W. Wickersham, Rev. A. W. Halsey, Rev. William T. Manning and Bishop William Lawrence. A letter from Jacob H. Schiff to the chairman of the House Committee on Appropriations was included:

> I have been a resident of Mt. Desert Island during the summer for the past fifteen years; have visited almost every nook and corner of the island, and in my travels all over the United States and in foreign countries, I have found no section that Nature has made more attractive than Mt. Desert Island. I really believe that the island is one of the finest gifts God has bestowed upon the people of the United States, and it is but right that they should show themselves worthy of this gift by seeing to its proper protection and preservation.

As Schiff and Dorr hoped, Congress joined the Mount Desert Island lands to the National Park Service. The Sieur de Monts National Monument became Lafayette National Park in February 1919, when President Wilson signed his name to the bill. (In 1929, it was renamed Acadia National Park.) A few days later, Dorr wrote to JDR Jr. to thank him for his help. "It is the first National Park to be created east of the Rocky Mountains, and the first created in this country by the gift of citizens."

Dorr's achievement was extraordinary, but it carried some searing personal costs. Although he was the superintendent of the new park, he began serving without pay, while his financial situation became more precarious than ever. In July 1919, a committee of over fifty permanent and summer residents raised a public appeal for $25,000 to pay Dorr for lands that he had purchased on behalf of the trustees and the new park.

To protect their lands, Eliot, Dorr and Rockefeller turned

from the isolated and exclusive summer colony of the rich and entered into a complex relationship with the federal government. Yet, on the surface, not much seemed to change. The new public park slipped easily into the private, elitist world. The "brain workers" that Dorr spoke of at the congressional hearing did not pour into the town. The multitudes from the cities—neither the native born nor the immigrant—did not converge on the island. In 1920, there were 150,000 visitors to the park, many in automobiles, but they hardly changed the tenor of the resort.

Within a few years, the railroads and steamships saw less and less traffic. The Maine Central would soon abandon Mount Desert Ferry and the trip across Frenchman Bay. Passengers would travel to Ellsworth and then by car or bus across the bridge to the island. Eliot sold his carriages and horses. Mrs. Bowen sent Larson, her erstwhile driver, to visit Detroit. Instead of horses, he now cared for cars.

Society life in Bar Harbor securely held to its own pace and pleasures. Each summer, with unequaled hospitality and aplomb, Mrs. Bowen sent out invitations to the privileged public of Bar Harbor—to "all the summer visitors, and to those of the natives I knew." The enticing invitation read, "Mrs. Bowen at home in her garden on pleasant Sunday afternoons in July and August from three until six o'clock." Sometimes as many as two hundred of the select visited her home to share the pleasures of Baymeath.

In 1920, Arthur Train's fantasy of fear had not come true. There had been no conflagrations, no railroad tracks on the island, no Foleys and no frenzied tours. Arthur Train was still there, but Moe Levy had not arrived. The few Jewish families in Bar Harbor—never more than five to seven at any one time—continued to live quietly and run their modest shops. Their religious life and Jewish communal activities remained sporadic, except in 1918, when as part of the nationwide relief campaign for eastern Europe, the Jews in Bar Harbor raised $2,000. Schiff helped them to meet their quota.

Jacob Schiff remained the one Jew who was accepted by the summer community. He was the only one who belonged to the Bar Harbor Swim Club and the only Jew who rented on a regular basis. Clearly Schiff felt at home. He visited with the Eliots. He climbed and tramped over the island and relished its beauty and grandeur. "Today we had one of those glorious Bar Harbor days," he wrote to his son Mortimer, "when one can see almost through the sky into heaven."

In recognition of Schiff's generous contribution to the Village Improvement Society, Dorr named a trail for him on Dry Mountain. And in recognition of his attachment to the island, Schiff enjoyed the honor and departed from his usual posture of philanthropic self-effacement. Refusing to allow any dedicatory plaques to honor his gifts to various institutions and causes, Schiff maintained that recognition should come only after a donor's death. But a trail on Mount Desert was different.

In September 1920, Schiff died after a year of poor health. "Mr. Schiff enjoyed the life here at Bar Harbor and was interested in the resort, being especially fond of the scenery here. He had many friends among the summer colony and was much respected by the residents of the town." Thus, the *Bar Harbor Times* wrote about Schiff's death in a front-page column. The long obituary echoed *The New York Times* in cataloging Schiff's outstanding business and philanthropic deeds.

Several months later, Charles W. Eliot paid homage to Schiff in the *Menorah Journal,* the publication for Jewish students in college. Eliot wrote of the "intimate friendship" between himself and Schiff. Proudly, Eliot referred to Schiff's generosity—amounting to $250,000—to Harvard's Semitic department and museum. "I have never met a keener intelligence, a more sympathetic yet discriminating maker of gifts large and small, a truer disciple of the nameless Good Samaritan, or a more grateful patriot, Jewish and American combined."

Their relationship involved an honest exchange of views on many subjects as well as a common love for Mount Desert. The two men, Eliot recalled, discussed "business ethics, labor union problems, international peace and the best way to develop and conserve for future generations the landscape beauties of Mt. Desert Island. We wrote to each other rather frequently, and in summer we walked together on the rough trails through the woods and up the hills of that wonderful island."

It was a unique friendship—one that flourished on Mount Desert—between the educator and the philanthropist, the brahmin and the German immigrant, between the Unitarian and the Jew. They were exceptions—in their liberalism, their active opposition to immigration restriction, their confidence and hopes for the future. In his belief in American diversity and improvement through education, Eliot championed the Jewish immigrant and encouraged Jewish students at Harvard. Unlike Schiff, Eliot even supported a Zionist state. Nonetheless, it would take several more decades before Mount Desert Island would be home to more than a handful of Jews within the Gentile population.

*On the Porch at Birchcroft, No. 2* by Carroll Sargent Tyson, 1911. This group portrait shows Tyson's sister, and father and mother, Carroll senior and Clara, on the porch of their cottage in Northeast Harbor.

Rosserne overlooks Somes Sound in Northeast Harbor. Designed by Fred Savage, the summer home originally built in 1891 for Rev. Cornelius Smith remains one of the island's finest examples of the shingle style.

Main Street, Bar Harbor, circa 1910

The Bar Harbor Swim Club, circa 1910

Charles W. Eliot on the piazza of his summer home, the Ancestral, in Northeast Harbor, circa 1920

George B. Dorr, steward of the national park on Mt. Desert Island

Mr. and Mrs. John D. Rockefeller, Jr., joined the park superintendent for a cookout at Grand Teton National Park in October 1931.

In 1910 the Rockefellers bought the Eyrie in Seal Harbor from Professor and Mrs. E. Lawrence Clark of Williamstown, Massachusetts, and considerably enlarged and transformed the summer cottage.

An uncharacteristically informal picture of Jacob H. Schiff and his wife, Theresa, date unknown

Ambassador Henry Morgenthau, Sr., and his wife, Josephine, in 1929, three years after buying Mizzentop

An interior view of Alf Pasquale's house, Dark Ledge, in Southwest Harbor, built in 1944

The view from the Smiths' restaurant at Pond's End shows Lyle Smith's tour boat on Long Pond.

Northeast Harbour. Maine.

16  Septembre  1899


·Madame Alfred Dreyfus

                Rennes                          France.

----------------------------------------------------------------

Madame;Le coeur du monde entier est vers vous.Le procès a mis en évidence

l'innocence et le noble caractère de votre mari,et le grand public qui a suivi

avec angoisse cette lutte,lui a rendu à lui,et à ses enfants,l'honneur pour lequel

il a jusqu'à présent lutté;pour lequel il lutte encore en France.

The letter sent from residents in Northeast Harbor to Mme
Dreyfus in support of her husband and family

# CHAPTER 10

# *The Highest Christian Circles*

In 1926, when Ambassador Henry Morgenthau, Sr., and his wife bought Mizzentop, a handsome, three-story granite cottage on Eden Street, they entered into Bar Harbor's exclusive summer colony with enthusiasm and ease. Six years after Jacob Schiff had died, Morgenthau became another exception in the enclave of upper-class Protestant life. He was the first Jew, married to a Jewish woman, the former Josephine Sykes, to own his own cottage. He came at a time of modest change in the community. At the same time, other new families were moving into the resort. When George Vanderbilt sold his home in the 1920's, it was the first major holding to change hands in over fifteen years. In quick succession, forty-seven cottages were sold. Included among the new buyers were the conspicuously wealthy Stotesburys and Kents from Philadelphia. There was much new blood—acceptable new blood—but Morgenthau was the only Jew.

For their first dinner party at Mizzentop, the Morgenthaus presented a distinguished guest of honor: Col. Edward M. House, the once powerful advisor to President Woodrow Wilson. For Colonel House, Morgenthau presented the cream of Mount Desert society, including Bishop Lawrence and his wife, the Dimocks, the Damrosches, the Farrands, the Schiefflins, the

Montagues, Mrs. Olga Stokowski and George Dorr. The day after the event, Morgenthau wrote to his son Henry Morgenthau, Jr., with pride and scant modesty: "Our dinner was, as House put it, 'a brilliant affair.' 25 nice people sat down to a sumptuous well-served meal and then moved into our library and listened with rapt attention to the Silent Colonel's first speech about foreign affairs that any of them had ever heard. He was very frank and answered a lot of questions and then gave the time and audience over to me."

Morgenthau, now in his mid-sixties, felt confident of gaining acceptance in Mount Desert society. Dignified and friendly, he came to them as a distinguished German Jew: a self-made man, rich from real estate investments in New York City, a member of the diplomatic establishment and a devoted guardian, in long standing, of Woodrow Wilson's presidential legacy.

In the 1920's it mattered little to Morgenthau that his ambassadorship to Turkey was considered to be a Jewish one—in fact the only one—given as a political reward to an important Jewish supporter of the President. Having been chairman of Wilson's finance committee in the 1912 campaign, Morgenthau had hoped to be appointed secretary of the treasury. When he was offered the position in Istanbul, he declined with disappointment and indignation. Friends persuaded him to accept the position anyway. Morgenthau found himself, during World War I, in a crucial position to aid the interests of the United States and its putative European allies. Furthermore, when the small Jewish population in Palestine was threatened with the end of all aid from European and American Jews, Morgenthau was able to save the community from extinction. From Istanbul, Morgenthau orchestrated relief efforts by Jacob Schiff and other Jewish leaders after the Ottoman Empire abandoned neutrality and joined forces with Germany and the Hapsburg Empire.

After three years of distinguished service, Morgenthau returned from Turkey and took on a series of diplomatic tasks, including a relief mission for the League of Nations to aid Greek refugees. He and his wife traveled widely, enjoyed a large circle of friends in the diplomatic world and maintained close connections to the Democratic party. He liked taking strong positions as an international statesman, loyal Democrat, philanthropist and self-confident Jew in America.

Along with men such as Schiff, Julius Rosenwald and Louis Marshall, Morgenthau could be counted upon by his Jewish peers to assume responsibilities for the welfare of Jewish institutions and needy individuals in a period of unprecedented challenge brought about by massive immigration to America and the dire disruption of Jewish life in eastern Europe during World War I. Under his leadership as cochairman in 1917 and 1918 of the largest American Jewish relief effort on behalf of European Jewry, national Jewish leaders reached for financial support into every Jewish community from Bar Harbor and Bangor to Los Angeles. The effort, which raised over $10,000,000, was a turning point in the organization of American Jewry.

Morgenthau, like many of his wealthy fellow German Jews in New York, belonged to the Reform congregation Temple Emanu-El. He attended services from time to time but was not an observant Jew. He was, however, a fervent anti-Zionist. "We Jews of America have found America to be our Zion," he wrote emphatically in his autobiography *All in a Life Time,* in 1922. "Therefore I refuse to allow myself to be called a Zionist. I am an American." Morgenthau felt so strongly on the issue that he made a special proposal to the British foreign secretary, Arthur Balfour, the author of the 1917 Balfour Declaration, which held out the promise of a Jewish homeland in Palestine. Morgenthau suggested to Balfour that Palestine become "an international non-sectarian reservation park, or republic" and that it would be possible to raise several hundred million dollars for public works in Palestine, with 90 percent of the money donated by Christians in America.

Morgenthau's autobiography praised the unlimited economic and political possibilities for American Jews and expressed little concern about the power and prevalence of prejudice. If the Jew sought a "social position," he might find it difficult. "But the social barriers are not insurmountable. Where they seem so, calm judgment will reveal that the social environment where this irrational prejudice exists is not worthy of the entrance of the Jew. Leave the intolerant to associate with their own kind. The Jew who has raised himself to the highest level will have put himself beyond the reach of prejudice and he will find himself welcomed in the highest Christian circles."

Mount Desert was a place to prove just that. As the Mor-

genthaus settled into summer life on the island, they were moving against the stream of social segregation and virulent
populist and patrician anti-Semitism. Morgenthau was both an
optimist and a realist. With his strong political instincts, he
knew what was happening to American Jews in the post-
Wilsonian world and about the severity of the quotas ending
the flow of Jewish immigrants from eastern and southern Europe.

Incensed by the bigotry and growing power of the Ku Klux
Klan, Morgenthau urged his young friend Franklin Delano
Roosevelt to win the Democratic nomination for President on
an anti-Klan platform. Thinking back to the impassioned
drama of William Jennings Bryan, Morgenthau called upon
Roosevelt to make his own "Cross of Gold" speech. To
Roosevelt, Morgenthau reported that he and his son Henry
Morgenthau, Jr., "were discussing the situation last night and
think you can be nominated as President and do your campaigning over the Radio. . . . You take the floor today and speak
agst [sic] Kukluxism. . . . Here is your chance seize it." Roosevelt
ignored Morgenthau's advice. Instead, William Pattangall, the
fiery Democratic candidate for governor from Maine, made the
Klan his issue at the national convention.

One wonders whether Morgenthau knew that the Klan
had made an appearance on Mount Desert. In 1923, two hundred people had gathered at the Neighborhood House in
Northeast Harbor to hear F. Eugene Farnsworth, head of the
Maine Klan, call for a local organization. The next year, Farnsworth returned to address an even larger crowd of six hundred
at the Congregational church in Bar Harbor. By that time,
however, the Klan's anti-Catholic and anti-Semitic rhetoric was
in decline in the state. Despite the large show of interest, the
Klan never took hold on the island.

Surely, Morgenthau was aware that many colleges and universities were imposing strict and severe quotas on the admission of Jewish students. Harvard led the way, as the number of
Jews rose to nearly 25 percent in the mid-1920's. Using the
social vicissitudes of the typical summer resort as a warning and
justification for protective action, President A. Lawrence Lowell called for a drastic change in Harvard's admission policy.
The analogy between college and resort was the most cogent
one for him in 1922: "The summer hotel that is ruined by

admitting Jews meets its fate, not because the Jews it admits are of bad character, but because they drive away the Gentiles, and then, after the Gentiles have left, they leave also. This happened to a friend of mine with a school in New York, who thought, on principle, that he ought to admit Jews, but discovered in a few years that he had no school at all. A similar thing has happened in the case of Columbia College. . . ." A ditty made the rounds on the same point:

> Oh, Harvard's run by millionaires
> And Yale is run by booze,
> Cornell is run by farmer's sons,
> Columbia's run by Jews. . . .

For Lowell and the presidents of the other Ivy League schools, too many Jews imperiled the growth and prosperity of their academic institutions based upon a satisfied Gentile population. Admission by merit alone led to an influx of academically ambitious Jews. "The contrasts between the two groups were striking," sociologist Jerome Karabel has written. "Where Jewish students looked to college as a vehicle of upward mobility, Gentile students viewed college as a means of adding a bit of polish to a status virtually assured; where Jews took grades very seriously, their Christian counterparts opted for the 'gentleman's club'. . . ."

During the heated controversy at Harvard over the imposition of quotas, ex-president Charles W. Eliot inveighed against the position of his successor. Ultimately, Eliot lost, as Harvard turned to new criteria for judging students: relying upon character, personality and geographical distribution. The revised standards called for information about family background that provided the means of recognizing and pruning out the aspiring Jews. Harvard imposed a quota of 15 percent, Yale 10 percent and Princeton only 3 percent.

Walter Lippmann, the political writer and journalist who rarely identified himself as a Jew, nevertheless castigated Harvard for its new policy. He bridled at Lowell's demeaning comparison between the great university and the summer resort. "In the place of Eliot," Lippmann wrote, "there sits a man who has lost his grip on the great tradition which made Harvard one of the true spiritual centers of American life. Harvard, with the prejudices of a summer hotel; Harvard, with the standards of a country club, is not the Harvard of her greatest sons."

Soon after Morgenthau moved into Mizzentop, he learned that Jewish exceptions at summer resorts could not always count on being acceptable. Morgenthau received a disturbing letter from Charles Riegelman, a well-respected and forceful attorney in New York, who was married to Morgenthau's niece Lilian.

> I do not know whether I have ever explained to you the feeling of uncertainty that we have about our membership in the Stockbridge Golf Club. I got in four or five years ago on the introduction of Edwin T. Rice, whom I know very well, and who, in turn, got Mr. Carl De Gersdorff, who was unknown to me, to second my proposal. I had no difficulty whatsoever in getting in because both of these men, particularly De Gersdorff, are very powerful in the Club. This was also prior to the time that the big drive began in the Berkshires against the Jews, which has resulted in even the Aspinwall refusing to take them as guests and which resulted in none of the hotels being permitted, as they had theretofore, to give cards to the various Berkshire golf clubs to Jewish guests. This drive began about three years ago, but resulted in no unpleasantness to us whatsoever ... although we do not do anything more than go down for golf and are careful not to attempt to participate in any of the activities. Accordingly, I have met and know very few members of the Club. One of the powerful members of the Club is your friend Norman Davis, who was President last year. I do not know him and had intended long ago to speak to you about this so that if any question should arise we might be assured of a friend at court.
>
> Now, to come to the real point, there is a boating club on the Stockbridge Bowl, called the 'Mahkeenack Boating Club,' which is a very pleasant place for bathing and boating, both of which we lack at our place. Mrs. Crane, whose husband is the clergyman in our town of Richmond ... mentioned to Lil a few weeks ago about this boating club that she had joined and

thought it would be nice if we joined it. Lil told her that we would be very glad to do this, but she wanted it made perfectly plain in advance that we were Jewish people, so as not to embarrass Mrs. Crane in proposing us or the people at the Club, should they feel that being Jews we were undesirable. Lilian asked her if she found any such feeling under no circumstances to propose our names. Shortly thereafter I received a bill for dues and was told that the matter of membership would come up on Labor Day at a meeting of the Governors. In order to make sure that Mrs. Crane had done what Lilian had asked her to, I saw Mr. Clukas, the Secretary of the Club, and I told him very frankly about us and what Lilian had asked Mrs. Crane to do. Unfortunately, Mrs. Crane had made no mention of the fact but had assumed that being members of the Stockbridge Club that we would be welcome in this Club. Mr. Clukas, as the Secretary, had assumed the same thing and for that reason had no hesitancy in sending us a bill and assumed that our name would go through the Governing Board without question. When I told him the facts he said that he had no notion as to whether there was any prejudice amongst the members of the Club or whether our being Jews would make any difference and he volunteered to sound out a few of the Governors before the meeting and if he found that there was objection he would not put in our name. He was very pleasant himself and seemed to think I had acted very decently about the matter. I noticed amongst the names of the Governors were Norman Davis and Newbold Morris. . . .

It occurred to me that if you thought it wise and were willing to do so that you might be willing to write Norman Davis before the meeting on Labor Day and tell him anything that you feel would be helpful in the situation. If he should feel it useless to do anything with reference to the Boating Club, I feel sure that if he knows that Lilian is your niece it would be helpful should any question arise at the Stockbridge Club. The latter is, of course, most important to us, for without it we would be rather unhappy up there. I have given you all of this at such length because I want you to know the whole situation so that you could advise properly and I hope that you will have no hesitancy whatsoever in telling me whether you prefer for your own reasons not to do anything about it.

Morgenthau immediately wrote to Davis asking that he help Riegelman in becoming a member of the club. Riegelman then went to see Davis and reported back to Morgenthau. Davis "was most gracious and pleasant about the whole business and I am mighty glad for many reasons that I wrote you and you wrote him." Morgenthau jotted a note back to his nephew, which closed the matter: "You evidently put on your very best front. I am very happy if I have been of some use to you and Lilian." What went on between Davis and Riegelman is not clear from the exchange of letters, but Riegelman and his wife never joined the Mahkeenack Boating Club. Whether they were asked and declined or simply withdrew their name to prevent any embarrassment is not known. They did, however, remain members of the Stockbridge Club, where, for many years, they were the only Jews.

Despite the mounting evidence of prejudice throughout American life, Morgenthau maintained his strong belief in acceptance and assimilation in America. "Any Jew in America," he had written in his autobiography in 1922, "who yearns for social position has only to cultivate his manners—there are no insurmountable discriminations here against true gentlemen. . . ." On the island, he did find acceptance, including membership in both the Kebo Club and the Bar Harbor Swimming Club. Arthur Train, the writer, invited the Morgenthaus for dinner, as did Max Farrand and his wife, Beatrix Farrand, the preeminent landscape designer and former Beatrix Cadwalader Jones. (Morgenthau soon engaged Beatrix Farrand to redesign his gardens.) Not only did he hand out ribbons at the annual horse show during his first summer at Mizzentop, but he also gave the Fourth of July address at Northeast Harbor under the sponsorship of Charles W. Eliot, Dr. Francis G. Peabody and Clifford Barnes. Enthusiastically, the Morgenthaus invited family and friends to visit the island to show them Bar Harbor society and the beauty of the island. "I have never possessed anything that has given me more pleasure than Miz-zentop," he wrote his daughter-in-law. "It is delightfully cool here. We are seeing considerable of the most interesting people and our gardens and house are much finer than we anticipated. I say 'gardens' because we have three separate ones."

The Morgenthaus' only disappointment was that Bar Harbor was too far from New York to be easily visited by family and friends. One other initial regret involved high prices in Bar Harbor. Mrs. Morgenthau took immediate action as she wrote the national office of the Atlantic and Pacific Tea Company. "I am a regular customer of yours in Bar Harbor. I am very well satisfied with the service here, etc. but in reading the Bangor newspaper, I find the A&P in that city may have more daily sales than your store in Bar Harbor. I am wondering why we do not have as many here."

One person whom Morgenthau was not able to see in the summer of 1926 was his friend Charles W. Eliot. At ninety-two, the educator had come to Northeast Harbor in deteriorating health. Morgenthau, who had seen Eliot the summer before, wrote of his poor condition: "We hear that Dr. Eliot is bedridden at present and has to be carried about so I think I am not going to call on him as I want to recall my pleasant recollection of the fine old gentleman when he was still active in his nineties." Eliot died just a few weeks later, in July, having enjoyed one of America's most extraordinary and exemplary careers in education and public life.

On the occasion of Eliot's ninetieth birthday in 1924, he had received tributes and testimonials from thousands of Harvard alumni, along with personal notes of gratitude from friends. George Dorr, who was hard at work on park matters under congressional review, wrote to Eliot about having to miss the large celebration in Cambridge: "If I do not come, I shall be present in spirit. Our friendship has been a pleasure, an encouragement and an inspiration to me these last twenty years, and one of my most valued and valuable possessions."

For John D. Rockefeller, Jr., Eliot occupied an equally special place. Despite years of working together, the two men maintained a fastidious formality. They never addressed each other by their first names or dropped their reserve, although frankness and sometimes brutal honesty, especially on Eliot's part, repeatedly surfaced. In 1917, Eliot advised the young Rock-efeller to relinquish his leadership of the Rockefeller Foundation.

> I feel in the strongest way that you ought not to live the kind of life that you have been living; that none but a peculiarly tough and robust person could endure it for any length of time; and that you do not possess that bodily or constitutional toughness. You have told me that you have difficulty with your sleep; and I observe that you have to be careful about your food and drink, and that you take medicines daily. A man who is in this condition at forty-three is sure to become worse as his age advances. . . .
>
> You work hard and long, often without enjoyment in your work; and you experience constant anxiety, not only about the success of your undertakings, but about your family, and especially your children. The worst breakdowns I have seen, and I have seen a good many, are not those which kill,—they are those which disable. . . . Your best advisor is, of course, Mrs. Rockefeller. If she does not agree with the substance of this letter, I shall feel like withdrawing it.

Notwithstanding those harsh words, Rockefeller expressed a striking tone of gratitude and intimacy, fostered by summer life on Mount Desert Island, on the occasion of Eliot's ninetieth birthday.

> Ever since I first came to know you, you have been an example and an inspiration to me in many ways. The uniform dignity and courtliness of your bearing, your unfailing courtesy, your splendid self control, your enormous capacity for work, the painstaking exactness with which you study the details of every problem upon which you pass judgment, your magnificent breadth of view, your clear insight and your keen vision have long commanded my profound admiration. I have counted it a high privilege to have the more intimate association with you which life on the Maine coast has made possible. The many informal visits which we have had together there for the purpose of

discussing matters of local interest have brought me into even closer relationship with you than the association in the philanthropic boards founded by my father. . . . This personal tribute to what your friendship has meant to me is the intimate message which I want to send you at this time.

Eliot's imaginative and democratic views about protecting the landscape and providing proper public use on the island significantly encouraged Rockefeller's support for public conservation. His philanthropic involvement with preservation began with the Hancock County Trustees of Public Reservations and led to significant involvements with Yosemite, Yellowstone, the Great Smoky Mountains National Park, and the Grand Tetons.

Rockefeller's national and global concerns—in medical research, education, public policy and conservation—never distracted him from caring protectively for Mount Desert. With the aid of Dorr, Frederick Law Olmsted, Jr., and Beatrix Farrand, Rockefeller designed fifty-seven miles of carriage roads. Using local contractors and engineers, he built handsome roads and sixteen fortresslike granite bridges that settled beautifully into the landscape. Many of the monumental, graceful spans were the work of architect William Welles Bosworth, whom Rockefeller employed at Pocantico Hills as well as for the restoration after World War I of Versailles, Fontainebleau, Chartres and Reims. Rockefeller also built two gatehouses of rustic French design to serve as stately adjuncts to the park. By the late 1930's, Rockefeller had spent over four million dollars on carriage and motor roads, land acquisitions and various improvements for the park.

With his tenacious commitment to the park, Rockefeller contributed to the democratic expansion of public access to Mount Desert. But his acts to benefit the larger public were sometimes contradicted in spirit and fact by private needs. Tucked within the larger sphere of benefiting the public—those for whom the United States government held Mount Desert lands in custody—Rockefeller was also engaged in another sphere of tightening exclusivity and intolerance.

The temptations to prejudice were great in the 1920's and 1930's. Rockefeller's wife, Abby Aldrich Rockefeller, a gracious

and serious woman, who often pushed her interests in directions that were different from those of her friends and family,
wrote of her concern to her eldest sons John, Nelson and Lau-
rance, all of whom were in college in the late 1920's:

> For a long time I have had very much on my mind and
> heart a certain subject. I meant to bring it up at prayers
> and then later have it for a question to be discussed at
> a family council; but the right time ... has never
> seemed to come. Out of my experience and observa-
> tion has grown the earnest conviction that one of the
> greatest causes of evil in the world is race hatred or
> race prejudice; in other words, the feeling of dislike
> that a person or a nation has against another person or
> nation without just cause, an unreasoning aversion is
> another way to express it. The two peoples or races
> who suffer most from this treatment are the Jews and
> the Negroes. . . .
>
> You boys are still young. No group of people has
> ever done you a personal injury; you have no inher-
> ited dislikes. I want to make an appeal to your sense of
> fair play and to beseech you to begin your lives as
> young men by giving the other fellow, be he Jew or
> Negro or of whatever race, a fair chance and a square
> deal.

She referred her sons to the Negroes' suffering from lynchings.
The "social ostracism of the Jew," she wrote, "is less brutal, and
yet it often causes cruel injustice and must engender in the Jews
a smoldering fire of resentment."

The private club was a prime example of that "social ostracism." On Mount Desert, clubs in Bar Harbor, Seal Harbor
and Northeast Harbor maintained a firm grip on exclusivity
and intolerance, with the Morgenthaus as the only exceptions.
Mrs. Henry Parkman, for many years a leading figure in Northeast Harbor and a member of the small and elite Cranberry
Club, explained her deep attachment to her summer home.
"Many people wonder just what it is that makes this place
unique, and creates the devotion of so many people." For her
there was the beautiful landscape, outdoor sports and Sunday
observances at church and the sunset service. Her final thought

was equally important: the sense of social safety. "We should often thank Bishop Doane for being 'mighty particular about what people he allowed to come,' for here we enjoy friendships to the full, and surely to a superlative degree in our Cranberry club."

The same closed and safe society prevailed in Bar Harbor. Louis Auchincloss wrote about his modest and "intelligent" parents, who lived out a "pastoral idyll in the very heart of Sodom and Gomorrah." As a grown man, no longer spending summers on the island, he wondered what made his serious mother tolerate the "silly side of fashionable summer life." The answer was quite simple: the power of the clan. "The summer colonies were tested and true. Secondly, Mother actually liked the huddled aspect of the watering places. She loved her sense of the tribe all around and close by."

Despite Abby Rockefeller's tolerant exhortations to her sons, the exclusive bonds held firm in the low-keyed Harbor Club in Seal Harbor. Her husband, along with Edsel Ford, had formed the Harbor Club in 1927 for swimming and tennis. The two men were the principal stockholders and financial supporters, with Roscoe B. Jackson and Charles McAlpin as minority owners. Invitations were sent to summer residents, primarily in Seal Harbor and Northeast Harbor, strictly on a summer-by-summer basis. Rockefeller and Ford contributed all of the capital costs and made up any deficits, while the other members paid only $100 per summer. With absolute certainty about the purposes and policies of the club, Rockefeller maintained his control for many decades. Until his death, Rockefeller enforced a ban on liquor at the Harbor Club and made clear to his fellow members that if the temperance rule were violated, he would cancel the lease. (For many years the club did not serve food— only bouillon at eleven in the morning.)

The harpist and composer Carlos Salzedo caused offense at the Harbor Club when he divorced and quickly remarried. He was not invited back to the club when Amy Montague, a Seal Harbor summer resident and the wife of the eminent lawyer Gilbert Montague, objected. Embarrassed and hurt, Salzedo plaintively wrote to Rockefeller. "In such a small community, a decision of like character is liable to be interpreted in various ways. . . . I do not believe that the governing members of the Harbor Club realize the offending character of their gesture.

In their minds there is undoubtedly a cause for such a gesture. It seems to me that my position, also my devotion to Seal Harbor, entitle me to an explanation." Rockefeller replied that the membership committee was free to add to and take names off its list as it so desired. Two years later, Salzedo started a music institute in Camden, Maine.

Once more, in 1933, the prickly issue of membership came up, again at the insistence of the vigilant Mrs. Montague. This time it involved another well-known and highly respected musician, the pianist Josef Lhévinne. He was not divorced, but he was Jewish—and an émigré from Russia. He had moved to the United States after World War I and joined the faculty of the Juilliard School of Music.

Amy Montague informed JDR Jr. that Mrs. Olga Stokowski had rented her cottage to the Lhévinnes, "professional pianists and competent artists but both Jews of by no means the highest grade." Already, she wrote in a tone of sharp annoyance, they had asked for membership in the Harbor Club for themselves and their pupils. "In view of the fact that persons of their race here, far more desirable than they, have not been invited to subscribe to the club, it seems to me impossible to make an exception in this case. . . ." She apologized for bringing such an "insignificant subject" to Rockefeller's attention. "I think Mrs. Stokowski greatly at fault,—in renting to persons who are undesirable and in putting the club in an awkward position, but to me, the issue is clear-cut, in view of the attitude we have taken is [sic] past cases of the kind."

Rockefeller was a deeply reserved and shy man who constantly battled to shield himself and his family from unkind press and public scrutiny. He searched for areas of privacy, moral certitude and social safety. Whatever prejudice he harbored found few instances of outward expression, and he may have been similar, in one aspect, to Herbert Saterlee's father in Louis Auchincloss's novel *The House of the Prophet.* When a young Jewish friend visited the Saterlee home, the elder Saterlee, although he had no intention of extending his circle of friends to include any Jews, behaved with "perfect politeness." His son remarked that "Father, after all, was a gentleman; he showed his prejudices only to those who shared them."

Put on the spot by Mrs. Montague's letter, Rockefeller's response revealed a subtle bias. "To invite these people to membership in the club would, as you point out, be a gross discourtesy and injustice to other Jews living in the vicinity to whom invitations have never been sent." He concluded tersely: "The situation is regrettable but in no way the fault of the club management." In the private world of the clubs—as opposed to the public world of beneficent philanthropy—the prejudice against the Jews held firm.

# CHAPTER 11

# *A National Possession*

IT IS LIKELY that Morgenthau was one of the Jews to whom Amy Montague and JDR Jr. vaguely referred as a "more desirable" member of the "race." The Montagues were dinner guests at Mizzentop. At Morgenthau's behest, Rockefeller gave the Federation of Jewish Philanthropies in New York an annual gift of $50,000 in the late 1920's. In the summer of 1933, when JDR Jr. contemplated including a German-sponsored building in Rockefeller Center, he went to Mizzentop for Morgenthau's advice. Morgenthau told Rockefeller that Germany, now led by Adolf Hitler, would soon go to war. The discussion helped JDR Jr. decide against inviting the Germans to build in Rockefeller Center.

Did Morgenthau detect any discomfort that Rockefeller and Amy Montague may have felt in the presence of a German Jew on the island? Probably not. He was ever confident and filled with enthusiasm for his summer home. Morgenthau asked Adolph Ochs, publisher of *The New York Times,* to visit Mount Desert in 1928. "I am sure we can make you comfortable and give you an opportunity to see what I consider the finest summer resort of America, if not of the world." In this exuberant—and appreciative—vein, Morgenthau continued to invite friends to Mizzentop throughout the 1930's. "We have so much to be thankful for," he wrote his wife, Josie, "that we should increase the joy it brings to us by sharing it with others. . . . Now remember these last years of ours are the Evenings of our lives after a very exciting exhilarating and complete day and let us make the best of it."

Yet some of his family felt uncomfortable with his anomalous position in Bar Harbor. His granddaughter, Barbara Wertheim, who later became the well-known historian Barbara Tuchman, visited her grandparents in 1932. Many years later, she wrote about her disquietude:

> In his fierce desire for proof of assimilation, he established his summer home, when he was in his seventies, in the WASP stronghold of Bar Harbor, Maine consorting with snobs to my acute embarrassment on my visits. Possibly they liked or admired him—he was a man of great charm, known as Uncle Henry to all acquaintances from FDR to the policeman on the beat—but what slights he may have endured I cannot tell. Yet he never for an instant attempted to play down his Jewish identity or remain passive in regard to his people . . . . Assimilation, for him, did not mean to cross over to Christianity; it meant to be accepted in Bar Harbor as a Jew: that was the whole point. He wanted to be a Jew and an American on the same level as the best. He wanted America to work in terms of his youthful ideals—and of course it did not.

All too obvious were the ways in which America and the world departed in the 1930's from Morgenthau's "youthful ideals." The Depression brought fear and havoc into the economic and social fabric of nearly every city and town. Intensified anti-Semitism constricted economic opportunities for Jews. Beyond the exclusive practices in colleges, clubs and resorts, employment notices boldly stated: "Jews need not apply."

Studies such as *Christians Only: A Study in Prejudice* by Heywood Campbell Broun and George Britt in 1931 and *Fortune* magazine's *Jews in America,* published in 1936, acknowledged that anti-Semitism was growing. According to the *Fortune* study, American anti-Semitism was still "feeble" in comparison to the outbreaks of it in Nazi Germany. Yet many Jews and non-Jews feared an "enormous increase in Jewish numbers in America will lead to charges that the Jews have monopolized the opportunities for economic advance and that these charges will pave the way for Fascism here as they paved the way for Hitler in Germany."

The specter of fascism at home was deeply troubling to American Jews, but the dangers in Nazi Germany caused even deeper dismay. Morgenthau, among many other Jewish leaders, actively worked to rescue Jews persecuted by the Nazis. He intervened with the State Department in the bureaucratic quagmire of indifference, visas and quotas.

Despite the Depression and disturbing changes abroad, summer life on Mount Desert continued unchanged in most respects. The Stotesburys, DuPonts, Blairs, Kents, Lippincotts, Dorrances, Distons, Fords, Palmers and Wanamakers enjoyed costume balls, sailing and dances at the Kimball House in Northeast Harbor and the Kebo and Bar Harbor clubs. An array of stores and services met the extensive needs of the summer population. In 1936, there were sixteen grocers, eleven beauty parlors, three furriers, fourteen clothing stores, four architects and six landscape architects in Bar Harbor. Regrettably, the Depression caused summer residents to reduce their donations to the island's hard-pressed institutions. The newly established Jackson Laboratory, dedicated to mammalian gentics, barely survived. The *Bar Harbor Times* and the Kebo Club required critical infusions of credit from the local banks.

Morgenthau remained part of the island's galaxy of rich and influential people. In 1932, he addressed the Pot and Kettle Club—although he was not invited to join—about the upcoming presidential election. (Neither Eliot nor Dorr was a member of the prestigious club whose members were thought to control 85 percent of the nation's wealth.) Over the next few years, Morgenthau enjoyed an enhanced status as a confidant of President Franklin Delano Roosevelt and as the father of the secretary of the treasury. The elder Morgenthau attended the festive opening of the Cadillac Mountain road, which Rockefeller had largely financed. Morgenthau and his wife indulged in local gossip and local pleasures, including seeing movies at the new Criterion theater in Bar Harbor. "A fine theatre," he wrote, "built by Ma's friend the bootlegger. He has turned respectable and put all his illgotten gains into a losing venture."

Along with Maine's governor Louis J. Brann and Bishop Lawrence, Morgenthau spoke before thousands of spectators at the third annual Visitor's Day in Bar Harbor. In a bleak state-wide economy, the pageant of music, speeches and historic floats was intended to show that Maine did not take visitors for granted. Leo Damrosch, the master of ceremonies, introduced Morgenthau with a touch of partisan jocularity: "Not only is he distinguished in his own right, he is the father of the secretary of the treasury. And, as I think the United States government is going to take away from me everything except my trousers, I hope, through him, to obtain the key to the treasury." With customary pride, Morgenthau sought to reassure his audience filled with stalwart Republicans: "I am enjoying a real immortality—just living on through my son. I enjoy the pure air and fine scenery in Maine while he and the others in Washington perspire through the summer to give us a good government. May I say to all semi-doubting Republicans that they need not be afraid? Prosperity is coming back. We all will share in it—and that is where true democracy prevails."

Among Morgenthau's many friends in Bar Harbor, George Dorr would be the least affected by Morgenthau's promise of prosperity. By the late 1930's, the superintendent and lifetime guardian of Acadia National Park was blind, nearly out of money, and living frugally in Storm Beach cottage, the guest-house at Oldfarm. For Dorr, the growth of Acadia National Park more than justified his generosity toward the island and his disregard for his own financial welfare. In the 1930's, he saw the expansion of the park to twenty-seven thousand acres, including the beautiful Schoodic Peninsula on the mainland opposite Mount Desert. New Deal recovery programs made sizable land acquisitions possible and provided men from the Civilian Conservation Corps to build an extensive network of trails and paths on the western side of the island. In 1941, almost 400,000 visitors came to the park.

Dorr was also partially responsible for the existence of two distinguished scientific institutions on the island. His inspiration and generous donations of land helped to establish the Mount Desert Biological Laboratory, originally known as the S. Weir Mitchell Laboratory. "It is all in delightful contrast to Bar Harbor's fashionable life," Dorr wrote proudly of the laboratory, "and far more in keeping with the true character of the region, rich in natural interest and the beauty of great scenery." Dorr also encouraged Clarence Little, an eminent scientist in the field of cancer research, to work on the island. Little resigned as the president of the University of Michigan in 1929 when Roscoe B. Jackson of Detroit promised to fund a new laboratory. Again, Dorr donated the land upon which the fledgling Jackson Laboratory was started.

In his late eighties and early nineties, Dorr retrieved memories of his personal and family history and recorded fragments of his autobiography. Thinking about the future of the park, Dorr asked John D. Rockefeller, Jr., which of his sons would continue Rockefeller's patronage. When JDR Jr. identified Nelson as the likely heir, Dorr presented the younger Rockefeller with an eighteenth-century Sheraton-style clock. It had come into Dorr's possession as a gift from Mrs. John Kane, who had generously donated Flying Squadron Mountain (originally known as Dry Mountain) and the tarn and gorge around it to the Hancock County Trustees of Public Reservations. "I shall like to think," Dorr wrote JDR Jr. in 1939 "as my journey ends, that this gift of Mrs. Kane's shall find a place with the on-coming generation and carry on to it, and others still, the memory of the Park's formation in the days before it was."

JDR Jr. responded with his customary grace. He took the occasion to write warmly of Dorr's accomplishments and of the long friendship between the two men:

> What a satisfaction it must be to you to reflect upon the immense contribution you have made to the permanent development of this Island and to its protection and preservation for the enjoyment of all the people! You have done a wonderful piece of work. No one knows better than I do how important it is and how unselfishly you have given of your time, your thought, your strength and your means to the accomplishment of the desired ends. I rejoice in what you have done and am proud to have been your silent partner in some phases of the work.
>
> The happy memory of our quiet visit together yesterday afternoon will remain with me all winter and I shall think of you often, and always with admiration and affection."

The following year Dorr sought to part with an even greater gift when he offered the main house at Oldfarm to the United States government as a permanent retreat for the President and his cabinet. At FDR's suggestion, Dorr gave his family home to Acadia National Park.

Dorr's health continued to fail. He could no longer buy books or new clothes. Local residents who read to Dorr in Greek and Latin found it was not an easy task, given Dorr's predilection for interrupting and constantly asking questions about sources. (Rockefeller, who offered to pay for the services of the readers, was kept informed of Dorr's condition and outlook.) Dorr's rich memories and ideals kept him from despair. In 1944, he died and his ashes were strewn over Frenchman Bay. In honor of his contributions, Flying Squadron Mountain was renamed for him. A simple brass plaque at Sieur de Monts Springs attests to Dorr's extraordinary strengths and gifts:

> GENTLEMAN SCHOLAR
> LOVER OF NATURE
> FATHER OF THIS NATIONAL PARK
>
> STEADFAST IN HIS ZEAL
> TO MAKE THE BEAUTIES OF THIS ISLAND
> AVAILABLE TO ALL

The park was secure, but the society that Dorr had lived in was not. Drastic economic change and World War II were undermining Bar Harbor's old way of life. The generations that had built the glorious summer resort were dying out, and no new leaders were emerging to carry on Dorr's tradition of boundless commitment and philanthropy. Few summer residents could get to the island during the war. Houses along the shore were blacked out. Lookouts, posted on the mountains and the coast, searched for enemy aircraft, submarines and spies. The navy took over the Mt. Desert Reading Room on the Bar Harbor waterfront. An air force base was located at Trenton across the narrows.

Louise de Koven Bowen no longer came to Hulls Cove. Not wishing to carry the expenses of her cottage, she had sold Baymeath for a small sum to Belgian refugees. Like Dorr, near the end of her life she looked back to the blissful decades around the turn of the century on Mount Desert. To her grandson William McCormick Blair, at war somewhere in Burma, she dedicated her history of summer days at Baymeath. "I cannot help but think how the world has changed since that time, our thought, our manner of living, the excessive expenditure of money, the style, the comforts and almost everything else seems to be different. The whole world seems to have been turned so topsy-turvy that one does not know what to do or to think."

She was right. The world was vastly different—for Henry Morgenthau as well as for her. Morgenthau's confidence in Jewish assimilation was less secure. His carefully nourished faith in America was less secure. Barbara Tuchman wrote that Morgenthau became a "reluctant pro-Zionist" as Germany exploded in unprecedented acts of persecution and as Europe and America failed to save European Jewry. He was converted to Zionism, Tuchman explained, by "the lack of protest, the elaborate do-nothing international conferences, the pious evasions, the passive connivance in which Hitler read his cue, the avoidance of rescue, the American refusal to loosen immigration quotas when death camps were the alternative, the refusal even of temporary shelter. . . ."

The family fought those forces of callous disinterest through Henry Morgenthau, Jr., the secretary of the treasury. Incensed and frustrated, particularly by the slow and obstructionist workings of the State Department, the younger Morgenthau drew upon the resources of his department, the power of moral suasion and his close relationship to FDR to establish the War Refugee Board in 1944. As the horrifying war came to its end, Morgenthau and the board worked assiduously to rescue the surviving Jews, carrying on his father's concern and dedication for providing relief for European and American Jewry.

Two years later and over a year after the end of the war, the elder Morgenthau died in November 1946. At his funeral at Temple Emanu-El in New York, Dr. Raymond B. Fosdick, president of the Rockefeller Foundation, gave the eulogy. "There is something truly magnificent," he said of Morgenthau, "about a life that is completely fulfilled—a life that ends great in years, great in achievement and great in its final dignity."

Morgenthau's connection to Bar Harbor had slowly slipped

away. His death was summarily noted by the *Bar Harbor Times*. "Mr. Morgenthau, together with Mrs. Morgenthau, were for many years summer residents of Bar Harbor where he was very well known and liked by other summer residents and natives alike." In no way did the words convey the happiness that the Morgenthaus had found on the island as part of its rich society.

That dazzling past was out of reach. Without the lavish resources of the Gilded Age and the 1920's, without inexpensive and underpaid labor of Irish maids and English gardeners, the summer empires of luxury were dismantled, auctioned or abandoned. (The most spectacular auction consisted of over 1,500 items from Mrs. Stotesbury's cottage in 1946.) Morgenthau's cottage was one of many that were for sale. Buyers were sought, but none came. Parts of Bar Harbor waited to expire. Instead, they burned up.

October 1947 was dry, hot and excessively windy. People on the island and throughout the whole state anxiously feared the worst. Fires broke out all over Maine, but none approached the catastrophe in Bar Harbor. The fire began on October 17 and did not officially burn out for an entire month. By then, 18,560 acres, or 29 square miles, had been destroyed, including 10,000 out of 25,000 acres in the park. All but 2 percent of the devastation occurred in Bar Harbor. Six hundred fire fighters were needed to meet the raging crisis. As the erratic fire spread through Bar Harbor from Hulls Cove to Thunder Hole, over the mountains and along the shore, it burned seventy local residences, sixty-seven summer cottages—one third of the total, including Morgenthau's Mizzentop—four hotels and the research facilities at the Jackson Laboratory. The damage was estimated at close to $10,000,000. Luckily, the town itself was spared.

Local and summer residents alike were courageous and calm as day by day they watched the fire spread and devastate their world. Mrs. Frank Rowell, a niece of John S. Kennedy, fled from her home in a car with the fire at her back. Alone, she drove through Bar Harbor to Otter Cliffs, Seal Harbor, Somesville and finally to safety over the narrows bridge. She glanced stoically at the island as she took the long shore route through Trenton on her way to Bangor. "Looking back on the Island was a sight never to be forgotten," she wrote soon after her dramatic escape. "The whole impression of the Island was more like a great volcano pouring fire down upon us and heaving great volumes of smoke and flame up to the heavens."

From New York, JDR Jr. anxiously followed the course of the devastation. Through his intervention, the secretary of defense enlisted air force, navy and army personnel to help the island meet the crisis. The carriage roads, JDR Jr. learned, had helped to control the blaze by giving access to trucks and creating crucial firebreaks. "When the fire first began to assume threatening proportions," he wrote to an inquiring friend, "we were naturally anxious about our own home at Seal Harbor which we love so dearly. As it grew in intensity, however, and threatened to engulf the Island, our only thought was of the beauty of the Island being thus destroyed and of course over and above all that, of the risk to human life and the destruction in the Bar Harbor area. . . . The people of the Island have shown the utmost courage and are dauntless as they face the future."

That future was painful to contemplate. Some commercial businesses lost 90 percent of their clientele. The furriers were gone, the architects and landscape architects dwindled in number. But relief came quickly to the town. The Friends of Bar Harbor, organized in many towns on the island, raised $50,000 to supply clothing and blankets to needy families. The federal government spent $400,000 for the cleanup. Rockefeller provided hundreds of thousands of dollars for additional work. Within a year, forty year-round residences had been rebuilt, but not one of the summer cottages or hotels.

Local leaders asked themselves what kind of community they wanted to rebuild. In response to official appeals, Rockefeller paid for the services of Louis Bartholomew, an urban planner from St. Louis. He arrived in November and issued his preliminary study six months later. Concerned with zoning, streets, building codes and schools, he also focused on the divergent interests of the local and summer populations. Noting that the summer residents represented nearly half of the assessed value of the town, he encouraged their return. They want "quiet, privacy and social contact with other members of the summer colony." As for the town itself, he had little good to say. "While the scenery is magnificent and the summer houses beautiful, the village of Bar Harbor is unattractive in character and appearance. . . . Most of the buildings are old, of frame construction and of undistinguished architecture."

The town adopted some of the zoning recommendations, but the summer colony remained a pale imitation of its former self. The Pulitzers, Thorndikes, Peltzes, Opdyckes and Brownings stayed on, still deeply attached to traditions and harboring a love for the island. Mary Roberts Rinehart, the well-known writer who had owned Farview before it burned in the fire, also returned. The town, she declared, "is a habit rather than a resort. It is really not a resort at all. It is a summer colony, where the second and even the third and fourth generations go for rest, for the sea and the mountains, for the coolness, and for the beauty of the island."

The old guard appealed for new blood—but still the right kind of blood. Richard Hale, a long-time summer resident and close friend of Dorr's, wrote a laudatory history of Bar Harbor two years after the fire. "Bar Harbor, for all the high standards it sets, accepts newcomers readily. The ways in which new blood comes in vary. Usually it is a matter of introduction by visiting friends, or residence at a hotel, then gaining a liking for Bar Harbor and buying." Still, Hale clung to old forms and safe connections. "This doesn't mean that John Doe can walk into Bar Harbor, ring anyone's doorbell and be invited in to make himself at home. It does mean that John Doe, when he has made proper contact, will feel at home quickly."

To feel at home in Bar Harbor in the 1950's, John Doe would have had to accept the influx of different kinds of tourists at the new motels. Anxious for business, Bar Harbor's motel owners broke down patterns of discrimination against Jews that were evident throughout the state. According to a B'nai B'rith study made in 1946, 65 percent of the hotels and motels surveyed in Maine engaged in discriminatory practices. Maine ranked the highest among the six New England states in "indications of discrimination." Those patterns continued through the end of the 1950's until the Maine legislature passed effective antidiscrimination legislation.

Acadia National Park attracted hundreds of thousands of tourists—rich and poor, Jew and Gentile. The tourists also gaped at the charred remnants of the rich life—an ill-kept outdoor museum of abandoned foundations and empty cottages. Store owners catered to a summer trade of popular tastes. Out of season, many of the businesses simply boarded up their shops after the trip to Bangor by car became an easy drive rather than a day-long challenge.

The slow pace and intimacy of small-town life, however, continued through the 1940's and early 1950's. Bar Harbor, with its static population of 3,500, remained a town of church-goers and keepers of modest-sized shops. When someone of local importance died, all the shops closed and the banks pulled their blinds. Everyone knew what church a family belonged to and who did not belong to any church. And everyone knew who the few Jewish families were: the Shiros, Sachsmans, Morris Franklins, Max Franklins, Adlers and Gordons.

Although several of the Jewish merchants continued to prosper, their small numbers dwindled further. There were Jewish families—but there was no Jewish communal presence. Many of the Jewish children moved away after high school so that they could make Jewish marriages. Most of the children who stayed married Gentiles from the area. Religious holidays were no longer celebrated in Bar Harbor, and only one family, that of A. M. Shiro, observed Jewish rites and kosher laws. When he wanted to make a minyan in the summer, Shiro would stand on the street looking for Jewish tourists who would join him in prayer. In the early 1950's, a few Orthodox Syrian Jews came to Bar Harbor to run linen shops for the tourists. The new Jews were shunned by the long-established Jewish families and never became part of the community.

In the postfire world, all groups in Bar Harbor made adjustments, although few forgot the old patterns of deference to the summer elite. The patricians retreated to their clubs and memories of days of glittering wealth and social pleasure. For little money, year-round residents bought prime properties that no one else wanted. Lacking a firm financial footing, for the first time the Kebo and the Bar Harbor clubs reluctantly accepted a handful of local members.

The dramatic change in tone and taste was symbolized by the fate of Beatrix Farrand's six-acre garden, Reef Point. Over thirty gardens on Mount Desert bore the mark of her imagination and skill. Dumbarton Oaks in Washington, D.C., and the Rockefeller garden in Seal Harbor were considered the major achievements of her fifty-year career. By the late 1940's, when many of her other celebrated gardens had been forsaken, she turned her sights and her fastidious attention to her own exquisite garden on the Shore Path.

Reef Point was her home. Making it a horticultural center was her dream. Farrand opened her experimental gardens and extensive library to a discrete and interested public. Tragically, like George Dorr, she outlived both her means and patrician times. When the Bar Harbor assessor refused to grant her relief from high taxes, she turned in fury on the town, the island and the state. She had her house torn down, sent her valuable library to the University of California at Berkeley and abandoned her garden.

Only through the work of Charles Savage, an immensely talented amateur landscape architect from Northeast Harbor, and the generosity of JDR Jr. were many of her plants and shrubs transferred to Northeast Harbor. Savage created two public gardens—the Asticou and Thuya—with the legacy from Reef Point. In 1985, Farrand's close associate, Robert Patterson, an accomplished architect and landscape designer, tried to explain her actions thirty years before. "It has sometimes been implied that there was an element of spite in the way Reef Point was brought to an end, but if there was, it was at the changing world and what Mrs. Farrand saw as a pervasive lowering of values."

Only in the handsome cottage communities of Northeast Harbor and Seal Harbor were Farrand's values, tastes and well-honed sense of philanthropy still to be found. Intellectuals and educators favored the area: among the most distinguished were the historian Samuel Eliot Morison, who had come for summers since childhood; Walter Lippmann, a relative newcomer; and Marguerite Yourcenar, the celebrated European author. The world of wealth and old Protestant families seemed little changed in the two subdued villages set between the shore and the mountains of Acadia National Park. There was little commercial life beyond the handful of stores on the main streets. Nothing showy, nothing to draw abundant trade.

The intricate networks of fine names, boarding schools, clubs, law firms and investment-banking houses held firm. Old money still mixed with the new as the best of Boston, New York, Philadelphia and Washington society gathered in Northeast Harbor and Seal Harbor. Prominent families, such as the Astors and the Belmonts, added new luster. Only family historians and social mathematicians could account for the marriages and remarriages formed within the summer colonies as well as a thick social fabric made of snobbery, superiority and scandals.

Throughout the 1950's, the clubs and hotels maintained exacting standards: Rockefeller's Harbor Club, the Seal Harbor Yacht Club, the Northeast Harbor Tennis Club and Swimming Pool, and the most exclusive of all, the all-female Cranberry Club, with its limited group of twenty-four lifetime members. The clubs and hotels were the primary keepers of the caste. Actually, Seal Harbor no longer had any hotels. Rockefeller had bought two of the old ones and taken them down to maintain a strictly residential community. The hotels in Northeast Harbor—especially the Asticou and Kimball House—maintained a homogeneous and familiar clientele in keeping with the *Social Register*. A small number of Jews sought entry into the hotels and inns. One proprietor recalled that one or two were allowed to come only in July, during the less-favored summer month. Another considered a few Jews no problem as long as they were "not aggressive and too forward and didn't show poor taste."

A new family had to be known by its associations and acceptable family connections. "Who is he?" and "Who are they?" were the crucial questions asked about a family that wanted to buy property and join the clubs. There were no restrictive covenants, but local brokers and residents rarely sold properties to Jews, knowing that they would not feel at home in the homogeneous communities.

While Bar Harbor sought the tourists and Northeast Harbor and Seal Harbor ignored them, hardly anyone noticed the small group of European Jewish immigrants who slipped into the western parts of the island, especially around Long Pond. These people had fled Hitler in the 1930's and the Nazi conquests in the 1940's. They came from the cosmopolitan bourgeoisie, from cities throughout Europe such as Frankfurt, Berlin, Vienna and Budapest. To get to America, they had followed convoluted passageways through Sweden, Holland, Russia and Palestine. As European Jews, they shared common interests and tastes, as well as a history of displacement and regeneration in America. They were not observant. None sought to develop any religious institutions on the island. Several, in fact, were married to non-Jews.

The European Jewish immigrants who gathered around the untouched beauty of Long Pond did not look to the island's clubs for social affirmation. They simply enjoyed the freedom of Acadia National Park, with its magnificent coast, ponds, trails and carriage roads. In Somesville and other communities on the western part of the island, as well as on the Cranberry Isles, they found the simplicity of New England country life.

Somesville had changed little over the past one hundred years. There were still a few inns, some stores, many modest houses and farms. The local population was still drawn from several old families—the Someses and Richardsons, to name but two. Many were still fishermen and carpenters, while others served the summer population. Over the years, several summer residents from other villages had established camps in the quiet and rustic setting around Long Pond and Indian Point, escaping—some for just a few hours or days, some permanently—from the relative formalities of life in Northeast Harbor and Bar Harbor. Their camps, although sometimes large and handsome, never dominated the landscape or changed the tenor of the communities. In the western part of the island, along with its proud traditions and memories, the hardships of Maine life still showed through the surface of daily life: poor incomes and the long, hard privations of winter.

Arriving on Mount Desert Island in the early 1950's, many of the Jewish émigrés were drawn by friends or family or through the vagaries of discovery on a journey through New England. In a landscape that reminded them of Europe, they found developers and speculators from whom they bought land cheaply. The conductor Max Rudolf was one of the first to come to the island. Fearful of the outbreak of anti-Semitic hostilities in his native Germany, Rudolf had taken his family to Prague in 1929, then to Gothenburg, Sweden, and finally to the United States in 1940. A casual question from a friend led Rudolf, the charming and highly intellectual artistic administrator of the Metropolitan Opera, and his family to the island in 1950. Mary Opdycke Peltz, a long-time summer resident of Bar Harbor and editor of *Opera News,* had asked Rudolf what he planned to do in the summer months ahead. He wanted to rent a cabin on a lake in Maine—nothing specific, just an idea. With great enthusiasm she recommended Long Pond and told him about Arthur Prey's cottages.

For generations, Prey's family had owned property on the Northern Neck at Long Pond. Unbeknownst to Mary Peltz, Prey had just sold his large holdings to Tom Flynn, a speculator from Ohio. Rudolf followed her advice and spent a month on Mount Desert. By that time, Flynn was desperate to sell lots in his newly formed subdivision. He was not alone. Mike Garber, a Jew from Connecticut, had come to know and love the island when he was stationed at the Trenton air base during the war. Within a few years, Garber acquired a great deal of land in Bar Harbor and around Long Pond. It did not matter to him or Flynn who bought the land or where their buyers came from, and it was from Flynn that Rudolf bought three parcels.

Alphonse Pasquale, a European-trained, German-speaking architect, was living on the island and was eager to design and build houses. Like Rudolf, he had escaped from a Nazi-dominated Europe. Pasquale first settled in New York, where he worked as a graphic designer. On a visit to Mount Desert, he met an old friend from Paris, Marguerite Yourcenar, the Belgian-born author. She convinced him to move to the island as she had done. The mountains and the sea entranced them both.

With Rudolf, Pasquale began his successful career of designing summer camps—over thirty of them—primarily for the Jewish émigrés who lived in New York most of the year. His talents and taste matched the modern European architectural sensibilities of his clients. He personally built many of the simple, rectangular, one-story, boxlike camps set in the woods or at the edge of the water. Expansive decks let the light and luminous scenery pour though large glass windows and doors. Mount Desert's traditional summer architecture of elaborate display, built with towers, bays, porticoes and porches, was not for Pasquale or his clients.

His own home overlooking the water in Southwest Harbor became a center for his Long Pond friends—both Gentiles and Jews. Yearly, the ebullient architect brought together scholars, musicians, engineers, analysts, photographers, doctors and art dealers to share his deep interest in art and music: the Rudolfs, Wylers, Tannenbaums, Hoffmanns, Leesers and Neus.

The immigrants had little contact with the social life of Seal Harbor and Northeast Harbor. The lone exception was Rudolf and his wife, Liese, who easily crossed the lines from Long

Pond to Northeast Harbor and Bar Harbor. They entertained their friends from the world of European and American musical culture, especially centered around the Metropolitan Opera. During each summer, the Rudolfs visited with the Peltzes in Bar Harbor and Mrs. August Belmont, one of the leading figures in Northeast Harbor society. She was much admired as the former actress Eleanor Robson and the wife of August Belmont III. The visits to Rudolf's camp were modest occasions of state, akin to visiting a dacha in the Russian woods. But Mrs. Belmont, a lady of aristocratic bearing and gracious charm, had her limits. She would not allow her car to be driven down the long, potholed dirt road to the Rudolfs' camp. Rudolf picked her up at the head of Long Pond and drove her back and forth.

Instead of a private club, the émigrés gathered at Pond's End, where the Smiths of Somesville—Zettie, Lyle, and their son, Bob—established a restaurant, specializing in Continental and Maine cuisine. Zettie and Bob cooked, while Lyle, the game warden on the island from 1928 to 1953, took tourists on excursions up and down the lake and rented rowboats to fishermen. The immigrants called Pond's End "New York on the Rocks." And even if the local people called Long Pond "Little Jerusalem," the Jews felt no prejudice. Just as summer residents had done for generations, the Jews romanticized the locals.

Beyond Long Pond, social changes were occurring in many places on the island. For the first time, in the 1960's, the Harbor Club accepted a number of Jewish members who had bought cottages in Seal Harbor. The Bar Harbor Club also changed its policy and allowed Jewish scientists who worked at the Mount Desert Biological Laboratory to join. Northeast Harbor, however, continued to maintain a singularly homogeneous and socially exclusive population.

The Jewish émigrés were part of that great democratic public that Eliot, Dorr and Rockefeller had worked for in creating the national park on the island they treasured. "The present generation," Dorr wrote a few years before he died, "will pass as my own has done, but the mountains and the woods, the coasts and streams that have now passed through the agency of the Park to the National Government will continue as a national possession, a public possession, henceforth for all time to come."

Gentiles and Jews—local summer residents as well as tourists and visitors—benefited from Dorr's mission of converting private land on Mount Desert to wise public use:

> It never will be given up to private ownership again. The men in control will change, the Government itself will change, but its possession by the people will remain whatever new policies or developments may come. . . . For the park the main thing is to open it as widely as may be to the people while yet keeping it from being a mere playground; to make it a source of real re-creation and save it from vulgarization. To make it something that will uplift and inspire its visitors, while giving them new health and vigor.

# III
---
# CALAIS

# CHAPTER 12

---

# *Claiming Their Place*

AT THE AGE of forty-nine, in December 1922, Joseph Unobskey suddenly died of a heart attack at his home in the small city of Calais, Maine, thousands of miles from Bresna, his birthplace in Russia. Because there was no Jewish cemetery in Calais, his body was placed in a simple pine box at the Scholl Funeral Home and sent by train to Bangor, nearly a hundred miles to the southwest, for burial. Joseph's wife, Sarah, and their sons, Arthur, William and Charles, followed the coffin to Bangor in their large Buick.

In the heart of winter, they did not take a chance on driving the narrow, hilly, unpaved "airline" route, although it was the most direct road between Calais and Bangor. Instead, they took Route 1, near the coast, winding laboriously through one small town after another for over one hundred fifty miles. They went through Machias, Cherryfield, and Ellsworth and passed within a few miles of the summer resort of Mount Desert Island, which the Unobskeys knew only by reputation as an exclusive gathering spot for some of America's richest Gentile families, with one small town where a few Jewish immigrant shopkeepers lived.

When the family finally arrived in Bangor, they sought to make interment plans. Unfortunately, they had come without

231

cash, carrying a check for an insufficient amount to pay for the preparation of the body and burial in Beth Israel's cemetery. Distraught and humiliated, Arthur, the eldest son at twenty-four, led the family in search of a Bangor Jew who would respect their word—take their check and advance money to the family. Only after arduous negotiations were the necessary funds found for the burial to proceed speedily according to Orthodox laws.

The Unobskeys regarded their treatment in Bangor as an unforgettable insult to their pride and honor. In Calais, they were known for their success, integrity and worthiness. Their word—their pledge—was their bond. A small obituary in the *Calais Advertiser* acknowledged that "by enterprise and industry," Joseph Unobskey had "built up a flourishing business." The paper asserted that he was a "man much liked by his co-religionists and by the public generally." Sarah, Joseph and their sons had labored at integrating into the city, among friends, neighbors and customers.

But Bangor's Gentiles were unaware of the Unobskeys' good reputation, and Bangor's Jews were little impressed by it. The Unobskeys were seen as just another family of provincial Jews from small towns in Washington, Aroostook and Hancock counties, intermittently drawn to Bangor for making Jewish marriages, celebrating religious holidays and burying their dead in one of the cemeteries owned by Bangor's synagogues.

Nor did Bangor's Jews understand the unusually tight bond firmly connecting Sarah Unobskey to her sons. Joseph, soft-spoken, slender and of medium height, had conveyed an aura of gentle passivity. It was Sarah and her sons who were unmistakably one in ambition and appearance. A picture of them taken a few years after Joseph's death reveals a strong front line: four short, stout people with dark wavy hair and strong pudgy hands. Much overweight, they look as if they are ready to burst forth out of their broad frames—Sarah in her long, plain black dress, and the three men in dark, pin-striped suits, following their mother's lead in standing erect, alert and confident.

Driven by shrewdness, tenacity and a paucity of money, Sarah had led the family to Calais in 1911. While their birth and emigration dates are fuzzy, the family's purpose never was. Living in Snovsk, Russia, in 1903, Sarah Unobskey demanded that her husband escape conscription in the Russian Army during the Russo-Japanese War and go to America. Joseph arrived at Ellis Island with 17 cents and one possession—a mink-lined coat. According to family legend, he borrowed $10, an amount required for entry by each immigrant, in exchange for his coat. In one version, the coat was returned; in the other, he was left with the 17 cents after he honorably returned the $10 but did not get the coat back.

Initially, Joseph worked in Boston in the fur business, as he had done in Russia. It is not clear whether Joseph found his way to Eastport, Maine, before or after Sarah arrived in 1905 with their two sons, Arthur and William. What is certain is that Sarah was attracted to cheap land in areas far from the large eastern cities. Like many poor Jewish immigrants, Joseph peddled goods around the rural Maine coast, selling bits of inexpensive clothing, pots, pans and anything else that allowed a profit. Finally, the family settled in Eastport and opened a small dry-goods store. There, another son, Charles, was born in 1906. In all, in Russia and the United States, Sarah bore nine children, only three of whom survived childhood.

Joseph and Sarah lived in Eastport for several years building their business and family. In 1906 Louis Unobsky, Joseph's brother, and Mary Unobsky, Sarah's sister, arrived in the United States. The two brothers had married sisters in Russia. Brought over by Joseph and Sarah, Louis and his wife started their own dry-goods store in Lubec, twenty miles from Eastport. (Unlike Joseph, Louis spelled his last name without an *e*.) The family consolidated further when Sarah brought over her half brother Morris Holland from Russia. For several years, he worked for Mary, his other half sister, and Louis in Lubec until he settled permanently in Calais where he worked for Joseph and Sarah.

The Unobskeys found Eastport, filled with fishermen and workers in the sardine plants, a difficult place. Arthur and Bill were frequently beaten up, taunted as Jews and forced to eat pork by gangs of young ruffians. In 1911, the Unobskeys became American citizens, an essential step in their resolution to remain and prosper in America. But they were not willing to be subjected to petty violence and prejudice. In the same year, the family sold their Eastport store and moved twenty-six miles to Calais, lured by the city's location as the regional center of trade between Canada and Maine. The city was also only ten miles from the St. Croix Paper Company, the large pulp and paper mill which opened in Woodland in 1905.

At the time, Calais was a small Jewish center that drew upon several immigrant families in St. Stephen (New Brunswick), Eastport and Lubec. One such Jew, Joseph Gordon, had left Minsk in 1906, traveled to New York and yearned for work beyond the harsh competitive turmoil of the Lower East Side. Looking for reasons to try his luck in Maine, Gordon wrote for information to an immigrant friend already living in Calais. "You'll never be a millionaire," Gordon's friend replied, "but you can do what you want here. Come down."

And down they came, as did the Unobskeys. The Unobskeys took out a bank loan and started a small clothing store in the Bernardini Block on Main Street. Variously called Unobskey's, Unobskey's Store, or Unobskey's New York Store, it was typical of the many competitive retail establishments throughout the state that sold inexpensive clothes. In the vernacular of the clothing industry, the Unobskeys were in the rag trade. In time, Unobskey's worked its way up to offering better-quality and higher-priced goods.

The hard-driving family were not the only clothing merchants in the city, but from the time they settled in Calais, they acted as if they were. They dismissed their competition from other successful stores, such as Levy's, but they never gave up the hot pursuit of customers. And although they regarded themselves as Orthodox, the Unobskeys departed from one of the most important laws by working on Saturdays, the Sabbath, driven by the pressing desire to succeed.

Their store carried any line of clothing that customers, mainly from Canada, would buy. Since Canadian goods were considerably more expensive and of poorer quality than American goods, shoppers came once a week, usually on Saturday or Saturday night, from as far away as Fredericton and St. John, over ninety miles away. The Unobskeys expanded their reputation for good service, fashionable and dependable merchandise, easy credit—interest-free for thirty to ninety days—and timely repayment of the family's numerous debts to the local banks.

They soon discovered that Calais was a tolerant city that harbored few suspicions about foreigners and no overt signs of anti-Semitism. Securely ensconced, the family unwittingly gained access to the magic formula that brought them respect and acceptance: they "believed" in Calais. Year by year, Sarah Unobskey borrowed as much money as she could from the local banks—the only source of capital she had—to expand her store, buy additional properties, and dig her roots into the city. In the process, she committed two of her three sons to a lifetime of business and civic responsibilities in Calais.

Sarah and her family made another discovery, one that was less encouraging: like many Maine cities and towns, Calais was suffering from an economy in decline. When other people were reluctant to invest in Calais and start new enterprises, Sarah and her sons let loose a fierce entrepreneurial spirit to build a successful family business—based on stores and real estate— and revive the city. One observer in Calais called the Unobskeys "gunslingers and gamblers," betting on the city's future.

They were hardly the first to do so. A little over a century before, bold and enterprising settlers, mostly of Scottish origin, were lured to the area by its extraordinary natural resources. Location was key to the history and hopes of Calais. From its earliest days through the late nineteenth century, the city was shaped by two factors: rich forests and the beautiful St. Croix River. It was Pierre du Guast, also known as Sieur de Monts, who had named the river in 1603. Traveling under the leadership of the great French explorer Samuel de Champlain past Nova Scotia and New Brunswick to the New England coast, Sieur de Monts and their small crew entered Passamaquoddy Bay and sailed up the twisting river, framed by gentle hills, to within a mile of what would one day become Calais. From this spot, Sieur de Monts directed Champlain to explore the coast. During his voyage, Champlain sailed to Frenchman Bay and named an island "l'Isle des Monts-deserts" or Mount Desert Island. Champlain also sailed up the Penobscot River all the way to the place which became the city of Bangor. A century and a half later, after numerous colonial disputes and wars, the Treaty of 1783 between the United States and Great Britain established the St. Croix River as the easternmost boundary between Canada and the Untied States.

By the late 1700's, a small number of settlers from Canada, Massachusetts and other parts of Maine had begun to exploit the forests, falls and river routes around Calais. Situated at the head of tidewater for navigation, fifteen miles from the mouth of the St. Croix River and thirty miles from the ocean, Calais started to flourish. A burgeoning lumber trade stimulated the development of sawmills and shipbuilding. In 1809, the residents incorporated the town of Calais along a narrow swath of land, fourteen miles from end to end, parallel to the St. Croix River.

The town, which was named by the Massachusetts legislature in tribute to France for her help in the Revolutionary War, created self-governing institutions, churches, roads, schools and fraternal organizations. Starting with the Congregational church in 1826, Calais erected thirteen churches for nine different denominations. They were handsome, large structures that loomed impressively over the town that lay on hilly land. Aspiring to excellence and distinction, several congregations employed architects, such as James Renwick and John Stevens, from New York and Boston.

Numerous fine homes were built in local vernacular patterns that called forth Greek Revival, Italianate and Federal styles; a few outstanding examples of Gothic Revival design still grace Main Street. They were built by Asher B. Bassford, an architect from Calais who designed the Greek Revival Calais Academy in 1851. Although it began as a private school for the wealthier members of the community, in 1860 it became the public high school for the city. By 1850, Calais was proudly proclaiming itself the "largest" city in the state "east of Bangor" and in the same year the nearly five thousand residents incorporated.

For several decades, lumber was gold in Calais, just as it was in Bangor. The trade spawned a generation of aggressive, shrewd men who owned and controlled vast tracts of land, mills, wharfs, ships, stores (where the men who worked their forests were compelled to buy supplies), railroads and banks. The St. Croix lumber trade was controlled by James Murchie, F. H. Todd, Henry F. Eaton and their three large, closely connected families. The industry in Calais peaked in the 1860's, enriched by trade with the West Indies, South America, Cuba and England.

Unexpectedly, the depression of 1873 marked the beginning of the downswing in the city. Severe unemployment, poor wages and the migration of population followed. In fact, by the mid-seventies, the best timber in the area had already been cut and the shipbuilding industry was in terminal decline, making Calais totally dependent on railroads that were part of the Canadian or New England networks. The Calais–Bangor connection, completed in 1898 along the shore route, was one of the last links in Maine's railroad system. The connection notwithstanding, without any strong industries, the city's population which had reached six thousand in the 1870's, stopped growing and then declined to five thousand people in the 1920's.

Maine's conversion to pulp and paper production was not initially injurious to most of the local lumber lords. F. H. Todd and Sons joined with backers in New York and Boston to establish the St. Croix Paper Company in Woodland. The plant emerged out of the forest, seemingly overnight, in 1905, and employed over five hundred people. Eventually, both the Todds and Murchies sold water rights on the St. Croix and great tracts of timberland to the paper company. By the end of World War I, however, the Murchies and Eatons had left the lumber business, and the International Paper Company bought the mill in Woodland. Several devastating mill fires along with the deterioration of the wharfs along the river completed the destruction of a once vibrant trade.

Yet Calais, whose history seems to parallel that of Bangor, developed a dynamic spirit that was unique. As the easternmost city in Maine, the city enjoyed a thriving relationship with Canadian cities and towns across the river and border. In calculating the wealth and vitality of Calais, one has to include the New Brunswick towns of St. Stephen, Milltown, and St. Andrews, whose cumulative populations and industries, such as the large St. Croix Cotton Mill, were of great benefit to Calais.

The open border fostered a more cosmopolitan society than was usually the case throughout Maine and, as the historian Harold Davis wrote, it engendered "a closely knit community of interests which was not disturbed seriously by tariffs or by international differences and tensions." Architects, businessmen, builders, laborers and landowners moved from country to country, easily changing their nationalities and residences over the years. Church congregations were drawn from both sides. Calais drew its water supply from St. Stephen, which was connected to Calais by trolley. The local hospital was in St. Stephen, as were two business colleges. Firemen on each side responded to calls from the other city. Six Calais mayors were Canadian or otherwise foreign-born.

In the 1880's, development of neighboring resorts in Canada and the United States stimulated the tourist and retail trades. Campobello, in Passamaquoddy Bay, was an island of farms and a few small fishing villages. Boston developers bought up property and promoted it to wealthy, upper-class clients such as the family of Franklin Delano Roosevelt. At St. Andrews in New Brunswick, businessmen affiliated with the Canadian Pacific Railroad built the large and handsome Algonquin Hotel as well as cottages for permanent summer residents.

Increasingly, summertime tourists appreciated Calais's beautiful, tranquil setting on the St. Croix River. During the rest of the year, however, Calais residents stoically tolerated its location and harsh climate. In 1875, Rev. I. C. Knowlton, searching for the best that could be said about the city's extreme northeastern location, wrote, "Though the climate has some very repulsive characteristics, the St. Croix valley is a healthy locality. The winters are long and extremely severe; the summers short and cool; and very little space is left for spring or autumn. . . ."

Notwithstanding the declining economy and severe climate, many educated and well-to-do men and women lived contentedly in the community. Cultural and scientific interests flourished. George Boardman, who made his fortune in the lumber trade, was an ornithologist of great renown. He gathered a remarkable collection of flora and fauna from the St. Croix valley, Europe and South America. In the late 1890's, he offered to donate his collection to the city. His biographer, Samuel Boardman, who was both a cousin and the editor of the *Bangor Daily Commercial*, explained the choice: "To be sure, Calais was but a small city and was in no sense an educational or scientific centre; but its people were intelligent, many were wealthy and all held Mr. Boardman in the highest esteem." When, for financial reasons, the city declined the offer of his collection, Boardman donated it to the New Brunswick government, which put it on permanent display in Fredericton.

From the turn of the century through the 1930's, Henry Eaton made Calais the most cultured of the region's cities and towns. He brought musical and dramatic performers to the city whenever they were not in demand elsewhere. He helped to found the St. Croix Chorus, of which he was an avid member, and along with many Calais residents, such as the talented cellist Ruth Ross, welcomed the annual visits of William Chapman. Each year the director of the Maine Music Festival trained a small Calais chorus to participate in the fall concerts in Bangor.

Residents enjoyed the security of traditional bonds among families and friends, the quiet pace of life, the handsome homes, beautiful trees and peaceful river, and the easy access to and from Bangor, Portland, Boston and New York on the two daily trains. Parents, cousins, aunts, uncles and unmarried sisters and brothers all partook of the social life of the city and were cared for by their families through old age. Although the most restless and ambitious sons and daughters moved to larger cities, those who stayed at home formed a tight community of extended families and common memories.

What was true for the native-born, however, did not pertain to the new immigrants. Their history in Calais began when they reunited their families from Russia and started looking to a future shaped by hard work and idealism. The Unobskeys did not indulge in nostalgia and pride. Instead, they looked ahead to revitalizing Calais.

There was reason to be optimistic in the 1920's. Calais, along with much of the state, enjoyed nearly a decade of unparalleled consumer spending, high employment and rising wages, especially at the unionized Woodland plant. Not only did the Unobskeys expand their retail establishment, but they also developed visions of what a thriving retail center in Calais could mean for their business and the city as a whole. In 1926, they made their first major real estate acquisition when they bought a property on Main Street adjacent to the clothing store. There they built a commercial block, which included a movie theater and four stores.

The Unobskeys thought on a grand scale, expecting the entire St. Croix valley to patronize their 870-seat State Theatre. (Ironically, the first movie shown was *The Moon of Israel*, starring Marie Corda and Arlette Marchal. According to the Unobskeys' advertisement, for 35 cents patrons could witness "the mightiest spectacle the world has ever seen.") Hardly one of the resplendent palaces that were springing up in cities and towns throughout America, the State Theatre was, nonetheless, a fine addition to Calais. Built in the modest, red-brick style of Main Street, the theater contained the latest in fireproof construction, attractive fixtures and a fine large stage.

The Unobskeys envisioned using the theater as a place for fashion shows and a platform for public events such as high school graduations. The paper hailed the opening in ways that must have pleased the Unobskeys and may even have emanated from their lips. "The theater will stand as a milestone in the progress of the Unobskeys, whose vision and determination made the undertaking possible."

The State Theatre, immensely popular as a new source of cheap entertainment, pumped up business for the Unobskeys' store nearby. Confidently, they enlarged the ladies' store and started a new men's clothing store. By the 1930's, they were handling a full line of merchandise—a mini department store for men, women and children that sold practically everything, except sets of dishes, and even those they gave away to good customers. Although the merchandise inched up in quality, the Unobskeys never cut out popularly priced clothing for their customers from the mills.

Despite the Crash of 1929 and the Depression, Sarah Unobskey continued to enlarge her holdings. In 1932, she built another structure on Main Street, taking a risky bet on an economic turnabout. The Unobskeys' two-story red-brick Professional Building contained eight offices for doctors and lawyers as well as three large retail stores. In Sarah's view, the city needed to provide an attractive place for professionals to work in. Metropolitan Life, which held the mortgage, also had its offices in the building.

Contracts multiplied, tenants were found, leases were negotiated and the family took on more debt. Sarah Unobskey not only had a "U" carved on her buildings in Calais, she also incised her tough and firm ways on all those with whom she dealt. A few businessmen in Calais never forgot or forgave the family for its aggressive business practices. In the eyes of Frank Beckett, who sold tobacco and groceries on Main Street and owned property contiguous to that of Unobskey's, she was a tough negotiator who couldn't be outmaneuvered. He was resigned to her ways. "You had to get up a lot earlier in the morning to outsmart her," he used to tell his fellow businessmen in the city.

She was her own architect and supervisor of all work done on her properties. In one well-known incident, she objected to the quality of the bricks bought by her contractor for the Professional Building. Without hesitation she told him they were defective and to send them back and find new ones. When he refused, she hired truckers to take the bricks from the building site in the middle of the night and dump them in the St. Croix River. The building was built with new bricks to her liking.

The city was well aware of the uncontested choices that Sarah made for her children—the roles she assigned them, the standards of behavior she imposed, and the status she sought for the family. She was not active in civic affairs, as two of her sons would be, but Calais residents saw her day after day as she worked in Unobskey's or moved through the city streets with her heavy gait, clothed in a simple long dress, never smiling, never loosening the stern expression on her face.

She was the commanding general of a small army of sons and relatives with whom and for whom she built the family business. In a bemused way, Arthur once remarked to his Lubec cousin Bert Unobsky: "Why she wants another building I don't know." The answer didn't matter. Arthur and Charlie loved the business—the stores and the real estate—as she did, and supported her decisions as to where and when the family would buy and build. The sons differed in their personalities but never in their dedication to her and to each other.

For many years, the family lived in the apartment above Ubosky's. When Arthur married, he bought a house on High Street, but Charlie lived with his mother until her death. He then moved in with Arthur's family, and Morris Holland, Sarah's half brother and his family moved into the apartment.

Sarah, who spoke Yiddish to her sons, defined her world by rigid moral judgments of right and wrong, good and bad. While she trained and led her troops for the combat of life, especially the commercial combat of a small city, she also fattened her sons and fed them to excess. She cooked traditional heavy Jewish foods—meats, stews, potatoes, noodles and strudels—and served them to the family on platters, according to one friend, as big as a skating rink. One wonders, was it to show that, unlike in Russia, the Unobskeys finally had enough money to feed the family? Or, haunted by the loss of six children, did she misguidedly overfeed the surviving offspring in a peasantlike defense against illness? Unfortunately, circulatory problems and heart disease undermined their health and caused two of them to die in their fifties.

None of her sons made independent choices about their careers or personal lives. Following her wishes, Arthur began working full time in the store after the eighth grade and did not finish high school. Sarah did send him to business school in St. Stephen to take shorthand and typing so that he would have useful skills in case the business failed. Charlie completed high school in Calais, attended business school and then went to work in the store. Sarah decided that Bill, the middle son, would be a doctor even though his interest was engineering. He was a splendid athlete who could easily have gotten a football scholarship to college. Yet Sarah, afraid that he would hurt himself, sent him to Tufts University because it did not allow its premed students to play football.

At first, Sarah intended that Bill practice medicine in Calais. Then she changed her mind and directed him to live in New York, where despite the difficulties of starting a practice during the Depression, he became a successful surgeon, joined the staff of the Hospital for Joint Diseases and eventually became its venerated chief of surgery. Among Sarah's instructions to Bill was that he serve the poor as well as those who could pay. "If a poor woman calls you, send the bill to me." In fact, as he became more successful, he, in turn, helped the family in Calais when they were short of funds.

Dutifully, Bill went home every summer for his ten-day vacation. The stories of Sarah's stern control were legion. On one occasion when Bill was home, he got a phone call from a patient on whom he had operated. In his convivial way, Bill had told her to call if she ever got to Maine from New York. Now she was waiting with a friend for Bill to come and pick her up in Machias, fifty miles away. Sarah was furious. Did he invite the woman to come to Calais? she asked Bill. His answer was beside the point. Nice girls, his mother insisted, would not have taken him up on his offer. Embarrassed, he brought them to Calais, but the next day Sarah forced them to leave. "Nobody sent for them and you are not going to be responsible," she told Bill. He frequently told the story on himself. "Never tell anyone to come to Maine. You can't just say to a New Yorker, 'Come to Maine.' They will take you up on it!"

The visit was a frivolous issue, but marriage was not. In Calais, everyone expected Arthur Unobskey would marry Tillie Gordon, one of Joseph Gordon's daughters, who had a vivacious personality and enjoyed living in Calais. Everyone, that is, except Sarah. There was no question that Arthur had to marry a Jewish woman, but she also had to be one who would meet Sarah Unobskey's social standards. The small community of Calais Jews was fine for the Unobskeys to pray and visit with. The Boxers, Levys, Gordons, Kramers, Ackers, Prilutskeys, Cohens, Krasneys, Matzes and the Unobskys from Lubec met for outings and often exchanged visits on Saturdays. But in 1930, because Tillie's father was still selling junk and scrap materials, the Gordon family lacked the status that Sarah considered essential for her son.

Sarah and Arthur looked all over the state and New Brunswick for a suitable wife. Finally, Sarah settled on the Rudman family from Bangor, whom she knew through her lawyer, Abraham Rudman. Lillian Rudman, a graduate of the University of Maine, was Abe Rudman's cousin. That Lillian was a quiet, contemplative and pretty woman and that Arthur was a gregarious man, far from handsome, who habitually placed himself at any center of activity, mattered little to their families. The two were married in Boston in 1931, and after their return to Calais, they both worked in the store. The move from a busy city to a small, tranquil community was a difficult one for Lillian, but she bore the change—and her place at the center of the Unobskey clan—with quiet grace.

As Sarah Unobskey imposed her will on her family, she also ruled over the small Jewish population around Calais. She was not the first in Calais to perpetuate Jewish observance and family life. From the time of the earliest Jewish families' arrival after the turn of the century, they struggled to establish a minyan for daily prayer and Sabbath observance. For the holidays, they hired the American Legion hall or, on one occasion, a house to serve as a synagogue. By the 1920's, as their numbers grew and most of the Jewish families developed moderately successful businesses, they sought to establish a synagogue. In 1923, an attractive, two-story Italianate house with bay windows, built by Joseph Kalish, was available for a price that included a $1,000 down payment. (Kalish, who had had a clothing store on Main Street in the 1870's and was once mayor of the city, was thought to have been a Jew.)

With one unalterable condition, Sarah Unobskey offered to donate the money and help secure a mortgage: the synagogue had to be named in honor of her husband, Joseph, who had died the year before. The bargain was a painful one for the Jewish families of modest means. No Jew around Calais was eager to start the unheard-of practice of naming a synagogue for a deceased member of the community. But Sarah insisted upon her terms. No name, no money.

Reluctantly, the Jewish families gave in. Congregation Chaim Yosef was inaugurated in 1926, the first and only synagogue in Washington County. The Unobskeys not only supported the synagogue financially but supervised its religious, philanthropic and social affairs. A relative recalled that Arthur forced his suppliers in New York and Boston to make contributions to the synagogue: if you wanted to sell dresses to Unobskey's you made a donation to Chaim Yosef. Morris Holland, Sarah's half brother, a quiet and gentle man, looked after the religious needs of the synagogue. Attendance was crucial. On harsh winter days, the Unobskeys sent a wagon to pick up male congregants to make a minyan.

Chaim Yosef was an Orthodox shul with eighty-eight seats. The rabbis trained boys for bar mitzvah. The girls who wanted a Jewish education—among them Jessie Gordon and Arthur's daughter Martha—were reluctantly allowed to listen to the instruction in the Torah and Hebrew language. Martha sat behind the rabbi's chair so he couldn't see her. There were community rooms upstairs and an apartment on the first floor for the rabbi. In the back of the house in the barn, the rabbi, who also served as the shohet, killed chickens according to kosher laws.

Surprisingly, it was not difficult for the tiny community to find rabbis, if only for short periods of time. In the aftermath of the severe immigration laws passed in the 1920's, coming by way of Canada and serving a congregation was one way around an almost impenetrable wall of restrictions. Several rabbis stayed only a year before moving on to other larger congregations in the United States. However, one distinguished and learned rabbi, Jacob Kalchein, remained for almost fifteen years where he was respected by his small Jewish congregation and the Calais community at large. One year, he was even called upon to participate in the graduation exercises for the Calais

Academy, which were held, as always, in the Unobskeys' State Theatre.

The congregants of Chaim Yosef bought burial rights in a Jewish cemetery in Bangor. They also formed a Ladies Aid Society, started by Esther Gordon, to which each Jewish lady contributed 25 cents a month to aid one or two poor Jewish families that had difficulty paying rent and buying food. The society also encouraged the men to make a daily minyan and prepare for holiday celebrations and the observance of yahr-zeits, or mourning services, marking the anniversary of the death of a loved one.

By the 1930's, the Jews around Calais formed a self-conscious community of approximately fifteen families. While clear differences emerged as to the degree of economic success and adaptability to American life, the poorest Jews around Calais were never left out or made to feel unwanted. Quite rightly, the entire community felt itself to be as far removed from the influences of eastern European Jewry as from the Jewish immigrant centers in the United States and even from Bangor itself.

Uniformly, the Calais Jews wanted to be identified as Orthodox regardless of their revisions of traditional practice. Some Jews, such as the Unobskeys, worked on Saturdays; others, such as Joseph Gordon, never did. But all observed the dietary laws at home, importing kosher meat from Bangor. Some, including Arthur and Charlie Unobskey, departed from the laws when they ate outside their home. But picnics were strictly kosher. Before preparing the food, everyone checked with Sarah to see whether she wanted meat or dairy dishes. To celebrate the holidays, the Jewish families came from Eastport, St. John, Lubec, and Woodland and stayed over in Calais for several days, bringing traditional Jewish foods from rye breads to soups to cakes for all to share.

From time to time, family and friends came to visit in the summer or Jewish strangers passed through the city, carrying "pushkies" (little boxes) for soliciting contributions for sundry Jewish organizations. Loafers, or "shnorrers," as well as Jewish businessmen, could stay in the Gordon house for fifty cents a day for lodging and kosher food.

Gentiles acknowledged and respected Orthodox Jewish

practices and, except for the Unobskeys when they lived in Eastport, none of the immigrants ever felt the sting of anti-Semitism. Robert Rosen, for many years a store owner and head of the single Jewish household in Woodland, belonged to every fraternal organization in the town. When he went to meetings of the Masons and Odd Fellows, the women would make a special salmon salad or sponge cake for him. During Passover, everyone in town knew that the Rosens would not eat or drink outside the house, or, if necessary, they would use paper cups at the drugstore.

All the Jews in the area joined together to rejoice over a birth or mourn a death. Such was the case in 1935 when, thirteen years after Joseph Unobskey's death, Sarah suddenly died of a heart attack at the age of fifty-seven. This time there was no uncertainty or humiliation when the family quickly went to Bangor for the funeral. At the home of Lillian Unobskey's parents, Sarah's body was prepared for burial according to Orthodox law. The rabbi from Calais as well as the "chief rabbi" of Bangor officiated at the service and interment.

The obituary, featured on page one in the *Calais Advertiser*, lauded Sarah as a "keen business woman . . . familiar with every phase of their varied business and the success of this firm was due in great part to her initiative and foresight." Sarah Unobskey's belief in Calais was praised as the *Advertiser* recalled her efforts to build the State Theatre and Professional Building: "She had faith in this city and although times were particularly hard, and against the advice of her sons, built the Unobskey Professional Building which has justified that faith."

Aspects of her Jewish identity and leadership were respectfully recognized. She was "active in the Jewish religious life of this community and was the major support of the Jewish Synagogue which is named after her late husband, Joseph Unobskey." She left her three sons, Arthur, Charlie and Bill "to mourn their loss." She left them, however, with much more than a sense of loss. Having shaped their lives and set their goals, she now bequeathed them a special obligation: to maintain the family's well-being—as Americans, Jews, merchants and developers—in Calais.

Main Street, Calais, circa 1910

Unobskey's, on Main Street, opened for business in 1911 and
continued in the same location through the 1970s.

St. Anne's Episcopal Church, built of wood in the Gothic style, and finished in 1853

The Unobskeys—mother and sons—circa 1930. *From left to right:* Charles, William, Sarah and Arthur Unobskey.

Congregation Chaim Yosef, established in the Joseph Kalish house in 1927, continued as an active congregation until 1974.

Arthur and Lillian Unobskey on their
honeymoon in Nassau in 1931

Arthur Unobskey driving Senator Margaret Chase Smith around
Calais. Lillian Unobskey sits to the left of the senator.

# CHAPTER 13

# *New Traditions*

AFTER SARAH UNOBSKEY's death, Arthur, her eldest son, was not content to function within her limited arena of the family and Jewish community. He forced his way into the heart of the "quiet and leisurely" Gentile city itself. As the self-proclaimed impresario and savior of the Unobskeys and Calais, he imperiously assigned roles and goals: to his brother Charlie, to his children, Joseph, Martha and Sidney, to his Uncle Morris Holland and his children, and to anyone else in the city who would accept his lead.

Unlike Russian Jews in Bangor, Arthur did not wait to be let into the Calais establishment. He pursued acceptance and pushed his way into a high position in the economic and social life of the city. In a lifelong process, Calais taught him what he needed to know about opportunity, tolerance and patriotism; it shaped his powerful identity as an American, an active Maine citizen, and a respected and self-respecting Jew.

He quickly gained the confidence to promote the interests of his family and city way beyond the boundaries of Calais itself. It was his family, especially Charlie and Morris Holland, who absorbed the shocks from Arthur's strong personality, blunt talk and imagination.

Arthur Unobskey acted as if Calais wanted a plan of war

251

and a bold general to lead it to another chance at economic well-being. The city itself was less sure of what was needed to revive its spirit. Many distinguished residents, moderately successful business establishments, fine homes—and beautiful, large trees—made Calais life as pleasing as it had been for the previous one hundred years, even if underneath that facade, the city was no longer prosperous.

In the mid-1930's, Calais lay on the uncomfortable edge of economic stagnation. The city had found no ways to recover from the decline of its lumber and shipping trade, the paucity of investments and its distance from urban and industrial centers. Its population remained small, with approximately five thousand people in Calais and fourteen thousand in the whole St. Croix valley area. The city slowly shrunk within its handsome nineteenth-century architectural frame. The looming, large, wooden churches were no longer filled. The Congregational church, for example, had no more than one hundred faithful parishioners for its three hundred seats. Even transportation had become more difficult: the passenger link with Bangor, Boston and New York was slowly being cut back by the Maine Central, which was losing out in the competition with the automobile.

In the late 1940's, the historian Harold Davis bleakly observed that farming, along with the area's moderate-sized established industries and tourism, would "probably be sufficient to maintain the present level of existence. For anything more than this a major economic miracle . . . will be necessary. Until then enterprising younger people will continue to seek their fortunes elsewhere, and the others, along with their elders, will go on spinning out their uneventful but not altogether unhappy lives along the St. Croix."

There were many in Calais who led uneventful lives, but Arthur Unobskey was not one of them. Making things happen, making the city come alive was Arthur's self-imposed mission. Behind his thrusts of activity—both civic and commercial—was the intrinsic need to sustain a market for the Unobskeys' stores and businesses. Arthur continually stoked the family's business machine: pursuing customers, selling quality clothing and merchandise, developing properties, and borrowing and paying back large bank loans. Tucked away on the Canadian border, the stores had to stimulate demand in the small, fragile local retail market and keep customers from shopping in Bangor and Boston.

With gusto, Arthur enlarged the family's connection to two industries dominated by American Jews in the mid-twentieth century: movies and clothing. The movie business at the State Theatre, which the Unobskeys leased from 1926 through the late 1950's to a St. Stephen firm, took care of itself. It was fashion that kept Arthur, and sometimes Charlie, on the run between Calais and New York. In the mid-forties, with full employment and wartime wages followed by strong postwar consumer demand, the store swept its clientele into the upscale clothing markets—selling names such as Hart Schaffner and Marx, Kimberly Knits, and Jonathan Logan and expensive dresses, wool coats, fancy lingerie, accessories, hats, bags and formal attire. The Unobskeys, however, never dropped the lines of modestly priced goods which provided the basis of their long-time success.

Arthur thrived on the frenetic pressure of the fast-paced Jewish world of wholesale clothing on Seventh Avenue, buying, catching the fashion shows, examining and sizing up the latest styles and fabrics. He savored the crackling ethnic humor and ghetto language of New York City but cared little about its theaters, the restaurants or the zoo.

He corralled family members to go with him to see the latest lines: his daughter, Martha, Bill's wife, Evelyn or his first cousin, Bert Unobsky from Lubec. Starting on the top floor of a building, they worked their way down the dreary floors filled with crowded offices and showrooms. One time with Bert, he watched the models with a pad and pencil, seemingly poised to order the desired styles. When the sales director pressed Arthur about what he was going to buy, Arthur told him he'd let him know as soon as he went back to the stockroom. "Everything looks good on these gals, but I want to see how they look on the hangers. That's how I have to sell them."

Arthur delighted in being known in the trade as the Jew from Calais, six hundred miles from New York, deep in rural Maine. He was one of the army of successful Jewish retailers with stores on Main Streets throughout America. But Arthur Unobskey was also a proud small-town Jew with his own Orthodox shul, kosher home and sons who would train for bar mitzvah. Although he came to the big city to buy the latest

goods, salesmen made semiannual trips, often at Arthur's insistence, to sign the contracts in Calais. There, they could see
his store and go to his shul, Chaim Yosef.

When they came to Calais, Arthur showed them off as they
made their presentations in Unobskey's, told their Jewish jokes,
boasted about their ambitious, successful sons and daughters
and joined in prayer at Chaim Yosef. One of the flashiest of the
salesmen, and the only one who came to Calais in a chauffeured
car, was Sam Newbart. Known to Arthur as the king of the
salesmen, Newbart sold coats, told Jewish jokes nonstop and
boasted that his brilliant cousin was writing a play about him.
(The relative was Arthur Miller and the play was *Death of a
Salesman*.)

Arthur Unobskey used the salesmen not only as his lifeline
to Jewish culture in New York but also as examples to his own
small community. When a Calais Jew was late for prayer,
Arthur told him: "If the salesmen can make it from New York
on time, you can make it from your house." He delighted in
bringing mementos back from New York. After each buying
trip, he roared into Calais on the Pullman train, carrying two
large boxes of fine pastries for his staff. For the family, he
bought whitefish and salamis from Barney Greengrass.

At the store, hired waiters and waitresses served the sweet
delicacies while Arthur held his own fashion shows—for his
own employees—just like the ones in the showrooms on Seventh Avenue. By touting the latest styles, fabrics and colors,
Arthur set the tone of enthusiasm and high-quality service that
he wanted his staff to convey to the customers. The staff at
Unobskey's was a large one, consisting, in its most prosperous
days, of sixteen employees, including three full-time seam-
stresses. Unobskey's augmented the salaries by paying commissions for goods sold. Some of the employees eventually worked
for the stores for over fifty years; many were supported financially in family crises, if the need arose; all were taken every
summer to the Algonquin Hotel in St. Andrews for a day's
outing.

Unrelenting hard work, first-class service, and quality
goods were the rules that enabled the Unobskeys and their staff
to dominate Main Street—the one and only street in Calais that
had any retail life. Inside Unobskey's, the mini department
store was a hub of activity controlled in every detail by Arthur

and Charlie. They walked the floors, doted on customers and kept their own books. Hawkishly, they watched their inventory, knowing every item and every price.

Unobskey's used a multitude of merchandising devices. Large ads in the *Calais Advertiser* hyped Unobskey's big-city connections and the excitement of new fashions: ARRIVING DAILY ALL CHOSEN PERSONALLY BY ARTHUR UNOBSKEY, WHO IS STILL IN NEW YORK SELECTING THE LARGEST AND MOST VARIED STOCK OF SPRING AND SUMMER CLOTHING EVER SHOWN BY UNOBSKEY'S.

The Unobskeys also held fashion shows at the State Theatre during the intermission of first-run, premier movies. The proceeds from the ticket sales benefited local charities. Sometimes the Unobskeys exhibited the latest fashions for women from the stores; sometimes they reached to Paris and rented couture clothes (via Seventh Avenue) for the occasion. Arthur served as the master of ceremonies. Favored and attractive customers modeled the clothes along a specially placed runway through the theater, while patrons were served refreshments and entertained with music.

Arthur even created the special events at which the latest high fashions could be purchased at his stores. Every year, he organized a dance, similar to those held in other cities, in honor of President Roosevelt's birthday to benefit the March of Dimes and the Calais Community Nurses. Invited by Arthur, the governor of Maine and the premier of New Brunswick were honored guests. Even when the temperature fell to twenty below zero, as it did for the event in February 1935, the patrons at the President's Ball danced in formal attire to two orchestras.

Unobskey's name spread through Washington County, claiming the store's place as the largest retail establishment in the region. Advertising was heavily employed in the regional newspapers, as were signs along the three routes that led to Calais. Along the "airline," the ninety-eight-mile direct route between Bangor and Calais, signs were planted every twenty miles: ONLY 90 MILES TO GO and then ONLY 70 MILES TO GO, and finally ONLY 10 MILES TO GO clicking off the miles along the monotonous and bumpy road that seemed to go nowhere but ended in Calais. Intrigued by the signs and exhausted by the ride, many people came into the store asking, "Who is this guy? Who is Unobskey? Who is this lost Jew?"

And as the tourists looked over Unobskey's, the Unobskeys

looked over the tourists. Arthur always watched for new customers and people who might be lured to stay in the city, adding to its small population and torpid commercial life. On one
occasion, Rabbi Samuel Sandmel, a renowned Hebraic scholar
and teacher at Hebrew Union College in Cincinnati, was driving toward the International Bridge to St. Andrews. He stopped
the car and told his wife, Frances, that he was going to find out,
after several years of wondering, if Unobskey was an Eskimo or
a Jew. The Reform rabbi, casually dressed and clean-shaven,
entered the store. In his soft Southern accent, Sandmel struck
up a conversation with Arthur, bought a tie, and quickly exchanged enough information for each to know that the other
was a Jew.

Arthur asked Sandmel what he did. When he proudly explained that he was a rabbi, Arthur pulled back, quickly
changed his tone and looked the Hebraic scholar and rabbi up
and down. Emphatically, Arthur shook his head. "You won't
do," he said in his uncompromising tone. Mystified and taken
aback by the abrupt dismissal, Sandmel asked Arthur what he
was referring to. "You won't do as the rabbi of Chaim Yosef."
In need of a new rabbi to serve the small Orthodox congregation, Arthur assumed that Sandmel had come into Unobskey's
looking to fill the next one- to two-year rabbinic stint in Calais.

The distinguished and amused rabbi may have been the
only person Arthur Unobskey ever discouraged from coming
to Calais. Each man who could be enticed to stay in the city was
a potential customer, a man with needed skills, services or capital to put into the faltering city—and maybe a Jew to add to the
daily minyan as one of the ten men required to say Kaddish
after the death of a family member. Arthur could never forget
that he had clothing to move, offices to rent, properties to lease,
debts to repay and a Jewish community to sustain.

Arthur Unobskey used his merchandising skills and status
in Calais to launch a career as a booster of civic and commercial
causes. With the intensity and hunger of an aspiring politician,
he toured the county and state at a dizzying pace, looking for
ideas, investments, capital, manufacturing concerns, entrepreneurs and professionals for Calais and the surrounding areas.

Charlie and Morris tended to many of the responsibilities
of running the stores while Arthur threw himself into projects
to improve the quality of life in the city and county. He devel-

oped a plethora of ideas and businesses, many of which gleamed with hope. Few of his optimistic visions came to fruition or met success. Along with several other men in Calais, Arthur started the Calais Federal Savings and Loan Association in 1932 to generate a pool of available capital for local entrepreneurs. In several instances, he acted as a one-man subsidy for people interested in living in Calais. Through his control of numerous properties on Main Street, he made deal after deal to encourage the presence of Newberry's, W. T. Grant and J. C. Penney, even though they meant competition for Unobskey's. Ever faithful to Sarah Unobskey's vision, Arthur was willing to let the competition play off itself as the price of building a dynamic retail center.

His civic enthusiasms blended firmly with the commercial ones. He headed a long list of organizations: chairman of the Washington County Industrial Committee, chairman of the Calais Chamber of Commerce, chairman of the Washington County Red Cross, a founder of the Student Loan Fund, a director of the Maine Publicity Bureau, a director of the Maine Development Commission, president of the Calais Rotary, chairman of the County War Bond and War Savings Campaign, and a member of the St. Croix Country Club, the center of the city's social life. Few possibilities for civic improvement escaped his attention, from lobbying to make St. Croix Island a national park, to pushing the state to upgrade Route 1, which ran through the city. And like P. T. Barnum and the Music Man, he promoted festivals, parades (there were at least six a year in which children wore costumes and uniforms), trips, and spelling, writing and reading contests—with cash prizes from Unobskey's. During World War II, as chairman of the salvage effort, he organized the city's children into teams to tear the city apart for scrap metal.

In 1947, in his most serious and prodigious campaign on behalf of Calais, Arthur raised over $100,000 for a combination gymnasium and auditorium for the high school. His effort was part of his ongoing concern for improving the city's educational and philanthropic institutions—the school, library and hospital in St. Stephen. As part of his strategy, he had encouraged Emma Eaton, who was the city's richest philanthropist, to donate land for a new high school.

In his enterprising and exacting way, Arthur Unobskey

constantly sought to stir the city out of its economic compla-
cency and state of resignation. He worked with a small core of
Calais business and professional men whom he deeply respected: John Trimble, the owner of the finest shoe store in the
city, Arlo Bates, the leading jeweler, C. Arnold Brown, a union
representative of the International Brotherhood of Papermak-
ers. Arthur also encouraged younger men, such as Francis
Brown, to take on civic responsibilities. Arthur appointed Francis secretary of the Rotary Club, and Charlie chose him to be
the city attorney. But human resources were limited within the
small population, especially when several distinguished and ca-
pable men—such as Harold Murchie, the chief justice of the
state's highest court—were not available to commit themselves
to the civic and commercial projects that the city needed.

Ahead of most of the Russian Jews in Maine, Arthur Unobskey in the 1930's made his entrée into the middle- and
upper-class society of his home city. Furthermore, Arthur's ambitious efforts brought him into contact with politicians and
government leaders in Maine, New England and Canada, a
highly unusual circumstance for any of Maine's Russian Jews.
One of the leading Gentile members of the community recalled
that Arthur participated "in most of the solid things that were
done when he was here." On further reflection, she said, "He
was in all of them, as a matter of fact. I can't think of any that
he would have missed. He was a very strong character and very
much interested in seeing that Calais had what it ought to have.
Once in a while he might antagonize somebody but he was very
well liked and recognized as somebody who was working for the
good of the town. . . . It was so obvious that he really had something worthwhile."

Above all else, the Passamaquoddy power project, or
Quoddy, was the focus of Arthur's energies and efforts from
the late 1940's until 1956. For many years, powerful visionaries,
politicians and utility interests had fought over the idea of gen-
erating vast amounts of energy from tidal flows in Passamaquoddy and Cobscook bays and, principally, those in the Bay
of Fundy, which rose and fell an extraordinary fifty feet twice
a day.

Franklin D. Roosevelt, campaigning for the vice-presidency
in 1920, was the first public supporter of the project. In Eastport, just a few miles from his family's summer home in Cam-

pobello, Roosevelt championed the ideas of Dexter E. Cooper, an engineering expert in hydroelectric power. Through the formation of water pools and the construction of dams, Cooper envisioned that Quoddy could generate unequaled quantities of energy for the needs of all of New England. He also proposed the development of aluminum and chemical plants in the area.

Cooper and Roosevelt successfully solicited electrical companies such as General Electric and Westinghouse for funds for further studies. Cooper moved the project slowly ahead by obtaining charters of incorporation from the legislatures in Maine and New Brunswick. Within a few years, however, Quoddy advocates confronted the powerful opposition of fishing interests in Canada and the United States and the hostile campaigns of the private utility companies. The Depression in 1929 marked the end of Quoddy's private funding.

The project remained dormant until Roosevelt moved into the White House in 1933. It took the resolute President several years of complicated political maneuvering to deliver for his Quoddy supporters. Roosevelt's deep concern for his beloved Campobello fit well into his administration's efforts to revive the economy through vast relief programs and power projects such as the Tennessee Valley Authority. Despite a projected cost of $60 million, the United States government embarked on the Quoddy project. In 1935 and 1936, while the Canadian government was unwilling to risk the wrath of its fishing industry, the Works Progress Administration spent $7 million on constructing two dams, building Quoddy Village to house 5,500 workers and undertaking extensive engineering studies.

Within a year, however, Quoddy became another bloody battlefield of New Deal policies. Opponents railed against the high costs and questioned the existence of markets for the energy. Partisan politics in Washington, D.C., and Augusta, along with the virulent hostility of Maine and New England utility companies, aborted the creation of a TVA-type authority for Quoddy. Facing reelection in 1936, the President shied away from identifying with the embattled program. William Pattangall, the outspoken chief justice of Maine's highest court, led the anti-Roosevelt and anti-Democratic forces; and when Maine voted for Alf Landon in 1936, Quoddy totally lost its political support from Roosevelt's administration.

Although Quoddy Village served as a Seabee base during the Second World War, the area's potential was ignored until the late 1940's, when C. Arnold Brown, Arlo Bates and Arthur Unobskey, along with Roscoe Emery and the Rev. Ernest Heywood of Calais, placed it, once again, on political agendas in Augusta and Washington. They looked longingly at the resources around the Passamaquoddy Bay and the Bay of Fundy: coal deposits in Nova Scotia, iron ore in Labrador and a deep harbor for shipping in Eastport. With these resources, American and Canadian industrialists could build massive steel, aluminum and chemical plants at the center of the hydroelectric power project.

With dismay, this cadre of concerned men watched Maine's textile industry move to the South, and the shoe industry lose its hold to foreign competition. Like men possessed, Arthur Unobskey, Roscoe Emery and others in the group traveled around the state spreading the Quoddy gospel of cheap and abundant energy, industrial development and employment for Maine workers. They sponsored meetings, sat on regional and international commissions, held numerous press conferences and spoke on radio programs. They promoted studies, touted technological advances and appealed to governors, senators, congressmen and members of Parliament—parties and politicians all over New England and eastern Canada.

Their moment of glory came in 1951 when a five-man delegation from the Washington County Chamber of Commerce, including Arthur Unobskey, went to Washington to lobby the New England congressional delegation. Their trip culminated in a meeting with President Truman in the Cabinet Room of the Executive Office Building. "Sit down, boys, and let's talk this over," the President said. The delegation appealed for federal sponsorship of a new survey for the power project. The *Calais Advertiser* proudly measured the positive results: "The President's friendly interest, his obvious planning for a survey and the fact that he gave the delegation so much time between such appointments as those with the Premier of France and General Eisenhower, gave the Quoddy group ample grounds for enthusiastic satisfaction with the conference."

For Arthur Unobskey, Quoddy meant a new kind of reward: he was no longer dreaming alone. The recently forged political alliances gave him greater status, especially as a political broker in Washington County. In 1951, Governor Frederick Payne appointed Unobskey to the prestigious Maine Development Commission. Although a lifelong Republican, he now switched his support from party to party in congressional and senatorial races according to the candidate's stand on Quoddy. If Arthur Unobskey was now a maverick, he was one who still maintained certain proprieties. When the Republicans visited the Unobskeys at their home, they entered through the front door for all to see; when Democratic candidates, such as Edmund S. Muskie, came calling, they entered, like the family, through the side door.

Despite the political machinations and fervent pronouncements of Quoddy supporters, including Senators Margaret Chase Smith and Owen Brewster, it is unlikely that Quoddy ever had any chance of being funded in Congress in the 1950's. The private utility and power companies, the "old forces," according to Senator Smith, were too strong. They killed the idea of a federally sponsored project—a "moondoggle," they said, that would compete with private sources of energy. Thus, New England remained the only area in the United States that did not have a public power project.

Yet, Unobskey never gave up hoping and pushing Senator Smith to work for the cause. Discreetly, he raised money for her campaigns, offered his home to her when she stayed over in Calais, and sponsored her appearances at Rotary and other local organizations when she wanted a forum to consolidate her support in Washington County. On her part, the venerated senator championed Quoddy in the Senate and throughout Maine and listened to Unobskey's views whenever he wanted to reach her. "When he calls me in Washington, I answer the call," she told Bert Unobskey in her soft, steady voice. "Do you know why? If I don't, he'll keep calling me until 3:30 in the morning."

According to the senator, Arthur Unobskey was "very direct, very honest and very civic-minded. He was very friendly, very courteous, never asking for anything personally for himself. He asked only for his area." Then, upon further reflection, she added, "Now I was reminded once in a while that he had stores and was looking for business and I agreed. But while he was looking for business he was looking for ways to improve the community."

When necessary, as with Senator Smith, he was courteous and deferential, but he was always persistent in advocating his cause, and was frequently gruff, demanding and imperious. He lived, said one of his friends, on the "slopes of Mt. Vesuvius." Those Calais residents who resented his commanding and prickly ways would say quietly to one another that he was just "trying to line his pockets." But they also conceded that in their poor, depressed and neglected area of Maine, improvements would not have come to them without the leadership and constant efforts such as those Arthur Unobskey provided. If you came from Calais, you were family to him; and, if you came from Maine, he would work on your behalf.

According to one of his Gentile friends, Unobskey's constant efforts in Rotary and other civic and service organizations overcame an inherent native suspicion about Jewish "money grubbers." Furthermore, the friend observed, it was the Unobskeys' exemplary behavior, charitable example and leadership of the minuscule Jewish community that "put out the anti-Jewish fires." This extraordinary degree of acceptance was easily noticed by Jews from other parts of the state. When George Ginsberg, a Jewish manufacturer from Bangor, met Jessie Baig in Calais, he was amazed to learn that she worked at the local bank. His frame of reference, in both business and social terms, was completely different: Bangor's Jews were unable to get jobs in their local banks; only a small number of them were invited into Rotary; and it was not until forty years after Arthur Unobskey was a member of the local gold club that Bangor's Jews were able to join a Gentile club.

The Jewish community around Calais was so small, one of its members remarked, that it was "not even a minority." At its high point in the early 1950's, it consisted of no more than twenty-six families. Most of the growth in Washington County occurred in Eastport during the Second World War, when the newly thriving sardine market attracted several new families, such as the Jacobsons and Stiebers. Nine Jewish families lived in Calais, seven in St. Stephen, five in Eastport and two in Lubec in the late forties.

With the small number of families, it was comparatively easy for Arthur Unobskey to unify, dominate and finance Jewish life in his area. He and Morris Holland set high standards. Bar mitzvahs were celebrated, as were all of the holidays. Daily minyans were held. Intermarriage was insistently discouraged. (For many years before his death, Charlie had a close relationship with the first-grade teacher in Calais. She was as strongly committed to her Baptist church as he was to remaining a Jew. Neither would convert, and they never married.) Through the 1950's, most of the families maintained kosher homes, despite the great difficulties in getting meat from Bangor.

The Jewish families in Calais, St. Stephen, Eastport and Lubec proudly made modest contributions to Israel and Maine's Jewish welfare organizations. They continued to care for each other, providing relief for families in need through the Ladies Aid Society. If there were difficulties with the law, as was the case with one Jewish family involved in smuggling, Arthur worked things out with the police and courts. Except for Arthur, Calais Jews took on the quiet, unaggressive mannerisms of their Gentile neighbors and were indistinguishable from the rest of the middle and upper classes in Calais.

What did Arthur Unobskey's Jewish identity mean to him? Although he was not deeply observant or learned, he maintained the formalities of religious practice that his mother and father brought from Russia. He continued the rites to honor their memory and to ensure the cohesiveness of the Jews in his area. His Jewish identity prompted a sensitivity to the needs of strangers; it also engendered deep gratitude for America's promise of opportunity and freedom, which differed so radically from what his family had experienced in Russia. Realistically, he recognized the existence of anti-Semitism. Knowing that there were many hotels in Maine, unlike the Algonquin in St. Andrews, that would keep him out, he simply would not go to resorts in the state, refusing to do something that he knew would be hurtful.

As the number of Jews increased during the Second World War, Arthur Unobskey insisted that they behave in honorable ways. He would not allow them to tarnish the hard-earned good reputations of the Jews in the area—and the reputation of the Unobskey family in particular. If any of the Jews, new or old, exceeded Arthur's limits, they were chastised and, if need be, expelled. A particularly painful episode involved an Eastport Jew who could not refrain from having relationships with some of the married women in the area. He was quiet, scholarly and close to indispensable to Arthur's well-being as an expert in making smoked salmon—lox and nova scotia—from salmon out of the St. John River. Arthur repeatedly lectured the man about his philandering until the man went too far and had an affair with the wife of one of the ministers in town. After the minister pleaded with Arthur to stop the relationship, he gave the Eastport man two days to leave town.

Fortunately, other family members deflected the resentment and jealousy that Arthur provoked. His brother Charlie— the soft-spoken, sweet-tempered politician—was the Unobskey who was elected as a Republican member of the city council; and year after year fellow councilmen voted him mayor. "Unanimous Unobskey" was what Charlie was called in the mostly uncontested elections. He was also the district commander of the American Legion and president of the Lions Club. And it was Arthur's uncle Morris, the tall, fair-haired, kind and dignified member of the family, who became a Mason and Odd Fellow.

This kind of acceptance never came to Arthur. Nor did he ever put himself to the test. With his overbearing ways, Arthur Unobskey probably would not have been elected to office. Nor was he invited into organizations, such as the Masons, that emphasized fraternal bonds and camaraderie. Not everyone, however, in the city quietly made his peace, directly with Arthur or indirectly through Charlie and Morris. Thomas DiCenzo, a contractor who moved to Calais in the 1940's, repeatedly clashed with Arthur and at one point punched him in the nose. Brought to court, DiCenzo was fined $50. Unrepentant, he asked the judge if he could pay $100 so he could hit Arthur again.

The family, especially the three Unobskey brothers, remained intensely close. Bill returned to Calais every summer for his ten-day vacation with his wife and his daughter Sukie. One of the Unobskey clan remarked that Arthur, Charlie and Bill were "like hugging bears in the forest when they got together." They took pride in each other's accomplishments: the successful stores in Calais as well as Bill's prominence as a leading surgeon in New York City. The "U" on the Calais buildings continued to stand for success, honesty and solid reputations.

Like Arthur and Bill, Charlie was a bon vivant—but a quiet and somewhat shy one. He loved to tell stories, play poker and gin rummy, and smoke cigars; above all, he enjoyed eating enormous quantities of food, especially sweets. Persistently, even when Charlie was mayor of the city, Arthur circulated among the local drugstores, imploring his friends at the soda fountains not to let Charlie eat sundaes.

Charlie endeared himself to Lillian and to Arthur's and Bill's children. Affectionate and generous, he paid for the college educations of Arthur's three children and Bill's daughter. He was never apart from Joe, Martha and Sidney when they were growing up, except for his stint in the army during World War II. Arthur, who deeply regretted that he was too old to serve, fulfilled his patriotic duty by standing guard as a spotter, watching for German spies several nights a week—winter and summer—on a tower a few miles from Calais. But Charlie was drafted despite the fact that he was overweight, had a double hernia and was flat-footed. Close to the ineligible age and in poor health, Charlie could have avoided the draft, but, as a relative observed, "There were so few Jews in the town that you didn't do things like that."

The army regretted its action the minute it took Charlie Unobskey in. He was perpetually exhausted and barely able to keep up with the training. At boot camp in the South, he suffered from the heat and long marches. With his unit one day, he marched past a Civil War monument that listed names of soldiers from Maine who had fallen in battle. Charlie's drill sergeant asked if there were any men in the company from Maine. Someone volunteered Unobskey. The officer ordered Charlie to come forward to see if he recognized any of the old Maine names. Not intending to be disrespectful, Charlie said that if he took another step, they could add his name to the list of dead soldiers from his native state. When his health broke just before he was to be shipped overseas, Charlie refused a medical discharge, insisting upon an honorable discharge as a matter of pride before returning to Calais.

Arthur was as involved with his children as he was with his brothers. He allowed for little emotional distance between himself and his children, identifying with their aspirations, ambitions and successes. Joe, Martha and Sidney embodied their father's fervent hopes for the future and the aggrandizement of the Unobskey name within Calais and beyond the city.

Education was one of the linchpins. As Arthur looked around Calais, he was acutely aware of which schools Calais men and women had attended: Henry Eaton went to Andover and Harvard; Harold Murchie to Dartmouth and Harvard Law School; and Barbara Murchie to Wellesley. Following their examples, Arthur sent his three children to boarding schools and college. But Calais remained the crucial reference point. He made his children understand that they were not to forget that they were Jews and from Calais—even when they entered the educational domain of America's Gentile educational aristocracy.

No one and no institution caused Arthur Unobskey to compromise his values and convictions—either on his own behalf or on that of his children. That assertiveness and inveterate self-confidence were strikingly on display when he first took Sidney to Phillips Academy in Andover, Massachusetts, to start his sophomore year. At Arthur's insistence, they met with G. Grenville Benedict, the dean of students. Proudly, Unobskey introduced Sidney and himself and unabashedly told the dean that he had dreamed all his life about having his son go to Andover.

They chatted easily and took care of pleasantries. Arthur then informed the dean that although Sidney was just starting at Andover, he would have to miss two days of classes during the first week and one in the second. Benedict was puzzled and asked why. Arthur told the dean that Sidney would observe Rosh Hashanah and Yom Kippur. Dean Benedict said that he understood Arthur's point, but no days off were permitted between September and Thanksgiving vacation—for any reason or for any religious group. Unmoved and unimpressed, Arthur conceded nothing. He shot back that Sidney would have to miss the days no matter what. The dean said no. Arthur said yes.

Finally, the exasperated dean stood up, towering over Arthur and turning red in the face. Once more, Benedict explained that the school lived by traditions that were over two hundred years old; no matter what, Andover did not allow days off for exceptional religious holidays. As Benedict pounded his desk, Arthur patiently reached over and placed his hand on top of the dean's. "Dean Benedict, this is a wonderful, wonderful day." The dean stopped short and asked why. "Congratulations, Dean Benedict," Arthur calmly and triumphantly said. "You have a new tradition!" As he left Benedict's office, Arthur could not drop the subject: "I will be back in the spring," he said, "and we will discuss Passover."

Andover was part of the master plan Arthur had devised

for all of his children. According to the scenario, Joe would go to Colby College, Harvard graduate school and return to Calais to run the Unobskeys' businesses; Martha would go to Walnut Hill and then to Wellesley, since Arthur thought that no co-ed school was as good as the best of the women's schools. Afterward, she would marry a doctor who would practice medicine in Calais. As for Sidney, after Andover he would go to Yale, then return to Calais, join the business and run for political office.

In 1954, crucial parts of his master plan were realized. In one weekend in June, Arthur, Lillian, Charlie, and Bill and his family proudly attended three graduations: Joe received a degree from the Harvard Business School, Martha graduated from Wellesley, and Sidney, on his way to attending Yale, graduated from Andover. Almost on schedule, during the next year, Martha became engaged to a doctor, Fred Goldner from Tennessee, who seriously considered opening a practice in Calais. In 1956, in a festive ceremony in the Unobskeys' fourteen-room home on Main Street, Martha and Fred were married by Rabbi Freedman from Bangor. Within a year, Martha and Fred had their first son, Arthur Goldner, when they were living in Nashville.

But the joys over the plans-come-true—the festive graduations, wedding celebrations, and expected grandchildren—were tempered by Arthur Unobskey's deteriorating health and bad news in Calais. His brother Charlie was ill, too. The business began to suffer as the two brothers could not give it the kind of attention that they had always demanded of themselves. Facing tough economic conditions, they moved the men's store out of its separate quarters and into the women's store.

On December 27, 1956, Arthur succumbed to heart and circulatory disease at the age of fifty-eight. "News of his passing was learned with profound shock and sorrow," wrote the *Calais Advertiser,* "in this city of which he was acknowledged to be one of the leading citizens throughout Washington county where he had long been active in every movement directed towards improving the condition of its people." Two long, front-page columns summarized Arthur's activities and eulogized his careers as a businessman and civic crusader. Up until the day he died, Arthur and the *Calais Advertiser* still believed in Quoddy. "His energy, resourcefulness and promotional ability were largely responsible for the advancement of the Quoddy Tidal Project survey measure to its present advantageous position, requiring now only favorable action by the House of Representatives."

In language that reflected the triumph of Sarah Unobskey's mission for her family, the paper observed: "To Calais he rendered services perhaps unmatched by any other of its citizens present or past. He spared no effort to increase its prosperity and attractiveness as a place in which to live, work and trade." The paper cited Arthur's role as the principal founder of Chaim Yosef, a director of the Maine Committee of the United Jewish Appeal and an "acknowledged leader" of Maine's Jews. "Warm hearted, generous, enterprising, enthusiastically energetic and gifted with a deep faith and love for his fellow man, he had hosts of friends in all walks of life. Among them were leaders in every department of activity in Maine. There was not a governor of the state in thirty years who was not happy to be included in this group."

In preparation for the funeral, the family departed from fundamental aspects of Orthodox laws that Arthur had meticulously followed when Joseph and Sarah had died. Instead of an Orthodox burial as soon as possible after death, for the first time, the body of an Unobskey was placed in an open casket in the family's living room in Calais. For three days, Arthur's friends and associates came to view the casket and pay their respects, a rite that the Gentile community expected, but hardly one that the Orthodox Calais Jews were accustomed to.

Several days after Arthur's death, the family, along with many friends, went to Bangor, where Rabbi Freedman conducted the funeral services and presided over the burial in the Beth Israel cemetery. On the day of the funeral, all of the stores in Calais were closed out of respect. After the interment, the family returned to Calais and sat shivah for the obligatory week of mourning.

Although Arthur's death had been expected for some months, the loss was deeply shocking. His children could hardly believe that the world would continue as before without their father's energetic, commanding presence. Burdened by disease and sadness over his brother's death, Charlie suffered ever-failing health. In 1958, he took a trip to Calais, France, where he was feted as a representative of its Maine namesake and continued on to Israel, fulfilling a lifelong dream. There but a few days, he died of a heart attack. His body was brought back by plane and buried in Bangor next to Arthur.

Just two weeks before Charlie died, the family suffered yet another devastating blow: The theater block burned down and Unobskey's was damaged. Suddenly, highly mortgaged properties and an overextended style of living could no longer be managed without Arthur and Charlie's skills and finesse. A handshake, a pledge, and Sarah, Arthur and Charlie's good name were all that the banks and insurance companies had required. Once they had passed away, the lenders quickly moved in to recoup their money and salvage their investments, while the children, Joe and Sidney, struggled to maintain the Unobskeys' investment and commitment to the city.

Throughout the late 1950's and 1960's, the two sons worked within the powerful shadow of their father, guided by the impact of his character, aspirations and optimism. But Arthur Unobskey's death in 1956 marked a decisive break in the Unobskey legacy and the family's commitment—and carefully honed sensitivity—to the needs of their adopted city.

Unfortunately, Arthur and Charlie Unobskey's deaths coincided with the continuing decline of the Calais economy. Quoddy never came to fruition. No new industries were started. Young adults continued to leave. Railroad passenger service was discontinued. Calais homes, many of them between fifty and one hundred years old, began to slide into disrepair and give the city a stark, depressed appearance. Empty storefronts dotted Main Street. The multitudinous overarching elms succumbed to disease, and much of the city was suddenly stripped of its verdant cover.

Many of the changes boded ill for the existence of the Jews in the area. As their children went to college and moved away and no new Jewish families settled in the area, their numbers were reduced to a handful who were unable to form minyans. In the summer of 1969, when Jessie Baig's mother died, the Jews had to rely upon visiting relatives to help form the group of ten men who would say Kaddish. On the seventh day, one of the Jewish men left town. In desperation, Jessie Baig called friends who owned the International Motel. "Look in your register," Jessie asked, "and see if there is a Jewish name on the list." The owner found a Goldberg from Staten Island. Jessie told the motel owner to call Mr. Goldberg and tell him that someone was coming down to pick him up. Ten minutes later, a startled gentleman from New York joined the Calais Jews in prayer.

In 1974, Congregation Chaim Yosef closed its doors for good. Unobskey's also shut down when Joe moved to Bangor. By the 1970's, a short but unique chapter in Maine history was over. Were there other places in the state that had provided such fertile ground for blending tolerance and ambition, uniting the native-born Mainers and the Russian Jewish immigrants? Probably not. Throughout Maine, Jewish immigrants had successfully established themselves on Main Street—in cities such as Waterville, Portland, Bar Harbor, Bangor and in towns in Aroostook and Washington counties. But few, if any, had achieved the Unobskeys' intense mixture of family closeness and pride, commercial flair, civic leadership, and Jewish commitment.

There are those who thought that Arthur's talents and energies were wasted in that small, remote city of five thousand people. But he knew otherwise. His immigrant parents, although poor, uneducated and barely acquainted with American ways, had deliberately chosen Calais as the place to integrate their family into American life. The choice was a good one. Through three generations, the Unobskeys thrived in the city that was enriched by an era of small-town confidence, security and patriotism. Inexorably, by the time of Arthur's death, that special time—which benefited and distinguished Calais's Gentiles and Jews alike—had drawn to an end.

# *Epilogue*

BANGOR, Mount Desert Island and Calais! The interactions between Jews and Gentiles in one place could not have occurred in the others. The confluences of personalities, traditions and economic and social conditions of these three Maine communities provide a valuable microcosm of American immigrant experiences. Outside the well-known (and well-researched) large urban centers, Russian and German Jewish immigrants in small towns and cities throughout the country made the most of America's extraordinary economic and political opportunities.

History records the struggles between possibilities and aspirations, obstacles and failures. In the confrontation in Maine of two different cultures and religions—the Protestant hosts and the Jewish immigrants—it may come as no surprise that Charles W. Eliot, John D. Rockefeller, Jr., Jacob H. Schiff and Henry Morgenthau, Sr., emerge as dominant figures. In the Maine context, however, we see the four men—the nationally renowned educator, the philanthropist, the investment banker and the diplomat—in the uncustomary, but strong sidelights of local history. With Sarah and Arthur Unobskey, George B. Dorr, Dr. Lawrence Cutler, Catherine Cutler, Abraham Rudman, Henry Wheelwright, Rev. Arlan A. Baillie, and Rabbis Henry Isaacs and Avraham Freedman, we discover the rele-

271

vance of little-known figures to the record of Gentile and Jewish accommodation in Maine. All these men and women richly
demonstrate the complex challenge of immigrant Jewish hopes
and limitations worked out in the midst of Protestant life.

The Jewish immigrants eagerly sought to become part of
America—to succeed economically and socially, but also to retain crucial parts of their religion, culture and traditions. The
possibilities for success differed from place to place and time to
time. Away from the densely populated, culturally engulfing
Jewish ghettos in New York and other Eastern cities, the Jews in
Maine boldly broke off from the mainstream of immigrant life
in the late nineteenth and early twentieth centuries. They were
in the vanguard of the collective thrust of all Jewish immigrants:
to leave the ghettos as quickly as possible, enter the middle class,
partake of American education and assume some of the mores
and manners of Protestant society. Becoming Americans and remaining Jews—this was the trick and the tension.

In each of the three Maine communities the terms were
different. The tiny, nonthreatening population of no more than
twenty-six Jewish families stayed within the limits of acceptance
in the small, liberal city of Calais. In Bangor, the few hundred
Jewish families met tolerance. But for decades, the conspicuous
minority also confronted firm economic and social segregation,
set by the Protestant leadership, that divided Bangor's population into unequal and tight ethnic enclaves. And, on Mount
Desert Island, with but a handful of exceptions, Jewish immigrants, rich and poor, German and Russian, were kept away
from the inner circles of the exclusive summer colonies.

It is my assumption that success for Sarah and Arthur
Unobskey was fixed to Main Street and bound to Calais. The
family's confidence and enthusiasm for Maine and American
life were rooted in acceptance, granted by Protestant leaders in
the Calais community. That strong sense of confidence traveled
well. Wherever Arthur went—to Seventh Avenue, Washington,
D.C., or Phillips Andover Academy—he pressed on with assurance in fulfilling his goals.

But viewed from the secure domains of their home and
clothing stores in Calais, the Unobskeys always distrusted the
bigger and more complex Jewish community in Bangor. In-
stinctively, Sarah and Arthur must have known that being the
dominant Jewish family in Calais was a far different achieve-

ment from attaining leadership of Bangor's Jewry. The Unobskeys would have had little patience with the slow pace of acceptance offered by Bangor's entrenched Protestant leaders. Remaining on the sidelines of that city's life until the 1960's was not something the Unobskeys were prepared to do. As for Mount Desert Island, Arthur Unobskey never went there. He knew by reputation that it was a place where he, as a striving Russian Jewish immigrant, was not welcome.

On the other hand, Bangor offered Lawrence Cutler enormous opportunities, unlike those available to Jewish merchants in the isolated city of five thousand Calais residents. Through the hospital, city government and university close by, the quiet, ambitious, professionally skilled and highly respected immigrant's son moved slowly and successfully into the upper middle class and on to the middle ground of Bangor's ethnic life. Like the Unobskeys and Jews throughout the rest of Maine, Lawrence and Catherine Cutler were never drawn to summer life on Mount Desert Island, with its display of rich ornamentation and social exclusion. The Cutlers knew that professional and social success in one of Maine's prominent cities did not make for success on Mount Desert Island.

It took the likes of a minuscule number of national Jewish figures, such as Schiff and Morgenthau, to succeed in entering the vacationland of the national WASP establishment on Mount Desert Island. Riding the crest of accomplishment at the financial and political centers of life in New York and Washington, Schiff and Morgenthau earned their way to respect and acceptance by Mount Desert's Protestant elite. Extraordinarily ambitious and successful, supremely confident and deeply optimistic about the promise of equality in American life, both Schiff and Morgenthau dared to be exceptions away from the safe centers of Jewish communal life in New York.

They found no overt anti-Semitism in Bar Harbor or in other parts of the island. They sustained no embarrassing rejections from exclusive clubs, such as they experienced or knew about in cities or other resorts. But Schiff and Morgenthau made their way on the island in single file. They had to. They were representative and token Jews. Deliberately, they separated themselves in the summer months from the numbers of Jews who would have posed a threat to the island's Protestant homogeneity and the intercity aristocracy.

Both men, however, had strong reason to sense that, in time, Mount Desert Island would grant a broader acceptance to Jews. Certainly, Eliot's preeminent career at Harvard and his unique and deep faith in the future integration of Jewish immigrants inspired confidence. His friendships with Schiff and Morgenthau deepened on Mount Desert Island. Furthermore, the democratic efforts of Eliot, Dorr and Rockefeller to commit their beloved lands on Mount Desert to public use—rather than making them an impregnable private reserve—presaged a more open and nondiscriminatory community.

To the generations coming to maturity in the 1980's and 1990's, the nature of Jewish immigrant life consists of vague, often nostalgic memories. Buried in the recesses of the past are stories about a hermetic and precarious Jewish existence in eastern Europe; the heroic commitment of the immigrants to improve their lives and those of their children by settling in a new land; and the complex, painful attempts to reconcile Jewish needs and American life.

Scrimping and saving, the immigrants rebuilt their Jewish lives. They brought their families to Maine and founded synagogues such as Beth Israel, Beth Abraham and Chaim Yosef as well as Jewish philanthropic and fraternal organizations. When invited, the immigrants eagerly joined the Elks, Odd Fellows, Masons, Rotary, the Tarratine Club, the Bar Harbor Club, the Kebo Club and the Chambers of Commerce in Bangor, Calais and Bar Harbor. They fervently supported national war-loan campaigns as well as sectarian relief efforts for Jews trapped in devastating wars in Europe and Israel. Most Jewish immigrants became good Republicans, while a few tried the Democratic party even before the New Deal. Seeking out the likes of Rev. Arlan Baillie in Bangor, the Eatons in Calais and Charles W. Eliot in Northeast Harbor, the immigrants and their children looked to their Protestant hosts for those who would transform neighborliness into genuine acceptance, tolerance into integration, tokenism into the eradication of the ethnic count.

Despite their small numbers, the Jews in Maine have not disappeared. But the terms of their complex balancing acts—reconciling Jewish ways and American life—have changed radically. They were once performed by the Unobskeys, Gordons, Goldens, Epsteins, Bergs and other immigrants who precariously built upon a common set of fears and aspirations, deprivations and hopes. Now, the children and grandchildren of the immigrants face challenges of religious identity in a world where strong traditions have vanished, along with exclusion based on anti-Semitism. Through the slow, cumulative effects of World War II, the civil rights movement and the financial needs of non-Jewish organizations, once-Protestant economic, social and cultural institutions have largely opened themselves to Jews.

The changes are striking. But the gains, bringing a sense of rootlessness and restless mobility, embody losses, too. The educated second and third generations of Calais-born Jews have moved away, leaving only one Jewish family, the Baigs, in the city in 1991. Chaim Yosef ceased functioning as a synagogue in 1974. Several years later, the building was sold. In 1989, it was torn down, leaving a vacant lot. In Bangor, Jewish life has followed the patterns of mainstream America: Jews participate in all aspects of the city's secularized and multiethnic life. Beth Israel changed from an Orthodox to a Conservative synagogue. Rabbi Isaacs's day school closed, but his small congregation remains vibrant. Beth El, a Reform congregation, made up of many families of mixed marriages, started meeting in the Unitarian church and hired a rabbi. The Jewish Community Center, long the unifying force in the Jewish community, closed its doors in 1990 because of insufficient interest and financial support. Other Jewish organizations fight hard for survival.

On Mount Desert Island today, there are many year-round Jewish families, but they have not established any religious institutions. Nevertheless, religious holidays and the Sabbath are observed in untraditional ways. Together, Gentiles and Jews have celebrated the Passover Seder at St. Saviours in Bar Harbor and St. Mary's-by-the-Sea. A Conservative rabbi, with a pulpit in New York, has a home in Southwest Harbor. Finally, almost every club on the island has some Jewish members. Whether or not they are correct, most Jews do not consider themselves—nor are they considered by others—as isolated ethnic exceptions in the island's Protestant realm.

# Endnotes

## CHAPTER 1: CITY TIDES

*Page*
19  "He that hath . . ." *Bangor Daily Commercial* (hereafter referred to as *BDC*), March 26, 1890, p. 1.

20  "Think where we . . ." Ibid.

20  New kinds of immigrants. In the 1870's, the Maine legislature passed laws to promote immigration from England, Norway, Sweden and other "desirable" countries in western Europe. The objective was to give one hundred acres of public land tax-free to men over twenty-one. A self-contained and prosperous Swedish colony was established in New Sweden in Aroostook County. But there was no other state-sponsored encouragement of immigration. Senate Document 785, 61st Congress, 3rd Session, *Report of the Immigration Commission: Immigration Legislation* (Washington, D.C.: Government Printing Office, 1910), v. 5879, p. 673.

20  Bulfinch. Deborah Thompson, *Bangor, Maine 1769–1914: An Architectural History* (Orono, Me.: University of Maine Press, 1988), p. 10.

21  "Wilderness acropolis . . ." James Mundy and Earle Shettleworth, Jr. *The Flight of the Grand Eagle: Charles G. Bryant, Maine Architect and Adventurer* (Augusta, Me.: Maine Historic Preservation Commission, 1977), p. 54.

21  Bryant led militia. *BDC,* February 2, 1901, p. 10.

*Page*

21    "Like a star . . ." Henry D. Thoreau, *The Illustrated Maine Woods* (Princeton: Princeton University Press, 1974), pp. 82–83.

22    "Astonished" at the "intelligence . . ." Bangor Board of Trade, "City of Bangor, 'Queen City of the East' " (Bangor, 1888), p. 12.

23    "In other words . . ." Ibid., p. 21.

23    Frank Putnam, "What's the Matter with New England? Maine: A Study in Land-Grabbing, Tax-Dodging, and Isolation," *New England Magazine,* Vol. 36, No. 5 (July 1907), p. 51.

23    "Lottery." David C. Smith, *A University of Lumbering in Maine, 1861–1960* (Orono, Me.: University of Maine Press, 1972), p. 11.

23    "It is a statistical . . ." Ibid., p. 173.

24    "Maine once owned . . ." William R. Pattangall, *Meddybemps Letters, Maine's Hall of Fame, Memorial Addresses* (Lewiston, Me.: Lewiston Journal Company, 1924), p. 189.

25    Value of timberlands. Putnam, p. 520.

25    "Oh, the boys . . ." Smith, p. 19.

27    "The Jew firm . . ." *BDC,* September 28, 1903, p. 7.

28    Lord in debt. *BDC,* December 9, 1905, p. 3.

29    For Bangor Irish see James Herbert Mundy, "Heroes By Appointment: The Fire Companies of Bangor, 1830–1860," Master's Thesis, University of Maine, Orono, June, 1970.

30    Labor unions. *BDC,* February 2, 1903, p. 2.

33    "Society people of . . ." *BDC,* December 11, 1890, p. 1.

33    "It seems as if . . ." Ibid., August 28, 1890, p. 1.

33    Bangor's historians have written selectively about parts of the city's past. The fine works by James B. Vickery, James H. Mundy, Earle G. Shettleworth, Jr., and George Savery Wasson are important contributions. But essential research needs to be done concerning the city's business community, local government, labor, philanthropic organizations, fraternal societies, timber and railroad development, and tax policies.

34    "I felt as if . . ." *BDC,* April 10, 1896, p. 8.

35    "The living, breathing . . . " *Bangor Daily News* (hereafter referred to as *BDN*), June 24, 1889, p. 21.

*Page*

35    "Cathedrals of Kitsch." *The New York Times,* January 24, 1989, p. 21.

36    National charity movements. Paul Boyer, *Urban Masses and Moral Order in America: 1820–1920* (Cambridge, Mass.: Harvard University Press, 1978), pp. 147–150.

36    "All kinds of . . ." *Bangor Whig and Courier,* March 25, 1891, p. 3.

37    "Alas! how much . . ." *BDC,* May 2, 1899, p. 3.

38    Population stagnation. According to the 1900 census, Bangor's population had increased by only 2,000 in ten years to 21,850, per *Twelfth Census of the United States, "Population"* (Washington, D.C.: Government Printing Office, 1901), p. 191. Of the total, 2,726 were foreign-born and 183 were "colored" (Ibid., p. 657). The next census figures, in 1910, showed a modest increase in the Bangor population to 24,803. The native-born white population was 14,512, with 4,280 foreign born. The "colored" population was 205. *Thirteenth Census of the United States, "Population,"* 2 (Washington, D.C.: GPO, 1913), p. 819.

38    "We are poked . . ." *BDC,* December 8, 1910, p. 8.

38    "Prosperous and happy." Bangor Historical Society, *Fiftieth Anniversary of the Bangor Historical Society, Bangor, Maine, 1914* (Bangor, Me.: 1914), pp. 5–6.

38    "The strong, able, virile . . ." Ibid.

39    "O wanderers from . . ." *BDC,* February 9, 1895, p. 5.


## CHAPTER 2: THE WANDERERS

41    Russian Pale. Zvi Y. Gitelman, *A Century of Ambivalence* (New York: Schocken Books, 1988), p. 39.

41    *Shtetlekh.* Morris Raphael Cohen, *A Dreamer's Journey* (Glencoe, Ill.: Free Press, 1949), p. 25.

41    "We have, knock . . ." Sholem Aleichem, *Tevye the Dairyman and the Railroad Stories,* trans. Hillel Halkin (New York: Schocken Books, 1987), p. 147.

42    "With God's help. . ." Ibid., p. 4.

42    "Master of the Universe . . ." Ibid., p. 6.

42    "Inner life and religious . . ." Cohen, p. 7.

*Page*

43 "Every Jew in Russia . . ." Lucille M. Epstein, Incomplete Master's Thesis, University of Maine, Department of History, 1940, p. 39.

43 Separate identity. Thomas Kessner, *The Golden Door: Italian and Jewish Immigrant Mobility in New York City, 1880–1915* (New York: Oxford University Press, 1977), p. 172.

44 Statistics on population. Senate Doc. Ibid. "Statistical Review of Immigrants, 1820–1910: Distribution of Immigrants," Vol. 5878, pp. 90–91.

44 "Liberal, optimistic, sober . . ." Paul Johnson, *A History of the Jews* (New York: Harper & Row, 1987), p. 369.

44 Activities of congregation. William J. Leffler, "A Study of Congregation Ahawas Achim, Bangor, Maine from 1849 to 1856, From the Minutes of the Congregation," Bangor Public Library and American Jewish Archives (hereafter referred to as BPL and AJA).

45 "Warmest friends of . . ." *BDC,* November 9, 1896, p. 2.

45 Riverside Park. Ibid., August 19, 1903, p. 7.

46 "Comparable economic and social . . ." Epstein, p. 29.

46 "On one occasion . . ." Ibid., pp. 25–26.

46 Russian Jews on their own. Ibid., p. 41. Beyond Epstein's fine study, accurate demographic and economic statistics are difficult to establish for the Jewish community from the 1890's through the 1950's. Some facts can be gained from the annual city business directory. But many of the 1890's census records burned, leaving only the statistical summaries. Furthermore, the records of Beth Israel Synagogue were accidentally destroyed in the 1960's.

47 "My father had . . ." Jordan S. Alpert, *The Alperts and Cohens of Bangor, Maine* (San Francisco: privately printed, 1990), p. 68.

47 "A familiarity possible . . ." Lura Beam, *A Maine Hamlet* (New York: Winfreed Funk, 1957), p. 150.

48 Peddler's license. Epstein, p. 49.

48 Witnesses for Jews. Conversation with Lucille Epstein Rich.

48 "A dealer in . . ." *BDC,* December 10, 1896, p. 3.

48 Residential patterns. Epstein, p. 43.

Page
49 "Ruthless underconsumption." Stephan Thernstrom, *Poverty and Progress: Social Mobility in a Nineteenth Century City* (Cambridge, Mass.: Harvard University Press, 1964), p. 136.

50 "Can I sleep . . ." Conversation with Epstein.

50 Plates upside down. Ibid.

50 "Sheer curiosity." Epstein, p. 54.

50 "Theirs was the polity . . ." John Higham, "Immigration," C. Vann Woodward, ed., *The Comparative Approach to American History* (New York: Basic Books, 1968), p. 93.

50 Fifty-seven families. *Twelfth Census of the United States, 1900, Schedule No. 1—Population, City of Bangor, Penobscot County.*

51 "Made Americans acquainted . . ." Oscar Handlin, "American Views of the Jews at the Opening of the Twentieth Century," *Publications of the American Jewish Historical Society*, 40 (June 1951), p. 327.

51 "Lazarus Goldstein . . ." *BDC*, February 28, 1890, p. 5.

51 "Masked ball, giving . . ." Pattangall, p. 304.

52 Jewish cemetery. It was not until 1907 that Beth Israel bought the cemetery from the order for $35. Congregation Beth Israel, *Diamond Jubilee, 1888–1963* (Bangor, Me.: 1963), p. 32.

52 "Rosh Hashonoh . . ." *BDC*, September 22, 1892, p. 2.

52 "Made welcome without . . ." Ibid.

52 "Wherever Jews are . . ." Ibid., September 11, 1893, p. 3.

53 "A Grand Ceremony." Ibid., May 5, 1894, p. 7.

53 "The melodious chanting . . ." Ibid., May 7, 1894, p. 2.

53 "Hindoo language." *Bangor Whig & Courier*, August 23, 1897, p. 4.

54 "In the center . . ." *BDC*, October 7, 1897, p. 9.

54 "Prominent Gentiles . . ." *BDN*, December 20, 1897, p. 2.

54 *Bangor Tax Records*, 1897, BPL.

55 "From a Gentile's . . ." *BDN*, December 20, 1897, p. 2.

## CHAPTER 3: A HUMBLE NICHE

56 JACOBS DISAPPEARS! Ibid., December 27, 1906, p. 2.

56 "Utmost misery, privation . . ." Ibid.

*Page*

57    "A good, pure place . . ." Ibid.

57    "The lowest type . . ." Ibid.

57    Jacobs disappeared. Ibid.

57    Tamer tale. *BDC,* January 27, 1906, p. 5.

58    "Something to be settled . . ." Ibid.

59    "Breathed in an atmosphere . . ." Ibid., July 20, 1906, p. 4.

59    ALL COONS LOOK . . . *Bangor Business Directory,* 1901 (Bangor, Me.: 1901), p. 5.

59    "There was a race war . . ." *BDC,* April 21, 1907, p. 10.

59    Number of Bangor Jews. *Twelfth Census of the United States, 1900, "Schedule No. 1—Population," City of Bangor, Penobscot County. Thirteenth Census of the United States, 1910, "Population," City of Bangor, Penobscot County.* Between 1899 and 1910, 1,485,641 Jews arrived in America from eastern Europe. *Annual Report of the Commissioner General of Immigration,* 1914 (Washington, D.C.: Government Printing Office, 1915), p. 101.

60    "The extent to which . . ." *BDC,* September 22, 1909, p. 9.

60    Residential statistics. Epstein, pp. 44, 73.

60    Occupational statistics for 1899. There were nine tailors, two clerks, two professionals who were rabbis, four in manufacturing (with two in clothing and two in bottling soda water), two skilled laborers and two who had junk shops. Ibid., p. 46.

60    Occupational statistics for 1910. Ibid., p. 74.

61    "A Hebrew lady . . ." *BDN,* May 8, 1900, p. 7.

61    "If you were clean shaven . . ." Epstein, pp. 55–56.

62    "Jewish baker." *BDC,* October 12, 1908, p. 5.

62    Debate about education. Stephen Steinberg, *The Ethnic Myth: Race, Ethnicity and Class in America* (New York: Atheneum, 1981), p. 136.

62    "Forms the transcendent . . ." Emelyn Foster Peck, "The Russian Jew in Southern New England," *New England Magazine,* 31 (1904–05), p. 28.

62    "Many children have . . ." *BDC,* May 29, 1920, Bangor Public Library Collection (hereafter referred to as BPLC).

*Page*

63 "There is no way . . ." Ibid.

63 "Bangor citizens may . . ." Ibid., October 3, 1902, p. 4.

63 "Every Hebrew is . . ." Ibid., September 17, 1907, p. 10.

64 "There are nearly 600 . . ." Ibid., July 5, 1906, p. 5.

64 "Instead, there stands . . ." Ibid.

64 "Grossly insulted." Congregation Beth Israel, p. 45.

65 "Situation is open . . ." Ibid., p. 46.

65 Jewish Women. See Sydney Stahl Weinberg, *The World of Our Mothers: The Lives of Jewish Immigrant Women* (Chapel Hill, N.C.: The University of North Carolina Press, 1988).

66 "Shall be deemed . . ." Congregation Beth Israel, p. 48.

66 Collecting money for Hebrew school. Catherine E. Cutler, "The First Forty Years of the Bangor Hebrew School: A History of It's [*sic*] Growth from 1907 to 1947," "Bangor Hebrew School: Fortieth Anniversary, 1907–1947," Bangor Hebrew Community Center, October 2, 1947, p. 32.

66 "For the most part . . ." Epstein, p. 59.

66 "Little is known . . ." Beth Abraham Synagogue, *Fiftieth Anniversary Commemorative Journal* (Bangor, Me.: 1983).

68 "Even in this country . . ." *BDC*, April 20, 1908, p. 7.

68 "Foreigners Outbreed Us . . ." Ibid., January 27, 1910, p. 10.

69 "Status panic." John Higham, "Social Discrimination Against Jews in America: 1830–1930," *Publications of the American Jewish Historical Society,* 47 (September 1957), p. 23.

69 "Blackest deeds . . ." *BDC*, May 23, 1903, p. 12.

70 "A committee of Hebrew bankers . . ." Ibid., August 31, 1905, p. 3.

70 "That the million or more . . ." Ibid.

70 "A Jewish rabbi . . ." Congregation Beth Israel, p. 53.

70 "I have as little . . ." *BDC*, February 19, 1902, p. 12.

## CHAPTER 4: CONVERGING WORLDS

72 "Blazing brands, sticky . . ." *BDN*, April 30, 1911, BPLC.

73 Bangor Historical Society holdings. In 1915, E. M. Blanding

*Page*

compiled a list—twenty-seven pages of tiny print—of the Society's losses. Bangor Historical Society, op. cit.

73 "Sefer Torahs and other . . ." Congregation Beth Israel, p. 58.

74 Property losses. *BDN*, November 25, 1911, BPLC.

74 "I walked home . . ." Mary C. Robinson, *Annals of a Happy Family* (privately printed, 1933), p. 115, BPL.

74 "You can make . . ." Committee on Civic Improvement, *Bangor City Plan: The Burned District* (Bangor, Me.: 1911), pp. 4–5.

75 "The members of the congregation . . ." *BDC*, May 18, 1911, BPLC.

76 "The balcony will . . ." *BDN*, June 8, 1911, p. 3.

76 "Brains and brawn . . ." Ibid., June 9, 1911, BPLC.

77 Lewen's advertisement. *BDN*, June 1, 1911, p. 12.

77 "Something absolutely new . . ." Congregation Beth Israel, p. 62.

78 "Collection of wards . . ." *BDN*, October 2, 1912, BPLC.

79 "For those who . . ." Congregation Beth Israel, p. 69.

79 "Religious ceremony . . ." Ibid., p. 64.

79 "Heart of the Hebrew . . ." Ibid., p. 68.

79 Schiff's support. Ibid., p. 60.

80 Taxpayers. *BDC*, November 15, 1913, BPL.

81 Jewish student census. The American Jewish population was 2,500,000 or 2.5 percent of the total population. *Menorah Journal*, "A Census of Jewish University Students," Vol. 2, No. 4 (October 1916), pp. 260–261.

81 "Objectionable Jew." Harold E. Stearns, "A Gentile's Picture of the Jew," *Menorah Journal*, Vol. 2, No. 4 (October 1916), p. 228.

81 "The cultured and liberal . . ." "The Gentile's Attitude Towards the Jews: As a Jew Sees It," *Menorah Journal*, Vol. 2, No. 5 (December 1916), pp. 174–175.

82 "Conditions on the . . ." *Menorah Journal*, Vol. 1, No. 3 (June 1915), pp. 196–197.

83 Immigrants' support for the war. Rita Mae Breton, "The Red Scare: A Study in Maine Nativism, 1919–1925," Master's thesis, University of Maine, Orono, 1972, p. 14.

*Page*

83   "Home guard, special police . . ." Ibid., p. 23.

83   "In the midst . . ." *BDC,* April 4, 1917, BPLC.

84   Bangor men in army. Ibid., March 30, 1918, BPLC.

84   Jewish contributions. Ibid., April 6, 1918, BPLC.

84   "Wonderful enthusiasm." *BDN,* April 11, 1918, BPLC.

84   "There are times . . ." Breton, p. 49. *BDC,* March 9, 1918, BPLC.
     See David C. Smith, *The First Century: A History of the University of
     Maine, 1865–1965* (Orono, Me.: University of Maine Press,
     1979), pp. 108–110.

84   "An inbred hatred . . ." *BDC,* April 23, 1918, BPLC.

85   "New blood was . . ." Marcus Eli Ravage, *The Jew Pays: A Narra-
     tive of the Consequences of the War to the Jews of Eastern Europe and
     of the Manner in which Americans Have Attempted to Meet Them* (New
     York: Alfred A. Knopf, 1919), p. 113.

85   "Mr. Kirstein is . . ." *BDC,* November 28, 1917, BPLC.

86   Bangor women offer jewelry. Congregation Beth Israel, p. 73.

86   "An appeal to the . . ." *BDN,* December 5, 1917, BPLC.

86   Size of contributions. Ibid.

86   "The city was proud . . ." *BDN,* March 5, 1918, BPLC.

86   "Receiving house for . . ." *BDC,* November 3, 1917, BPLC.

87   "One of the results . . ." Ibid., June 24, 1918, BPLC.

87   "After 20 centuries . . ." Ibid.

87   "Royal reception . . ." *BDN,* June 1, 1918, BPLC.

88   "We buried Kenneth . . ." Ibid., June 4, 1918, BPLC.

89   "Bangor's Happiest, Noisiest . . ." Ibid., November 12, 1918,
     BPLC.

89   "Though conscious of . . ." Robinson, p. 122.

90   "For the first time . . ." *BDC,* November 12, 1918, BPLC.


## CHAPTER 5: PASSAGE BETWEEN THE WARS

97   Wasson novels. Mildred Wasson, *The Big House* (Boston: Hough-
     ton Mifflin Company, 1926). Wasson, *Churchill Street* (New York:
     Coward-McCann, Inc. 1928). *The Strange Woman* by Ben Ames

*Page*

Williams also took place in Bangor. The book, however, was not about Bangor. It used the city only as background to present the story of an abused woman. Ben Ames Williams, *The Strange Woman* (New York: Houghton Mifflin, 1943).

98  "Faded spinster culture . . ." Wasson, *The Big House,* p. 74.

98  "We're just parasites . . ." Ibid., pp. 112–113.

98  "Hamlin had deteriorated . . ." Ibid., p. 18.

98  "Amount to anything . . ." Ibid., pp. 112–113.

98  "Ever sat in the . . ." Ibid., p. 213.

98  "Who is this party . . ." Ibid., p. 147.

99  "As assimilation improved . . ." John Higham, *Send These to Me: Jews and Other Immigrants in Urban America* (New York: Atheneum, 1975), p. 166.

101  Klan members. Breton, p. 177.

101  Portland Klan members. *BDC,* January 22, 1923, BPL.

101  Aid to parochial schools. Breton, p. 185.

101  "There are no more . . ." *BDN,* April 9, 1923, BPLC.

103  "The time has come . . ." *BDC,* July 8, 1929, p. 10.

103  Newberry's opening. *BDN,* March 13, 1920, BPLC.

103  Investors at city hall. *BDN,* November 6, 1925, BPLC. Frank Gordon was forced to sell the *Commercial* to Col. Harry F. Ross of Bangor and Eraston Tefft of New York. Ross derived his wealth from his wife's family's lumber business. Tefft was a stockbroker in New York.

104  "Very active." Ibid., January 30, 1925, BPLC.

104  1921 occupational statistics. Epstein, pp. 75, 83.

105  Residential statistics. Ibid., p. 81.

105  Abandoning Jewish observance. Congregation Beth Israel, p. 70.

105  Intermarriage rate. Epstein, p. 88.

106  Kirstein gifts. *BDC,* November 17, 1922, BPLC.

107  English-speaking teachers. Cutler, p. 33.

107  "That he had attended . . ." *BDC,* March 15, 1920, BPLC.

107  "Chose those numbers . . ." *BDC,* May 18, 1923, BPLC.

*Page*

108 "Sprague, Sawyer, Smith . . ." *BDN,* April 8, 1921, BPLC.

109 "Of quiet, undemonstrative . . ." *BDC,* July 19, 1922, BPLC.

110 "It stands under . . ." Fannie Harlow Robinson, *D.A.R.* (private printing, 1968), p. 266.

112 "Discussed the ways . . ." *BDN,* April 19, 1933, BPLC.

113 Civil Works Administration. *BDC,* December 7, 1933, BPLC.

114 "A presiding genius . . ." *BDN,* January 3, 1939, BPLC.


## CHAPTER 6: SORE PROBLEMS OF SOCIAL PREJUDICE

117 Souvenir program. Antoinette Torrey, Dr. H. O. H. Levine, Mimi Stern and Geraldine Watson, "Bangor: First Formal Visit of a First Lady of the Land to Bangor," May 20, 1941.

117 "Affair was one . . ." *BDN,* May 21, 1941, p. 1.

117 "Sponsoring organization." Ibid.

118 "We are determined . . ." Bangor Jewish Community Center, "Community News" (January 1, 1940), p. 2.

118 Federal investments in Dow. Charles Ranlett, "History of Aviation in Bangor, Maine, Including Dow Air Force Base," Thesis, Bowdoin College, 1954, pp. 26–31.

119 Bangor men killed in service. Felix Ranlett, librarian at the Bangor Public Library, produced a book honoring the dead soldiers. Each individual was memorialized by a short biography written in beautiful calligraphy. Placed in the public library, a page is turned every day to show the picture of another person. Ranlett, the author of the histories of All Souls Church, the Rotary and the Public Library, succeeded E. M. Blanding as Bangor's institutional historian.

119 "There are too many . . ." Bangor Jewish Community Center (November 15, 1945). My assumption is that Dr. H. O. H. Levine, the director of the center, wrote the statement.

122 "Our task right now . . ." Rev. Arlan Andrew Baillie, "Selected Sermons, February 1945–October 1946" (Bangor, Me.: privately printed).

122 "Minority peoples who . . ." Ibid.

122 School board. It was not until the late 1960's that the city elected the school board.

*Page*

124　"For many years . . ." *BDN*, June 6, 1956, p. 1.

124　Statistic on Jewish occupations. Catherine Cutler, "Final Report of the Jewish Community Council, Self-Survey" (April 1951), p. 46.

124　Population statistics. Ibid., pp. 43–45.

125　"Common meeting ground . . ." Ibid., p. 9.

126　"Had to be done." Interview with Rev. Arlan Baillie, May 1989.

126　"Especially effective as . . ." Congregation Beth Israel, p. 107.

129　Jewish marriages. Cutler, "Final Report," p. 43.

129　"What passions are aroused . . ." William S. Cohen, "Clara's Eyes," *Of Songs and Seasons* (New York: Simon & Schuster, 1978), p. 136.

## CHAPTER 7: BREAKING THROUGH

131　"A considerable number . . ." Cutler, "Final Report," p. 49.

135　"He was the first . . ." *BDN*, October 1, 1970, p. 1.

136　"Race, color, religion . . ." Director of Legislative Research, *Acts and Resolves as Passed by the Ninety-Ninth Legislature of the State of Maine* (Augusta, Me.: Kennebec Journal, 1959) p. 363.

137　Funeral chapel. Beth Israel obtained additional land near Mount Hope. Even the uncrowded Webster Avenue cemetery was placed on a sound financial basis. The Kirstein family raised $75,000 for perpetual upkeep of the cemetery.

140　Master Plan. Bangor City Planning Board, "A Master Plan: Bangor, Maine," 1951.

141　"Poverty, crime, war . . ." Bangor City Planning Board, "Preliminary Report on a Housing Analysis and Program for Bangor" (1955), i.

142　Authority's mandate. Bangor Urban Renewal Authority, "Urban Renewal Plan for the Kenduskeag Stream Urban Renewal Area, Maine R-7" (1964), pp. 2–3.

142　"It was a street . . ." Cohen, p. 23.

144　"Bangor's historical background . . ." "Comprehensive Plan Summary," (Bangor, Me., 1970), p. 22.

146　"The ancient laws . . ." Cutler, "The First Forty Years," p. 32.

## CHAPTER 8: A SUMMER EMPIRE

*Page*

151 "An erroneous idea . . ." *BDC,* July 13, 1897, p. 1.

152 "He longs for . . ." Pattangall, p. 297. Patangall struck on many fronts. Bass "supports a summer cottage at Bar Harbor, enlivening that resort of fashion and beauty by quarreling with the market men about the price of butter, milk and eggs, and much as he hates to spend those valued dollars which he has spent a life time in accumulating, contributes liberally and ostentatiously to every form of public entertainment given in honor of the summer guests. So far, however, his great ambition has been slightly recognized." Ibid., pp. 297–298.

152 "Thou favored isle . . ." Henry Walton Swift and Dacre Bush, "Mt. Desert in 1873" (Boston: J. R. Osgood & Co., 1873).

153 "Though fresh as ever . . ." Ibid.

153 "To the lover of . . ." *The Coast of Maine: Campobello to the Isles of Shoals* (Boston: Henry G. Peabody, 1889).

154 "Wooden barracks." Bishop William Lawrence, *Memories of a Happy Life* (Boston: Houghton Mifflin, 1926), p. 192. By comparison, the Adirondacks had built hotel rooms for 8,000 people, the Catskills had 5,000, Old Orchard Beach 3,000, Rangeley Lake 1,500 and the White Mountains 8,000. Edward Hungerford, "Our Summer Migration," *Century,* 20 (1881), p. 570.

154 "Squillionaires." Joseph Alsop, *The Rare Art Traditions: The History of Art Collecting and Its Linked Phenomena Wherever They Have Appeared* (New York: Harper & Row, 1982), p. 333.

154 "Old gentry." E. Digby Baltzell, *The Protestant Establishment: Aristocracy and Caste in America* (New York: Random House, 1964), p. 112.

154 "The cottages or villas . . ." W. B. Lapham, *Bar Harbor and Mt. Desert Island* (Augusta, Me.: Maine Farmer, 1888), p. 113.

155 Intercity aristocracy. Baltzell, *The Protestant Establishment,* p. 113. Not only the rich were coming to the island. Friedrich Adolph Sorge, a German-born Socialist, spent many summers at Mt. Desert Island. In a letter to Friedrich Engels, Sorge invited Engels to visit in Maine, but Engels never came.

155 "How astonishing are . . ." Mrs. Burton Harrison to Fairfax Harrison, August 1889. Mrs. Burton Harrison Papers.

156 Baymeath. Louise de Koven Bowen, *Baymeath* (privately printed, 1944).

*Page*

156 "It is the fashion . . ." Roger G. Reed, "A Biographical Dictio-
     nary of Architects in Maine: Bruce Price, 1845–1903" (Maine
     Historic Preservation Commission, 1986).

156 Emerson and the shingle tradition. Roger Reed, *A Delight to All
     Who Know It: The Maine Summer Architecture of William R. Emer-
     son"* (Augusta, Me.: Maine Historic Preservation Commission,
     1990).

156 The art of "floriculture." Edith Wharton, *Italian Villas and Their
     Gardens* (New York: DaCapo Paperback, 1988), vi.

156 "It is a common sight . . ." *BDC*, September 26, 1905, p. 3.

156 "The drives about . . ." Elizabeth Ingleheart, "A Biographical
     Dictionary of Architects in Maine: Frederick Law Olmstead,
     1822–1903" (Maine Historic Preservation Commission, 1988),
     p. 9.

157 "A young lady . . ." *BDC*, October 10, 1896, p. 9.

157 "Intelligent, lively and entertaining," R. W. B. Lewis, *Edith Whar-
     ton: A Biography* (New York: Harper & Row, 1975), pp. 39–40.

157 The navy was too weak to fight. Barbara W. Tuchman, *The
     Proud Tower: A Portrait of the World Before the War, 1890–1914*
     (New York: Macmillan Company, 1966), p. 133.

157 "It is *so* . . ." Mrs. Burton Harrison to Fairfax Harrison, June 22,
     1889. Harrison Papers.

158 "Many people familiar . . ." Mrs. Burton Harrison to Burton
     Harrison, August 1889.

159 "White wings." *BDC*, December 7, 1905, p. 4.

159 The township of Mount Desert on Mount Desert Island includes
     the villages of Northeast Harbor, Seal Harbor, Pretty Marsh,
     Somesville and Otter Creek.

159 "One who engages . . ." Charles W. Eliot, "The Forgotten Mil-
     lions: A Study of the Common American Mode of Life," *Century
     Magazine,* Vol. 40, No. 4 (August 1890), p. 563.

160 Ministers now regularly performed christenings. Charles W.
     Eliot, "The Right Development of Mount Desert" (privately
     printed, 1903), Jesup Memorial Library.

160 "If they [the summer residents] . . ." George E. Street, *Mt. Desert:
     A History,* ed. Samuel A. Eliot (Boston: Houghton Mifflin, 1926),
     p. 276.

Page
160 Swim club for summer residents only. Robert Pyle, "Northeast Harbor," *Mount Desert: An Informal History,* ed. Gunnar Hansen (Mount Desert, Me.: Town of Mount Desert, Maine, 1989), p. 82.

160 "When I made my request . . ." Emily Phillips Reynolds, "Down Memory Lane" (Portland, Me.: Maine Printing Co., 1975), p. 59.

160 "Keep out of the . . ." Ibid., p. 2.

160 "Oh, Larson . . ." Bowen, p. 50.

161 "Just as the white . . ." Baltzell, *Protestant Establishment,* p. 118.

161 "It is noticeable . . ." Charles W. Eliot, *The Durable Satisfactions of Life* (New York: Thomas Y. Crowell, 1910), pp. 64–65.

161 "The competency on which . . ." Street, pp. 288–289.

162 Henrietta G. Rowe, *The Maid of Bar Harbor* (Boston: Little, Brown, 1905).

162 "Strong, brave and resourceful . . ." Arthur Train, "The Viking's Daughter," *The Best Maine Stories: The Marvelous Mystery,* ed. Sanford Phippen (Augusta, Me.: Lance Tapley, 1986), p. 39.

163 "For I've danced . . ." Alick J. Grant, "Her Letter," *Sherman's Guide, Business Directory and Reference Book* (Bar Harbor, Me.: W. H. Sherman, 1890), pp. 107–108.

163 "Wild place where . . ." Marion Lawrence Peabody, *To Be Young Was Very Heaven* (Boston: Houghton Mifflin, 1967), p. 20.

163 "The intimacy established . . ." Robert Grant, "A Plea for Bar Harbor," *Outing,* Vol. 6, No. 5 (August 1885), p. 519.

163 "Much foreign blood . . ." Ibid., p. 524.

165 "Observed of all . . ." Peabody, p. 322.

165 "No later than the age . . ." Louis Auchincloss, *A Writer's Capital* (Minneapolis: University of Minnesota Press, 1974), p. 36.

165 "Cultivate manly, Christian . . ." Frank D. Ashburn, *A Portrait: Peabody of Groton* (Cambridge, Mass.: The Riverside Press, 1967), p. 68.

165 "Gentleman of the Jewish faith . . ." Ibid., p. 192.

166 "Sharpen the informal . . ." John Higham, *Send These to Me: Jews and Other Immigrants in Urban America* (New York: Atheneum, 1975), p. 148.

*Page*

166 "In the lower levels . . ." H. G. Wells, *The Future of America* (New York: Harper & Row, 1906), p. 134.

167 "Devoid of public . . ." Oscar and Mary Handlin, "The Acquisition of Political and Social Rights by the Jews in the United States," *American Jewish Yearbook* 56 (Philadelphia: Jewish Publication Society of America, 1955), p. 73.

167 "There were moments . . ." Wells, p. 135.

167 "I am required . . ." Lee Max Friedman, *Jewish Pioneers and Patriots* (Philadelphia: Jewish Publication Society of America, 1942), p. 273.

167 "We do not like Jews . . ." Marc Lee Raphael, *Jews and Judaism in the United States: A Documentary History* (New York: Behrman House, 1983), p. 261.

167 "In recent years . . ." Philip Cowan, *Prejudice Against the Jews* (New York: Philip Cowan, 1928), p. 29.

168 "There are many people . . ." Ibid., p. 34.

168 "Loud and pushing." Ibid., p. 51.

168 "Hardly touch the evil . . ." Ibid., p. 96.

168 "I often talk . . ." Ibid., p. 101.

169 "To support a Coney . . ." Eliot, "The Right Development of Mt. Desert," p. 7.

## CHAPTER 9: VISIONARIES

170 "It was on July . . ." "The Isle of Mt. Deserted: Pleasures and Amenities of Life at Bar Harbor in 1920 After the Automobile Invasion, A Prophecy by Arthur Train." *BDC*, August 27, 1907, p. 3.

170 "Thriving town with . . ." Ibid.

172 "Aggressively ambitious, adventurous . . ." James P. Warburg, *The Long Road Home: The Autobiography of a Maverick* (New York: Doubleday, 1964), p. 10.

172 "A Jew, and the Jews constituted . . ." E. Digby Baltzell, *Philadelphia Gentlemen: The Making of a National Upper Class* (New York: Free Press, 1958), p. 20.

173 "A strange mixture . . ." Warburg, p. 11.

*Page*
173  "I wish you joy . . ." Ibid., p. 42.

173  "Each car was a house . . ." Edward M. M. Warburg, *As I Recall* (privately published, 1978), p. 20.

174  "His address was practical . . ." *Bar Harbor Record* (hereafter referred to as *BHR*), August 26, 1908, p. 5.

174  "Echtes Bar Harbor wetter" E.M.M. Warburg, p. 21.

174  "Today I had the most . . ." Frieda Schiff Warburg, *Reminiscences of a Long Life* (New York: privately published, 1956), p. 59.

175  "The heart of the entire . . ." Letter included in the exhibition, "The Dreyfus Affair: Art Justice and Truth," Jewish Museum, fall, 1987.

175  Anti-Semitic conversations. Precilla Mary Roberts, "The American 'Eastern Establishment' and World War I: The Emergence of a Foreign Policy Tradition," doctoral dissertation, University of Cambridge, n.d. AJA, p. 31.

176  "Some time ago . . ." Jacob H. Schiff to Charles W. Eliot, April 29, 1902, Eliot Papers, Box 112, Folder 159. Harvard University Archives (hereafter referred to as HUA).

176  "By a misfortune . . ." James Mott Hallowell to Eliot, May 17, 1902. Eliot Papers, Box 112, Folder 159. HUA.

177  "I would like to say . . ." Schiff to Eliot, January 2, 1906, Eliot Papers, Box 245. HUA.

179  "Mr. Franklin is . . ." *Bar Harbor Souvenir,* 1906.

179  "In his long residence . . ." *People and Places: Lubec—Jonesport—Ellsworth—Machias and Bar Harbor,* 1906.

179  "There is a nobbiness . . ." *Bar Harbor Souvenir,* 1906.

180  "One of the oldest . . ." Ibid.

180  "This store has . . ." Ibid.

180  "The event of circumcision . . ." *BHR,* July 10, 1905, p. 5.

181  "Well, Mrs. Povich . . ." Howard Simon, *Jewish Times: Voices of the American Jewish Experience* (Boston: Houghton Mifflin, 1988), p. 9.

181  "It is to escape . . ." Eliot, "The Future of Mt. Desert," pp. 13–14.

182  "City millionaires . . ." *BDC,* January 27, 1909, p. 2.

*Page*

182  "Can nothing be done . . ." Charles W. Eliot, *Charles Eliot, Land-scape Architect* (Boston: Houghton Mifflin, 1902), p. 315.

182  "By what means . . ." Eliot to Parke Godwin, August 12, 1901. Eliot Papers, Jesup Memorial Library.

183  "Yaas, that's him . . ." Lawrence, p. 295.

183  "Of course you should never . . ." Ibid., p. 297.

183  "To acquire, by devise . . ." George B. Dorr, *The Story of Acadia National Park* (Bar Harbor, Me.: Acadia Publishing Co., 1985), pp. 5–6.

186  "Our idea as to the . . ." House of Representatives, Subcommittee of the Committee on Public Lands, "Mt. Desert National Park," May 30, 1918. Hearings, p. 12.

187  "I have been a resident . . ." Jacob H. Schiff, *Jacob H. Schiff: His Life and Letters,* ed. Cyrus Adler (Garden City, N.Y.: Doubleday, Doran, 1928), II, p. 324.

187  "It is the first . . ." George Dorr to Rockefeller, March 3, 1919. Rockefeller Family Archives (hereafter referred to as RFA), Homes, 2, Box 113, "Public Reservations." Rockefeller Archive Center (hereafter referred to as RAC).

188  "All the summer visitors . . ." Bowen, p. 51.

189  "Today we had . . ." Schiff to Mortimer Schiff, August 1917, Schiff Papers, Box 450.

189  "Mr. Schiff enjoyed . . ." *Bar Harbor Times* (hereafter referred to as *BHT*), September 29, 1920, p. 1. Having been sold in 1914, the local newspaper was now known as the *Bar Harbor Times*.

189  "I have never met . . ." Charles W. Eliot, "Jacob Schiff," *Menorah Journal,* Vol. 7 (February 1921), p. 21.

189  "Business ethics, labor . . ." Ibid., p. 20.

## CHAPTER 10: THE HIGHEST CHRISTIAN CIRCLES

197  Forty-seven cottages were sold. Cleveland Amory, "Bar Harbor," *Holiday Magazine* (July 1951), p. 40.

198  "Our dinner was . . ." Henry Morgenthau, Sr., to Henry Morgenthau, Jr., July 10, 1926, Henry Morgenthau, Sr., Papers.

199  "We Jews of America . . ." Henry Morgenthau, Sr., *All in a Life Time* (Garden City, N.Y.: Doubleday, Doran, 1922), p. 404.

*Page*

199  "An international non-sectarian . . ." Henry Morgenthau, Sr., to Arthur Balfour, February 4, 1922. Morgenthau Papers.

199  "Social position . . ." Henry Morgenthau, Sr., p. 400.

200  "Cross of Gold . . ." Henry Morgenthau, Sr., to Franklin Delano Roosevelt, June 28, 1924. Morgenthau Papers.

200  Klan interest on Mount Desert. *BHT,* April 9, 1924, p. 9.

200  "The summer hotel . . ." Steinberg, p. 245.

201  "Oh, Harvard's run . . ." Heywood Campbell Broun and George Britt, *Christians Only: A Study in Prejudice* (New York: Vanguard Press, 1931), p. 73.

201  "The contrasts between . . ." Jerome Karabel, "Status-Group Struggle, Organized Interests, and the Limits of Institutional Autonomy," *Theory and Society,* 13 (January 1984), p. 8.

201  "In the place of Eliot . . ." Ronald Steele, *Walter Lippmann and the American Century* (Boston: Atlantic Monthly Press, 1980), p. 195.

202  "I do not know . . ." Charles Riegelman to Henry Morgenthau, Sr., August 23, 1926. Morgenthau Papers.

204  "Was most gracious . . ." Riegelman to Henry Morgenthau, Sr., August 31, 1926. Morgenthau Papers.

204  "You evidently . . ." Henry Morgenthau, Sr., to Riegelman, September 2, 1926. Morgenthau Papers.

204  "Any Jew in America . . ." Henry Morgenthau, Sr., p. 404.

204  "I have never possessed . . ." Henry Morgenthau, Sr., to Elie and Henry Morgenthau, Jr., June 18, 1926. Morgenthau Papers.

205  "I am a regular customer . . ." Mrs. Henry Morgenthau to Great Atlantic and Pacific Tea Co., July 1, 1926. Morgenthau Papers.

205  "We hear that Dr. Eliot . . ." Henry Morgenthau, Sr., to Helen and Mortimer Fox, June 25, 1926. Morgenthau Papers.

205  "If I do not come . . ." Dorr to Eliot, March 18, 1924, Eliot Papers, Box 409. Eliot. HUA.

206  "I feel in the strongest . . ." Eliot to Rockefeller, February 10, 1917, RFA, Friends and Services, 108EL5, Box 59, Charles Eliot. RAC.

206  "Ever since I . . ." Rockefeller to Eliot, April 8, 1924, RFA, 2 Friends and Services, Box 59, Charles Eliot. RAC.

*Page*

207  Rockefeller's national philanthropy. Peter Collier and David Horowitz, *The Rockefellers: An American Dynasty* (New York: Holt, Rinehart & Winston, 1976), pp. 149–150.

207  Rockefeller's donations to park. John D. Rockefeller, Jr., to Harold L. Ickes, March 14, 1935. Ann Rockefeller Roberts, *Mr. Rockefeller's Roads: The Untold Story of Acadia's Carriage Roads & Their Creator* (Camden, Me.: Down East Books, 1990), p. 155.

208  "For a long time . . ." Mary Ellen Chase, *Abby Aldrich Rockefeller* (New York: Macmillan Company, 1950), pp. 79–80.

208  "Social ostracism . . ." Ibid.

208  "Many people wonder . . ." Mrs. Henry Parkman, "A Glimpse of Northeast Harbor in the Nineties." Northeast Harbor Library.

209  "Pastoral idyll . . ." Auchincloss, *A Writer's Capital*, p. 26.

209  "Silly side . . ." Ibid, p. 25.

209  Rockefeller would cancel the lease. Raymond B. Fosdick, *John D. Rockefeller, Jr.: A Portrait* (New York: Harper & Brothers, 1956), p. 261.

209  "In such a small . . ." Carlos Salzedo to Rockefeller, July 18, 1929, RFA, 2 Homes, Box 74, Seal Harbor Club. RAC.

210  Lhévinne "was shy and almost without competitive impulse." His wife, Rosina, also a pianist, became one of the most renowned teachers in America. *The New Grove Dictionary of Music and Musicians,* ed. Stanley Sadie, 10 (London: Macmillan, 1980), p. 712.

210  "Professional pianists . . ." Amy Montague to Rockefeller, June 20, 1933, RFA, 2 Homes, Box 74, Seal Harbor Club. RAC.

210  "Perfect politeness . . ." Louis Auchincloss, *The House of the Prophet* (Boston: Houghton Mifflin, 1980), p. 53.

210  "To invite these people . . ." Rockefeller to Montague, June 26, 1933, RFA, 2 Homes, Box 74, Seal Harbor Club. RCA.

## CHAPTER 11: A NATIONAL POSSESSION

212  German building in Rockefeller Center. John E. Haar and Peter J. Johnson, *The Rockefeller Century: Three Generations of America's Greatest Family, John D. Rockefeller, John D. Rockefeller, Jr., John D. Rockefeller III* (New York: Scribner, 1988), p. 401.

*Page*

212 "I am sure we can . . ." Morgenthau to Adolph Ochs, July 28, 1928. Morgenthau Papers.

212 "We have so much . . ." Morgenthau to Josie Morgenthau, June 10, 1932. Morgenthau Papers.

213 "In his fierce . . ." Barbara W. Tuchman, *Practicing History: Selected Essays* (New York: Alfred A. Knopf, 1981), p. 217.

214 "An enormous increase . . ." Fortune, *Jews in America* (New York: Random House, 1936), pp. 19–20.

214 Stores in Bar Harbor. Edward Lee Marmon, *Taking Care of Business Down East: The History of the Bar Harbor Banking and Trust Company, 1887–1987* (Graphic Chronologies, 1987), pp. 119.

214 "A fine theater . . ." Morgenthau to Helen and Mortimer Fox, June 10, 1932. Morgenthau Papers.

215 "Not only is he . . ." August 16, 1937, Scrapbook, Jesup Memorial Library.

215 "It is all in delightful . . ." Dorr Papers.

216 "I shall like to think . . ." Dorr to Rockefeller, September 9, 1939. RFA, Homes, Box 93, George Dorr. RAC.

216 "What a satisfaction . . ." Rockefeller to Dorr, September 15, 1939, RFA, Homes, Box 93, George Dorr. RAC.

218 "I cannot help . . ." Bowen, p. 9.

218 "The lack of protest . . ." Tuchman, *Practicing History,* pp. 211–212.

218 Henry Morgenthau, Jr., and War Refugee Board. Lucy S. Dawidowicz, "American Jews and the Holocaust," *The New York Times Magazine,* April 18, 1982.

219 "There is something truly . . ." *The New York Times,* November 28, 1946, p. 27.

219 "Mr. Morgenthau together . . ." *BHT,* November 28, 1946, p. 1.

220 "Looking back on . . ." Notes by Mrs. Frank Rowell, RFA. 2 Homes, Box 88, Mt. Desert, October 1947. RAC.

220 "When the fire first . . ." Rockefeller to Mrs. Eliot Crown, November 7, 1947, Homes, 88, Fire. RAC.

220 "Quiet privacy . . ." Louis Bartholomew, "Bartholomew Report, Preliminary Report on the Town Plan," July 1948, 8. RFA. RLC, Homes, Box 175, p. 88. RAC.

*Page*

220  "While the scenery . . ." Ibid., p. 10.

221  "Is a habit rather . . ." Mary Roberts Rinehart, "Phoenix in New England," *Town and Country* (July 1949), p. 91.

221  "Bar Harbor for all the high . . ." Richard Hale, *The Story of Bar Harbor: An Informal History Recording One Hundred and Fifty Years in the Life of a Community* (New York: Ives Washburn, 1949), p. 180.

221  Restricted hotels in Maine. Anti-Defamation League Report, New England Regional Office, "Memorandum," Boston, September 5, 1946, in American Jewish Committee Library.

223  "It has sometimes been . . ." Robert Patterson to Editor, *BHT*, Feb. 18, 1985. In collection of Mrs. Robert Patterson, Mount Desert, Maine.

227  "The present generation . . ." Dorr Papers.

228  "It never will be . . ." Ibid.


## CHAPTER 12: CLAIMING THEIR PLACE

232  "By enterprise and industry . . ." *Calais Advertiser* (hereafter referred to as *CA*), December 25, 1922, p. 5.

235  Champlain's discoveries. Samuel Eliot Morison, *The Story of Mount Desert Island* (Boston: Atlantic Monthly Press, 1960), pp. 9–10.

236  "Largest city east of . . ." "A Biographical Dictionary of Architects in Maine: Asher B. Bassford, 1805–1887," Vol. II, no. 3 (Augusta, Me.: Maine Historic Preservation Commission, 1985).

236  St. Croix lumber merchants. Harold A. Davis, *An International Community on the St. Croix (1604–1930)* (Orono, Me.: University of Maine Press, 1950), p. 270.

237  International Paper Company. Ibid., p. 274.

237  "A closely knit . . ." Ibid., p. x

238  "Though the climate . . ." Rev. I. C. Knowlton, *Annals of Calais, Maine and St. Stephen, New Brunswick* (Calais, Me.: J. A. Sears, 1875), p. 115.

238  "To be sure . . ." *Samuel Lane Boardman, The Naturalist of the Saint Croix: Memoir of George A. Boardman* (Bangor, Me.: 1903), p. 99.

*Page*

238 "The mightiest spectacle . . ." *CA*, December 28, 1927, p. 5.

240 "The theater will stand . . ." Ibid., p. 2.

246 "Keen business woman . . ." Ibid., November 20, 1935, p. 1.

246 "Active in the Jewish . . ." Ibid.


CHAPTER 13: NEW TRADITIONS

251 "Quiet and leisurely" Davis, p. 307.

252 "Probably be sufficient . . ." Ibid.

255 "Arriving Daily . . ." *CA*, February 27, 1935, p. 6.

259 Federal expenditures for Quoddy. Raymond Moreau, *Passamaquoddy Tidal Power: An Analysis*, University of Maine Master's Thesis, 1977, p. 22.

260 "Sit down, boys . . ." *CA*, February 15, 1951, p. 12.

261 "When he calls . . ." Interview with Senator Margaret Chase Smith, March 12, 1986, Skowhegan, Maine.

261 "Very direct, very honestly . . ." Ibid.

267 "News of his passing . . ." *CA*, December 28, 1956, p. 1.

268 "To Calais he rendered . . ." Ibid.

272 Desire of immigrants to leave the ghetto. Ben Halpern, "America Is Different," ed. Marshall Sklare, *The Jews: Social Patterns of an American Group* (New York: Free Press, 1958), p. 36.

# Bibliography

Abbreviations for manuscript collections:

AJA: American Jewish Archives, Cincinnati, Ohio.

FDRL: Franklin Delano Roosevelt Library, Hyde Park, New York.

HUA: Harvard University Archives, Harvard University Library, Cambridge, Massachusetts (Charles W. Eliot Papers).

JML: Jesup Memorial Library, Bar Harbor, Maine (George B. Dorr Papers, Charles W. Eliot Papers, Mrs. Burton Harrison Papers).

RAC: Rockefeller Archive Center, North Tarrytown, New York. (John D. Rockefeller, Jr., Papers).

(All material cited from Eliot papers by permission of Harvard University Archives. All material cited from Morgenthau Papers by permission of the family. All material cited from Rockefeller Papers by permission of Rockefeller Archive Center.)

Aleichem, Sholem. *Tevye the Dairyman and the Railroad Stories.* Trans. Hillel Halkin. New York: Schocken Books, 1987.

Alpert, Jordan S. *The Alperts and Cohens of Bangor, Maine.* San Francisco: privately printed, 1990.

Amory, Cleveland. "Bar Harbor," *Holiday Magazine* (July 1951): 41–47, 114–116, 118–119.

301

————. *The Last Resorts.* New York: Harper, 1952.

*Annual Report of the Commissioner General of Immigration, 1914.* Washington, D.C.: GPO, 1915.

Anti-Defamation League Report, New England Regional Office, "Memorandum," Boston: September 5, 1946. American Jewish Committee Library, New York.

Ashburn, Frank D. *A Portrait: Peabody of Groton.* Cambridge, Mass.: The Riverside Press, 1967.

Auchincloss, Louis. *The House of the Prophet.* Boston: Houghton Mifflin, 1980.

————. *A Writer's Capital.* Minneapolis: University of Minnesota Press, 1974.

"A Visitor's Guide to St. Saviours Episcopal Church, Bar Harbor, Maine." Compiled by Rev. Edwin A. Garrett, III.

Baillie, Arlan Andrew. "Selected Sermons, February 1945–October 1946." Bangor, Me.: privately printed.

Balmori, Diana. *Beatrix Farrand's American Landscape: Her Gardens and Campuses.* Sagaponack, N.Y.: Sagapress, 1985.

Baltzell, E. Digby. *Philadelphia Gentlemen: The Making of a National Upper Class.* New York: Free Press, 1958.

————. *The Protestant Establishment: Aristocracy and Caste in America.* New York: Random House, 1964.

————. *Puritan Boston and Quaker Philadelphia: Two Protestant Ethics and the Spirit of Class Authority and Leadership.* New York: Free Press, 1979.

Bangor Board of Trade. "City of Bangor, 'Queen City of the East.' " Bangor, Me.: 1888.

Bangor City Planning Board. "A Master Plan: Bangor, Maine." Bangor, Me.: 1951.

————. "Preliminary Report on a Housing Analysis and Program for Bangor." Bangor, Me.: 1955.

Bangor Historical Society. "Fiftieth Anniversary of the Bangor Historical Society, Bangor, Maine, 1914." Bangor, Me.: 1914.

Bangor Jewish Community Center. "Community News." Bangor, Me.: 1940–1952.

Bangor Urban Renewal Authority. "Urban Renewal Plan for the Kenduskeag Stream Urban Renewal Area, *Maine R-7.*" Bangor, Me.: 1964.

*Bar Harbor Souvenir,* 1906.

Barrett, Richmond. *Good Old Summer Days: Newport, Narragansett Pier, Saratoga, Long Branch, Bar Harbor.* Boston: Houghton Mifflin, 1952.

Bartholomew, Louis. "Bartholomew Report, Preliminary Report on the Town Plan," July 1948. RAC.

Beam, Lura. *A Maine Hamlet.* New York: Winfreed Funk, 1957.

Best, Gary. *Jewish Leaders and the Jewish Problem in Eastern Europe, 1890–1914.* Westport, Ct.: Greenwood Press, 1982.

Beth Abraham Synagogue, *Fiftieth Anniversary Commemorative Journal.* Bangor, Me.: 1983.

"Biographical Dictionary of Architects in Maine: Asher B. Bassford, 1805–1887," Vol. II, No. 3 (Augusta, Maine). Maine Historic Preservation Commission, 1985.

Boardman, Samuel Lane. *The Naturalist of the Saint Croix: Memoir of George A. Boardman.* Bangor, Me.: 1903.

Bowen, Louise de Koven. *Baymeath.* Privately printed, 1944.

Boyer, Paul. *Urban Masses and Moral Order in America: 1820–1920.* Cambridge: Harvard University Press, 1978.

Breton, Rita Mae. "The Red Scare: A Study in Maine Nativism, 1919–1925." Master of Arts, University of Maine, Orono, 1972.

Broun, Heywood Campbell and George Britt. *Christians Only: A Study in Prejudice.* New York: Vanguard Press, 1931.

Chase, Mary Ellen. *Abby Aldrich Rockefeller.* New York: Macmillan, 1950.

*Coast of Maine: Campobello to the Isles of Shoals.* Boston: Henry G. Peabody, 1889.

Cohen, Morris Raphael. *A Dreamer's Journey.* Glencoe, Ill.: Free Press, 1949.

Cohen, William S. "Clara's Eyes," *Of Songs and Seasons.* New York: Simon & Schuster, 1978.

Collier, Peter and David Horowitz. *The Rockefellers: An American Dynasty.* New York: Holt, Rinehart & Winston, 1976.

Collier, Sargent. *Acadia National Park: George B. Dorr's Triumph.* Farmington, Me.: 1965.

Committee on Civic Improvement. "Bangor City Plan: The Burned District." Bangor, Me.: 1911.

———. "Comprehensive Plan Summary." Bangor, Me.: 1970.

Congregation Ahawas Achim, Miscellaneous Documents, Bangor Public Library.

Congregation Beth Israel. *Diamond Jubilee, 1888–1963.* Bangor, Me.: 1963.

Cowan, Philip. *Prejudice Against the Jews.* New York: Philip Cowan, 1928.

Crawford, F. Marion. *Bar Harbor.* New York: Charles Scribner's Sons, 1896.

———. *Love in Idleness: A Tale of Bar Harbor.* New York: Macmillan, 1894.

Cutler, Catherine. "Final Report of the Jewish Community Council, Self-Survey." Bangor, Me.: April 1951.

———. "The First Forty Years of the Bangor Hebrew School: A History of It's [sic] Growth from 1907 to 1947." "Bangor Hebrew School: Fortieth Anniversary, 1907–1947." Bangor Hebrew Community Center, October 2, 1947.

Davis, Harold A. *An International Community on the St. Croix, 1604–1930.* Orono, Me.: University Press, 1950.

Dawidowicz, Lucy S. *The Golden Tradition: Jewish Life & Thought in Eastern Europe.* New York: Holt, Rinehart & Winston, 1967.

Director of Legislative Research. *Acts and Resolves as Passed by the Ninety-Ninth Legislature of the State of Maine.* Augusta, Me.: Kennebec Journal, 1959.

Dorr, George B. *The Story of Acadia National Park.* Bar Harbor, Me.: Acadia Publishing Co., 1985.

Duncan, Alastair and Neil Harris. *Masterworks of Louis Comfort Tiffany.* London: Thames and Hudson, 1989.

Eagle, Morris N. "Jewish Life in the United States: Perspectives from Psychology." In Joseph Gittler, *Jewish Life in the United States: Perspectives from the Social Sciences.* New York: University Press, 1981.

Eckstorm, Fannie Hardy. *The Penobscot Man.* Somersworth, N.H.: New Hampshire Publishing Co., 1972.

Eliot, Charles W. *Charles Eliot, Landscape Architect.* Boston: Houghton Mifflin, 1902.

———. *The Durable Satisfactions of Life.* New York: Thomas Y. Crowell, 1910.

_____. "The Forgotten Millions: A Study of the Common American Mode of Life." *Century Magazine,* Vol. 40, No. 4 (August 1890): 556–564. (Vol. 40 in old listing, Vol. 18 in revised).

_____. "The Right Development of Mount Desert." Privately printed, 1903.

_____. "Jacob Schiff." *Menorah Journal,* Vol 7, No. 1 (February 1921): 16–21.

Epstein, Lucille M. Incomplete Master's Thesis, University of Maine, Orono, Dept. of History, 1940.

Fortune. *Jews in America.* New York: Random House, 1936.

Fosdick, Raymond B. *John D. Rockefeller, Jr.: A Portrait.* New York: Harper & Brothers, 1956.

Friedman, Lee Max. *Jewish Pioneers and Patriots.* Philadelphia: Jewish Publication Society of America, 1942.

"The Gentile's Attitude Towards the Jews: As a Jew Sees It," *Menorah Journal,* Vol. 2, No. 5 (December 1916): 271–276.

Gitelman, Zvi Y. *A Century of Ambivalence.* New York: Schocken Books, 1988.

Godfrey, John Edwards. *The Journal of John Edwards Godfrey: Bangor, Maine 1863–1869,* ed. James B. Vickery. Rockland, Me.: Courier-Gazette, 1979.

Godwin, Edwin Lawrence. *Reflections and Comments, 1865–1895.* New York: Charles Scribner's Sons, 1895.

Goldman, Guido. *A History of the Germanic Museum at Harvard University.* Cambridge, Mass.: Minde de Gunzburg Center for European Studies, Harvard University, 1989.

Goldstein, Sidney. "Jews in the United States: Perspectives from Demography," *American Jewish Yearbook, 1981.* New York: American Jewish Committee, 1981: 3–60.

Grant, Alick J. "Her Letter," *Sherman's Guide, Business Directory and Reference Book.* Bar Harbor, Me.: W. H. Sherman, 1890.

Grant, Robert. "A Plea for Bar Harbor," *Outing,* Vol. 6, No. 5 (August 1885): 515–524.

Haar, John E., and Peter J. Johnson, *The Rockefeller Century: Three Generations of America's Greatest Family, John D. Rockefeller, John D. Rockefeller, Jr., John D. Rockefeller III.* New York: Scribner, 1988.

Hale, Richard. *The Story of Bar Harbor: An Informal History Recording One Hundred and Fifty Years in the Life of a Community.* New York: Ives Washburn, 1949.

Halpern, Ben. "America Is Different." In Marshall Sklare, ed., *The Jews: Social Patterns of an American Group.* New York: Free Press, 1958.

Handlin, Oscar. *Adventures in Freedom: Three Hundred Years of Jewish Life in America.* New York: McGraw-Hill, 1954.

――――. "American Views of Jews at the Opening of the Twentieth Century." *Publications of the American Jewish Historical Society* 40 (June 1951): 323–344.

――――, and Mary. "The Acquisition of Political and Social Rights by the Jews in the United States." *American Jewish Yearbook,* 56. Philadelphia: Jewish Publication Society of America, 1955: 43–98.

Hansen, Gunnar. *Not a Common House: A History of St. Mary's-by-the-Sea.* Privately printed, 1981.

Harrison, Mrs. Burton. *Recollections Grave and Gay.* New York: Charles Scribner's Sons, 1912.

Helfrich, G. W. and Gladys O'Neil. *Lost Bar Harbor.* Camden, Me.: Down East, 1982.

Helibut, Anthony. *Exiled in Paradise: German Refugee Artists and Intellectuals in America, from the 1930s to the Present.* New York: Viking Press, 1983.

Higham, John. "Immigration." In C. Vann Woodward, ed., *The Comparative Approach to American History.* New York: Basic Books, 1968: 91–105.

――――. *Send These to Me: Jews and Other Immigrants in Urban America.* New York: Atheneum, 1975.

――――. "Social Discrimination Against Jews in America: 1830–1930." *Publications of the American Jewish Historical Society,* 47 (September 1957): 1–33.

――――. *Strangers in the Land: Patterns of American Nativism, 1860–1925.* New York: Atheneum, 1965.

House of Representatives, Subcommittee of the Committee on the Public Lands. "Mt. Desert National Park." May 30, 1918. Hearings.

Hungerford, Edward. "Our Summer Migration," *Century,* 20 (1881): 569–587.

Huth, Hans. *Nature and the American: Three Centuries of Changing Attitudes.* Berkeley, Ca.: University of California Press, 1957.

Igleheart, Elizabeth. "A Biographical Dictionary of Architects in Maine: Frederick Law Olmsted, 1822–1903." Maine Historic Preservation Commission, 1988.

Johnson, Paul. *A History of the Jews.* New York: Harper & Row, 1987.

Kaiser, Harvey H. *Great Camps of the Adirondacks.* Boston: David R. Godine, 1982.

Karabel, Jerome. "Status-Group Struggle, Organized Interests, and the Limits of Institutional Autonomy," *Theory and Society,* 13 (January 1984): 1–40.

Kazin, Alfred. "The Past Breaks Out." In William Zinsser, ed., *Inventing the Truth: The Art and Craft of Memoir.* Boston: Houghton Mifflin, 1981.

Kessner, Thomas. *The Golden Door: Italian and Jewish Immigrant Mobility in New York City, 1880–1915.* New York: Oxford University Press, 1977.

Knowlton, Rev. I. C. *Annals of Calais, Maine and St. Stephen, New Brunswick.* Calais, Me.: J. A. Sears, 1875.

Lane, Franklin K. *Letters of Franklin K. Lane: Personal and Political,* ed. Anne Wintermute Lane and Louise Herrick Wall. Boston: Houghton Mifflin, 1922.

Lapham, W. B. *Bar Harbor and Mt. Desert Island.* Augusta, Me.: Maine Farmer, 1888.

Lasch, Christopher. *The World of Nations: Reflections on American History, Politics and Culture.* New York: Alfred A. Knopf, 1973.

Lawrence, William. *Memories of a Happy Life.* Boston: Houghton Mifflin, 1926.

Leffler, William J. "A Study of Congregation Ahawas Achim, Bangor, Maine from 1849 to 1856, From the Minutes of the Congregation." Bangor Public Library and AJA.

Levine, Steven B. "The Rise of American Boarding Schools and the Development of a National Upper Class." *Social Problems,* 28 (October 1980): 64–94.

Lewis, R.W.B. *Edith Wharton: A Biography.* New York: Harper & Row, 1975.

Marmon, Edward Lee. *Taking Care of Business Down East: The History of the Bar Harbor Banking and Trust Company, 1887–1987.* Graphic Chronologies, 1987.

Michaels, Theresa. "A Guide to the History of Acadia National Park

Hiking Trails." Senior Project. College of the Atlantic, Bar Harbor, Maine, 1987.

Moreau, Raymond. "Passamaquoddy Tidal Power: An Analysis." Orono, Me.: University of Maine. Master's Thesis, 1977.

Morgenthau, Henry. *All in a Life Time*. Garden City, N.Y.: Doubleday, Doran, 1922.

Morgenthau, Henry, III. *Mostly Morgenthau, A Family History*. New York: Ticknor and Fields, 1991.

Morison, Samuel Eliot. *The Story of Mount Desert Island*. Boston: Atlantic Monthly Press, 1960.

Mundy, James H. *Hard Times, Hard Men: Maine and the Irish 1830– 1860*. Scarborough, Me.: Harp Publications, 1990.

————. "Heroes by Appointment: The Fire Companies of Bangor, 1830–1860." Master's Thesis, University of Maine, Orono, June, 1970.

Mundy, James H., and Earle G. Shettleworth, Jr. *The Flight of the Grand Eagle: Charles G. Bryant, Maine Architect and Adventurer*. Augusta, Me.: Maine Historic Preservation Commission, 1977.

*New Grove Dictionary of Music and Musicians*. Stanley Sadie, ed. 10. London: Macmillan, 1980.

Parkman, Mrs. Henry. "A Glimpse of Northeast Harbor in the Nineties." Northeast Harbor Library.

Pattangall, William R. *Meddybemps Letters, Maine's Hall of Fame, Memorial Addresses*. Lewiston, Me.: Lewiston Journal Co., 1924.

Peabody, Marion Lawrence. *To Be Young Was Very Heaven*. Boston: Houghton Mifflin, 1967.

Peck, Emelyn Foster. "The Russian Jew in Southern New England." *New England Magazine*, 31 (1904–05): 24–33.

*People and Places: Lubec—Jonesport—Ellsworth—Machais and Bar Harbor*. 1908.

"Pot and Kettle Club." Bar Harbor, Me.: 1987.

Putnam, Frank. "What's the Matter with New England? Maine: A Study in Land-Grabbing, Tax-Dodging, and Isolation." *New England Magazine*, Vol. 36, No. 5 (July 1907): 515–540.

Pyle, Robert. "Northeast Harbor." In Gunnar Hansen, ed., *Mount Desert: An Informal History*. Mount Desert, Me.: Town of Mount Desert, Maine, 1989.

Ranlett, Charles. "History of Aviation in Bangor, Maine, Including Dow Air Force Base," Thesis, Bowdoin College, 1954.

Raphael, Marc Lee. *Jews and Judaism in the United States: A Documentary History.* New York: Behrman House, 1983.

Ravage, Marcus Eli. *The Jew Pays: A Narrative of the Consequences of the War to the Jews of Eastern Europe and of the Manner in Which Americans Have Attempted to Meet Them.* New York: Alfred A. Knopf, 1919.

Reed, Roger G. "A Biographical Dictionary of Architects in Maine: Bruce Price, 1845–1903." Maine Historic Preservation Commission, 1986.

———. *A Delight to All Who Know It: The Maine Architecture of William R. Emerson.* Augusta, Me.: Maine Historic Preservation Commission, 1990.

Reily & Associates. "The Carriage Roads at Acadia National Park: Resource Study," June 1988. Acadia National Park Headquarters, Bar Harbor, Maine.

Reynolds, Emily Phillips. "Down Memory Lane." Portland, Me.: Maine Printing Co., 1975.

Rifkind, Carole. *Main Street: The Face of Urban America.* New York: Harper & Row, 1977.

Rinehart, Mary Roberts. "Phoenix in New England." *Town and Country* (July 1949): 31–33, 90–92.

Roberts, Ann Rockefeller. *Mr. Rockefeller's Roads: The Untold Story of Acadia's Carriage Roads & Their Creator.* Camden, Me.: Down East Books, 1990.

Roberts, Precilla Mary. "The American 'Eastern Establishment' and World War I: The Emergence of a Foreign Policy Tradition." Doctoral Dissertation, University of Cambridge, England. n.d., AJA.

Robinson, Fannie Harlow. *D.A.R.* Private printing, 1968.

Robinson, Mary C. *Annals of a Happy Family.* Privately printed 1933. Bangor Public Library.

Rowe, Henrietta G. *The Maid of Bar Harbor.* Boston: Little, Brown, 1905.

St. Louis, Lyla E. *A Warden's Way: The Story of Lyle Smith, Maine's "Flying Warden."* Unity, Me.: North Country Press, 1991.

Schiff, Jacob. *Jacob H. Schiff: His Life and Letters,* Cyrus Adler, ed. 2 vols. Garden City, N.Y.: Doubleday, Doran, 1928.

Senate Document 785, 61st Congress, 3rd Session. *Report of the Immigration Commission: Immigration Legislation.* Washington, D.C.: Government Printing Office, 1910. Vols. 5878, 5879.

Shakland, Robert. *Steve Mather of the National Parks.* New York: Alfred A. Knopf, 1951.

Shettleworth, Earle G., Jr. *Summer Cottages of Islesboro.* Islesboro, Me.: Islesboro Historical Society, 1989.

Silk, Leonard, and Mark Silk. *The American Establishment.* New York: Basic Books, 1980.

Silk, Mark. *Spiritual Politics: Religion and America since World War II.* New York: Simon & Schuster, 1988.

Simon, Howard. *Jewish Times: Voices of the American Jewish Experience.* Boston: Houghton Mifflin, 1988.

Smith, David C. *A History of Lumbering in Maine, 1861–1960.* Orono, Me.: University of Maine Press, 1972.

————. *The First Century: A History of the University of Maine, 1865–1965.* Orono, Me.: University of Maine Press, 1979.

Solomon, Barbara Miller. *Ancesters and Immigrants: A Changing New England Tradition.* Cambridge, Mass.: Harvard University Press, 1956.

Stearns, Harold E. "A Gentile's Picture of the Jew," *Menorah Journal,* Vol. 2, No. 4 (October 1916): 224–276.

Steele, Ronald. *Walter Lippmann and the American Century.* Boston: Atlantic Monthly Press, 1980.

Steinberg, Stephen. *Ethnic Myths: Race, Ethnicity and Class in America.* New York: Atheneum, 1981.

Street, George E. *Mt. Desert, A History,* Samuel A. Eliot, ed. Boston: Houghton Mifflin, 1926.

"Sunrise County Architecture: Significant Buildings of Washington County." Machiasport, Me.: Sunrise Research Institute, 1979.

Swift, Henry Walton, and Dacre Bush. "Mt. Desert in 1873." Boston: J. R. Osgood & Co., 1873.

Thernstrom, Stephan. *Poverty and Progress: Social Mobility in a Nineteenth Century City.* Cambridge, Mass.: Harvard University Press, 1964.

*Thirteenth Census of the United States,* "Population." Vol. 2. Washington, D.C.: Government Printing Office, 1913.

Thompson, Deborah. *Bangor, Maine 1769–1914: An Architectural History.* Orono, Me.: University of Maine Press, 1988.

Thoreau, Henry D. *The Illustrated Maine Woods.* Princeton, N.J.: Princeton University Press, 1974.

Torrey, Antoinette, Dr. H. O. H. Levine, Mimi Stern and Geraldine Watson. "Bangor: First Formal Visit of Mrs. Franklin D. Roosevelt (This Is the First Formal Visit of a First Lady of the Land to Bangor). May 20, 1941."

Train, Arthur. "The Viking's Daughter." In Sanford Phippen, ed., *The Best Maine Stories: The Marvelous Mystery* Augusta, Me.: Lance Tapley, 1986.

Tuchman, Barbara W. *Practicing History: Selected Essays.* New York: Alfred A. Knopf, 1981.

————. *The Proud Tower: A Portrait of the World Before the War, 1890–1914.* New York: Macmillan, 1966.

*Twelfth Census of the United States,* "Population." Washington, D.C.: Government Printing Office, 1901.

*Twelfth Census of the United States, 1900, Schedule No. 1—Population, City of Bangor, Penobscot County.*

Uminowicz, Glenn. "Sport in a Middle-Class Utopia: Asbury Park, New Jersey, 1871–1895." *Journal of Sport History,* Vol. II, No. 1 (Spring 1984): 51–73.

Vickery, James. *An Illustrated History of the City of Bangor, Maine formerly the Plantation of Conduskeag or Kenduskeag in ye country of Arcadia on the River Penobscot, combining narratives of ye ancient sites and persons.* Bangor, Me.: Bangor Bi-Centennial Committee, 1976.

Warburg, Edward M. M. *As I Recall.* Privately published, 1978.

Warburg, Frieda Schiff. *Reminiscences of a Long Life.* New York: Privately published, 1956.

Warburg, James P. *The Long Road Home: The Autobiography of a Maverick.* New York: Doubleday, 1964.

Wasson, George Savery. *Sailing Days on the Penobscot.* Salem, Mass.: Marine Research Society, 1932.

Wasson, Mildred. *The Big House.* Boston: Houghton Mifflin, 1926.

————. *Churchill Street.* New York: Coward-McCann, 1928.

Wecter, Dixon. *The Saga of American Society: A Record of Social Aspiration, 1607–1937.* New York: Charles Scribner's Sons, 1937.

Weinberg, Sydney Stahl. *The World of Our Mothers: The Lives of Jewish*

*Immigrant Women.* Chapel Hill, N.C.: University of North Carolina Press, 1988.

Wells, H. G. *The Future of America.* New York: Harper & Row, 1906.

Wharton, Edith. *Italian Villas and Their Gardens.* New York: DaCapo, 1988.

Williams, Ben Ames. *The Strange Woman.* New York: Houghton Mifflin, 1943.

Wilmerding, John. *American Light: The Luminist Movement, 1850–1875, Paintings, Drawings, Photographs.* Harper & Row, National Gallery of Art, 1980.

# Index